D1756957

Gower College Swansea

Unwanted

RECENT TITLES IN

UNWANTED

Muslim Immigrants, Dignity, and Drug Dealing

Sandra M. Bucerius

OXFORD
UNIVERSITY PRESS

Oxford University Press is a department of the University of Oxford.
It furthers the University's objective of excellence in research, scholarship,
and education by publishing worldwide.

Oxford   New York
Auckland   Cape Town   Dar es Salaam   Hong Kong   Karachi
Kuala Lumpur   Madrid   Melbourne   Mexico City   Nairobi
New Delhi   Shanghai   Taipei   Toronto

With offices in
Argentina   Austria   Brazil   Chile   Czech Republic   France   Greece
Guatemala   Hungary   Italy   Japan   Poland   Portugal   Singapore
South Korea   Switzerland   Thailand   Turkey   Ukraine   Vietnam

Oxford is a registered trademark of Oxford University Press
in the UK and certain other countries.

Published in the United States of America by
Oxford University Press
198 Madison Avenue, New York, NY 10016

Library of Congress Cataloging-in-Publication Data
Bucerius, Sandra M.
Unwanted : Muslim immigrants, dignity, and drug dealing / Sandra M. Bucerius.
pages cm
Includes bibliographical references and index.
ISBN 978-0-19-985647-3 (hardcover : alk. paper)   1. Crime—Germany—Sociological aspects.
2. Muslim youth—Germany. 3. Drug traffic—Germany. 4. Immigrants—Germany—Social
conditions. 5. Muslims—Cultural assimilation—Germany. 6. Germany—Emigration and
immigration—Social aspects. I. Title.
HV6977.B826 2014
363.45088'2970943—dc23
2014005208

9 8 7 6 5 4 3 2 1
Printed in the United States of America
on acid-free paper

To the "Bockenheimer Jungs" -
who made me see the world with different eyes.

CONTENTS

ACKNOWLEDGMENTS

During the years it has taken to complete this work I have moved from Germany, to the United States, and finally, to Canada. I have benefitted from many people, both academic and personal friends, across two continents, who supported and encouraged me to write this book. Some of these people have played a more formal role as mentor, whereas others lent their support by keeping my mind off the book when I was stuck (many of these people are probably unaware of how much they helped me). While it would be impossible to mention everyone who falls into the latter category, especially all the personal friends who have supported me during my research, data analysis, and when completing this book, I am thankful to all of you. I shall mention the most notable ones here: thanks to Matthias Schelwies for being my oldest friend and the one I can always turn to; to Miriam Philipp, Nina Voigt, and Kathrin Voigt for all your mental support throughout my data collection and for so many great moments; to Victoria Dadet for being the best room-mate ever throughout my data analysis; to Bettina Lotsch for one million conversations about academia and beyond over cheesecake; and to Arndt Krueger for his unwavering friendship and listening to my random thoughts about my research (and other things) at all times. Thank you for everything—I miss you all!

When starting my field work, I wanted to use a local community youth center as point of access for my research. The social workers at that facility were initially not convinced of my idea and recommended that I should do research on a population that has more things in common with me. I am very thankful that they eventually changed their minds and allowed me to use their community youth center. It was there where I met and came to know most of the young men who inform this book.

Of course, academic works require funding and financial support. The Frankfurt Graduate School of Social Sciences and Humanities provided me with a generous scholarship that made my time as a graduate student much more manageable. I was also extremely fortunate to be funded by the

German National Academic Foundation (Studienstiftung des deutschen Volkes), a scholarship foundation that not only provided me with financial support but also with outstanding mentorship and opportunities for conference travel. Further, it allowed me to form networks and friendships with exceptional German graduate students who provided their support throughout the years (and allowed me to rant when frustrated); most notably Johannes Becker, Andreas Wolf, Bertolt Meyer, Aneka Flamm, and Florian Zickfeld. Thank you for all your advice regarding this research, academia, and most importantly, life in general.

I am also deeply indebted to two academic institutions (and the scholars affiliated with them) that received me as a visiting PhD student. First, I am grateful to the John Jay College of Criminal Justice in New York, and in particular, David Kennedy, Ric Curtis, Jeremy Travis, David Brotherton, the deceased Jock Young, Larry Sullivan and my fellow academic peers and friends Misha Lars (thanks for countless discussions about resistance—I miss you!), Sue-Lin Wong, David Caspi, Charles Lieberman, and Christiane Bernard. I am grateful to all of you, and my time at John Jay remains very close to my heart.

Second, I am thankful to the NYU School of Law and, particularly, Jim Jacobs, David Garland, and the Lunch Talk crowd at the Centre for Research in Crime and Justice. Over the years, both Jim and David have imparted their sage advice and support for me and my work—thank you kindly.

In addition, I am also very appreciative of the Centre of Criminology and Sociolegal Studies at the University of Toronto and the wider University of Toronto community who provided me an unrivalled first job and support network. Countless colleagues and academic peers in Toronto commented on various aspects of my work and attended the different talks that I gave at the University of Toronto. There are too many people to mention, but in no particular order, thank you to Mariana Valverde, Rosemary Gartner, Anthony Doob, Scot Wortley, Anver Emon, Candace Kruttschnitt, Audrey Macklin, Matthew Light, Phil Triadafilopoulos, Anna Korteweg, Randall Hansen, Matthias Koenig, Jeffrey Kopstein, Markus Dubber, Jeffrey Reitz, Kevin O'Neill, Ronit Dinovitzer, Shyon Baumann, Josee Johnston, Judith Taylor, Patricia Erickson, Daniel Mueller, Jooyoung Lee, Michal Bodemann, Kelly Hannah-Moffat, Paula Maurutto, Maria Seyun Jung, Akwasi Owusu-Bempah, Jane Sprott, Holly Campeau, and Brenna Keatinge. I am also thankful to all the MA and PhD students in the 2011 and 2012 classes who read and commented on the draft manuscript—their thoughtful feedback was truly helpful and appreciated.

I switched appointments in the final stages of this book and am very grateful to my new colleagues in the Department of Sociology at the

University of Alberta for welcoming and providing me with an excellent environment to finish my manuscript. Particularly, I am grateful to Harvey Krahn, for ensuring a swift and smooth transition from the University of Toronto to the University of Alberta. Thank you to Kevin Haggerty for being a source of both delightful conversation and thoughtful mentorship in the department. My sincere thanks also go to my team of truly outstanding research assistants who read the manuscript and provided me with invaluable feedback: Katherine Hancock, Marta Urbanik, James Joosse, Kelsi Barkway, and Katharina Maier.

At different points in time, Jody Miller, Godfried Engbersen, Keith Hayward, Frank Zimring, Scott Decker, Sveinung Sandberg, Iddo Tavory, Jeff Ferrell, Sudhir Venkatesh, Christian Joppke, Ruud Koopmans, Raphael Beer, Rosella Selmini, Wilson Palacios, Helga Cremer Schaefer, Isabell Diehm, Frank-Olaf Radtke, Christian Pfeiffer, Waverly Duck, and some anonymous reviewers commented on parts of the manuscript or my work. The support and critical feedback that they provided deeply enriched my work. I am grateful to all of them. Likewise, I was fortunate enough to present my research at different conferences and institutions and appreciate all the feedback I received over the years.

I am also so greatly thankful to my editor at Oxford University Press, James Cook, and his assistant, Peter Worger for believing in me and this book, for their ongoing support of this project and their patience in working with me as a first time author. Likewise, I am thankful to Jayanthi Bhaskar of Newgen Publishing and the OUP team of copy-editors. My two copy-editors Linn Clark and Beth McAuley have also provided expert advice and have done an outstanding job copy-editing and commenting on various drafts. Thank you!

I do not know where I would be without the unwavering friendship and support of Carolyn Greene and Natasha Madon—two of my closest academic friends. Thank you for everything and more! Ron Levi has been a fantastic sounding board, mentor, and close friend. Thank you for always giving me advice on my work and beyond. For years, Luca Berardi has provided me with insightful feedback on my work and this manuscript. Thank you for reading and commenting on the manuscript at different stages, for always asking the right questions about my data, and for your friendship! I am profoundly thankful to Rosemary Gartner and Anthony Doob for their outstanding support of my work and career, their many comments on my research, their friendship, and their insights into academia. There were many moments where I would have been lost without your guidance.

I am sincerely grateful to Sara Thompson for all of her support and advice over the years. Your friendship and boundless eagerness for new mutual projects constantly keeps me going and motivated. I could not ask for a better collaborator, and more importantly, for a better friend—love you lots!

In 2005, when attending my first American conference, David Kennedy spontaneously invited me to spend some time at John Jay in New York. Only two months later, his Center for Crime Prevention and Control proved to be an incredible host institution and David provided me with great research and learning opportunities. Most importantly, he tremendously helped me to think through my data and made sure that New York became my home away from home. Thank you kindly, David!

I honestly do not know how to possibly do justice to everything Michael Tonry has done for me. Thank you for your ever-lasting support, mentoring, and honest feedback at all times. Most importantly, thank you for providing me with so many learning opportunities. You keep me on my toes, and I am forever grateful.

Ric Curtis has been an outstanding mentor and friend during my graduate studies (and beyond) and has taught me how to write articles for a North American audience. Ric, I know I would not be where I am today without your guidance and input, and I feel tremendous gratitude to you. Ethnography is a craft, and I have never been more impressed than observing your ethnographic skills in the field. I hope you like the book!

I owe my supervisor and friend Henner Hess my deepest and most sincere gratitude. Not only did he encourage me to conduct this research in the first place, but he was also an ever-present sounding board and trenchant critic who argued many points with me. While we disagree at times, he has never stopped believing in and supporting this project and me whole-heartedly. He was instrumental in my journey across the pond and introduced me to the North American academic world. Henner, I feel tremendously blessed to have had the opportunity to be mentored and "academically raised" by one of the smartest people around. I just wish we could see each other more often!

My parents and brother as well as my husband's family have always encouraged me to follow my heart in all of my endeavors. I would not be the same person and scholar without their steadfast support and encouragement—thank you for everything! Likewise, I am tremendously thankful to my husband, soul-mate, and best friend Albert, and our three fantastic little boys, Lukas, Samuel, and Benjamin, for their unfailing love and understanding, and for providing me with endless support (and time) for this project.

Last but most importantly, this book would have never been written without the young men whose stories I share in this book. I was incredibly fortunate that they allowed me to participate in some aspects of their lives and to share very intimate moments. While I am tremendously grateful to all of them, I want to highlight three of the young men who have grown very close to my heart and who played a major role in this research: Ozgur, Akin, and Aissa. These three never stopped challenging me in the field and made sure that I would learn from them and about them—and they constantly encouraged me to write this book. I hope that my interpretations of the young men's lives and struggles will do them justice.

Unwanted

Introduction

> You really want to understand why we do this? Germans play piano, and *Kanaken* deal drugs. It's always been that way; it will always be that way. That's all you need to know.
>
> —Akin[1]

Veli dropped out of school just six months from graduation. Even though I was fully aware of the institutional discrimination against immigrants, especially young men, in the German school system and the formal job market, I couldn't help but blame him. About two weeks after I had first heard the rumors about him quitting, I ran into him on the street:

> SANDRA: Why on earth did you quit school? You were so close to finishing. . . .
>
> VELI: I am just really annoyed by this cunt [teacher] for a very long time. She always makes all these stupid Nazi remarks and talks shit about the guys [referring to the other young men]—as if she knew anything. Well . . . and now Jo came along and basically asked me whether I wanted to be part of this deal he has going. So I am just thinking: "Fuck it. I'm never going to make that much money again."

While I understood that he was annoyed by his teacher's discriminatory and stereotypical remarks, I couldn't help thinking, "You're so close to finishing—just suck it up."

I had expected him to finish, and I was angry and disappointed that he did not. Veli knew this, and so for the past few weeks, he had avoided coming to the youth center and had also made sure not to run into me at night. I had helped him with his schoolwork over the past year, tutoring him for several hours every Friday afternoon, and knew that from an academic standpoint, he could easily have graduated. While talking to him on the street, I caught myself thinking about the time I had wasted and that I could have spent differently, had I known that he would quit in the end. But this wasn't about me.

I had to remind myself that these young men did not really have the option of becoming lawyers or doctors. They could only hope for low-paying jobs in the formal economy or slightly better-paying jobs in the informal economy. It was within this context, surrounded by macro-level forces that limit the participation of immigrants in the labor market, that young men like Veli decided to seize the many and more lucrative opportunities available to them in the illegitimate sphere. When I asked Veli a year later about his decision, he underlined precisely this point:

> SANDRA: Don't you regret having quit? Do you sometimes think, "Well, I should have stayed on for these six more months"?
> VELI: Well, yeah . . . of course, I've thought about that before. Especially when I see you and just remember how you tried to teach me French, remember that? All these fucking French lessons. . . . I'll never forget that. But really, Sandra, what would I have done? I would have had my *Abitur* [a high school degree that allows you to study at a university] and then? Just look at the guys who learned a trade and even have good grades . . . or even Özgur, like the only one with an Abitur and everything . . . and you still don't get a job. You're still the foreigner. And you know, I am not even a Turk. . . . I'm even blond . . . but I am still a foreigner. Why should I pay taxes and work my butt off for this country? I will never, ever make as much money as I can with a few good deals. And then, you know, Croatia, amazing house and chilling in the sun! That's the way to go, Sandra.

The promise of fast money and the possibility of "being somebody" certainly made the drug market a tempting alternative to the formal economy. More importantly, however, at some point in their lives, the young men realized that staying in school would not have made a difference, as Veli commented:

> Well, had it not been for the cunt and had she not always pulled that Nazi shit, I'd now have my Abitur. Guaranteed. I mean, my grades would not have been a

problem at all, right, Sandra? You know that! But you know, it would not have made a difference either way. And it's just that everyone does this shit. It's . . . it's . . . so normal!

When I started my fieldwork, drug dealing was anything but normal to me. So, naturally, when I first set foot into a local community youth center in Frankfurt, Germany—known at that time to be a hangout for drug dealers—I didn't have a real vision of how fieldwork there would go and what kind of drug dealing activities I would be able to observe.

I began my research in the early summer of 2001 with the plan to study the illicit economy to determine the workings of the low- and mid-level drug trade in Germany. I did not specifically intend to study male drug dealers who were Muslim or immigrants; however, largely as a result of the particular site I chose, the majority of the dealers I met had these characteristics. I wasn't entirely surprised to find that most of the young men at the youth center were second-generation Muslim immigrants. This group is one of the most socially excluded populations in German society and a regular target of discrimination (Brettfeld and Wetzels 2003; Bommes 1996, 4–5; Gesemann 2006, 25; Gomolla and Radtke 2009); as a result of this, I argue, it has long been overrepresented in criminal statistics and criminological research in Germany (Baier et al. 2009; Albrecht 2011).

Very quickly, I became increasingly interested in the social, economic, and political situations of the young men—the social exclusion they were facing and the future they envisioned for themselves—rather than the drug market itself. In this book, I describe in great detail how the young men experienced various forms of exclusion on a daily basis, and in which ways these distinctive exclusionary practices not only helped forge strong cohesion among them but also allowed them to rationalize their participation in the drug trade as a reaction to this exclusion. To understand the various paths that second-generation immigrants may choose, and keeping in mind the prominent role that the quality of the host country's reception (actual or perceived) plays for social integration, it is revealing to examine the young men's narratives about German society. What did they think about Germany and their own chances in the country? Did they feel any sort of belonging to the country? And what was the relationship between their feelings and their involvement in the drug trade? How did they reconcile between their religious affiliation and their drug-dealing activities?

I hope that readers will find this book to be a fine-grained analysis of the relationships among immigration, social exclusion, and drug dealing. More importantly, I hope it will not be used to strengthen existing stereotypes of second-generation Muslim immigrants in Germany or elsewhere, or of marginalized populations in general. I have tried to provide a full, nuanced, and honest portrayal of the lives of the young men I studied; in some cases, as will become apparent, this called for an analysis of actions and beliefs that some might find repulsive or disheartening. My hope is that by framing their stories, activities, and ideologies using both theory and context, I will not exclude and stigmatize them further, but rather, will be able to clarify the macro-level factors that have profoundly shaped their lives and actions. Overall, then, throughout this book, I try to clarify the relationship between structural forces and individual actions—not just for young Muslim men in Germany, but for marginalized populations in all Western societies.

STREET CULTURE IN AMERICA AND GERMANY

In 2001, the fifty-five young men that I got to know at the local community youth center were between the ages of 16 and 31 years, with a mean age of 23. The great majority had a guest-worker background, meaning that their parents had been recruited by Germany as low-skilled workers in the 1960s and early 1970s to fill jobs in the booming German economy that no one else wanted to do (see chapter 1). As in many other European countries, Germany's guest-worker program was only intended to allow workers into the country temporarily, but many stayed and settled. Because these guest workers were never intended to immigrate permanently, Germany had no plans in place to integrate their children. The young men discussed in this book were part of a generation of perpetual foreigners for whom, as youth, no one was really prepared and, who, ironically, as adults, are now too old to benefit from recent integration policies. Accordingly, they are often labeled the "lost generation" (Beauftragte der Bundesregierung für Migration, Flüchtlinge und Integration 2007).

While many researchers rightly argue that feelings of hostility toward Muslims have increased since the events of September 11, 2001 (something the young men affirmed during my research), even before that, they were not well regarded in Germany. For example, in a survey conducted in 1995, only 15 percent of all West Germans and 7 percent of all East Germans indicated that they would "feel comfortable" having a Turk as a family member (Koch and Wasmer 1997, 465). Tied to this feeling are also rampant stereotypes about the criminal and violent *Kanaken*—a derogatory term widely used for second-generation male Muslims or "Turks," as they are generally assumed to be. In Germany, the term "Muslim"—technically a religious affiliation—is conflated with being ethnically Turkish.[2] As Cafer said: "Everybody just calls you 'foreigner' in Germany or, even better,

'Turk.' No matter whether you're Moroccan, Albanian, Iranian—'He has black hair, oh, he has to be a Turk.'" The image of Muslims in Germany is less associated with being "Arab," as it is in many other Western countries, and more with being a "non-assimilated Turk," independent of ethnic background. In short, Muslims are the least-liked immigrant group in Germany (Lynch and Simon 2002).

The extent to which this context mattered for the young men I wrote about in this book became very clear when, after completing my research in 2006, I moved from Frankfurt to work with colleagues who were studying marginalized populations in New York City. Against the backdrop of a different city, let alone continent, the importance and uniqueness of the social context in which the young men of Frankfurt lived became obvious. Over the course of five years, I had developed a nuanced understanding of the actions of the young men in Frankfurt, which were heavily influenced by their social position as children of former guest workers and their experiences of being marginalized second-generation Muslim immigrants in a country that is officially Christian (the ideals of the melting pot and multiculturalism, as adopted in the United States or Canada, are not supported in Germany). It is within this context that the young men made their day-to-day decisions.

The marginalized people I met in New York and the young men I knew in Germany shared some common experiences, such as street life, a marginalized position in society, and ongoing attempts to forge an identity within their neighborhood or group. However, the young men in Germany lived in one of the world's most advanced social welfare states, yet they were denied citizenship, so their social and political situation differed considerably from those of the populations in New York. Most American research has focused on marginalized populations living in the "American ghetto"—meaning neighborhoods with high spatial concentrations of poverty (Wilson 1987). In contrast to this typical ghetto setting, the young men in Germany were not spatially isolated. Most German cities are not residentially segregated like American cities, so the population in any given German neighborhood is usually quite diverse, with subsidized housing located alongside middle-class homes. Bockenheim, the Frankfurt neighborhood in which the young men grew up and where the community youth center was located, was actually a very desirable neighborhood. It had many little shops, local cafés, and bars, and was home to university professors and businesspeople as well as those classified as socio-economically disadvantaged.

Despite these structural differences, the young men in Frankfurt were socially isolated and economically excluded in ways that were similar to those described in many American studies. The difference was that they were isolated *within* a desirable neighborhood where so much was available but out of reach for them and their families. Living in a social welfare state, these young men will never be subjected to the extreme poverty that characterizes the most disadvantaged neighborhoods in the United States, but their isolation within middle-class surroundings reminded them daily of their marginalization and magnified their frustration. Because of their daily confrontation with people who could afford much better lifestyles, their relative deprivation was obvious to them—and, I would argue, even more obvious than if they had been isolated in a ghetto.[3]

Similar to American drug dealers and gang members, the young men in Frankfurt can be described as what Vigil (1997) called "multiply marginalized," despite living in a social welfare state. This marginalization included social factors (discrimination on the streets or bias in the criminal justice system), economic factors (disadvantages in the German school system and in the job market), and political factors (the denial of citizenship to second-generation immigrants)—as well as a double rejection from both the young men's host and home societies (Vigil 1988, 14). Their parents were former guest workers in Germany who had settled permanently, but even though the young men had been born in Germany, they never felt welcomed there. The experience of being "unwanted" certainly shaped their lives.

That feeling of being unwanted was further amplified by the German reluctance to extend the political correctness applied in other contexts to immigrant populations in Germany. This is important to understand. Some readers may assume that Germany's history might prompt German society to be sensitive about its treatment of minorities. However, political correctness largely characterizes conversations about the Jewish population and is not extended to the same degree to other minority groups in the country. It is not uncommon for German politicians to question whether Germany is ready for a vice-chancellor who looks "Asian"[4] or to openly accuse Muslim immigrants of exploiting the German welfare state and living in "parallel societies" (i.e., refusing to integrate into the mainstream and potentially being criminal). The often blatantly racist rhetoric around Muslim immigrants in the media and the public shaped these young men's feelings toward Germany as well as how they perceived their own role in society.[5]

Many of the young men became involved in the drug trade at the age of 12 or 13 and started dealing more heavily in their early adolescence, around age 16 or 17. When I met them, some of the teenagers were still in school and planned to graduate, only dealing a little on the side, but they were all fully involved in the drug trade by the time they reached their twenties. In Germany, parents' socio-economic background predicts their children's school performance more than anything else. In other words, children from poor socio-economic backgrounds are disadvantaged from the outset. Along those lines, the young men in this book were certainly not upwardly mobile (Portes, Fernández-Kelly, and Haller 2009) and maintained the same disadvantaged position held by their parents for themselves and future generations. About half dropped out of school at a fairly young age or stayed through high school but never graduated. With one exception, those who did graduate did not qualify to go to university, and only about a quarter learned a trade through vocational training (see chapter 3). As they told me, they had quickly learned that they would never make much money through the limited opportunities they had in the formal economy. And, living in Frankfurt—the financial hub of Germany—they were not content with just getting by. The young men, in fact, had extravagant tastes in cars, clothes, phones, and other status symbols. But despite their costly lifestyle, almost all of them still lived at home in close quarters with siblings and parents and did not plan to move out until later in life.[6] Because of their small apartments, and because bringing friends home was not part of their culture, they spent most of their time in the streets, at cafés or bars, or at the community youth center. Most of this time was spent simply hanging out in their neighborhood, Bockenheim, talking about girls, TV, politics, friends, and daily life.

As in the American context, the social marginalization experienced by the young men encouraged a street culture (see, e.g., Maher 1997; Miller 2000; Bourgois 2003; Bourgois and Schonberg 2009; Whyte 1943). Under conditions of widespread social and economic exclusion, groups of young people (often labeled as youth gangs, drug-dealing circles, or just street groups) can easily serve as "surrogate family, providing friendship, companionship, protection, identity, and entertainment" (Vigil 2007, 110). The streets, and the groups that form there, offer marginalized young people an identity, a home, and the opportunity to gain respect—a possibility often denied to multiply marginalized populations. For these young men, creating their own niche and identity within German society meant identifying with Bockenheim. Unable to fully comply with the rules of either German mainstream society or their parents' generation, they did not identify as either German or as members of their particular ethnic group. Instead, they identified as "Bockenheimers."

Identification as a Bockenheimer often translated into an effort to guard the neighborhood against certain types of crime and certain kinds of individuals. Contrary to popular belief (see Pattillo 1998), the relationship between drug dealers or gang members and their neighborhood can be mutually advantageous: local gangs or drug dealers may protect the neighborhood from other criminals or particular crimes that violate their code of ethics. The young men, for example, forbade crack dealing within the neighborhood and expelled junkies from the area.

The young men's shared experience of exclusion not only helped forge strong cohesion among them but also encouraged their mutual identification as both Bockenheimers and Muslims. Even the few young men in my sample who were not Muslim by birth adopted a sort of quasi-Muslim identity that was accepted by everyone. At the same time, they negotiated their drug-dealing activities while trying to adhere to their perceived cultural and religious obligations. They saw themselves as "good" drug dealers (as opposed to "real" criminals), adhering to certain distinctions between pure and impure drugs, customers, and ways of doing business that they claimed were in line with Islamic values. In this way, they performed what Lamont (2000) calls "boundary work." By distinguishing themselves from those individuals who were seen as "worse," they created a positive sense of self. Still, they knew that their actions did not comply with what was expected of good Muslims, so they planned to be good after they stopped dealing. In this way, both their drug-dealing activities and the life they envisioned as following that stage of their life were influenced by their (perceived) religious beliefs and values, providing and reinforcing moral and social norms (Durkheim 2001) and a form of social control and cohesion (Sandberg 2010).

STRUCTURE VERSUS AGENCY: THE STRUGGLE OF ETHNOGRAPHERS

Analyses of marginalization almost always include the issue of whether, or to what extent, people who follow unconventional and illegal lifestyles and are involved in street culture have a choice. The young men I got to know were not mere victims of structural forces, marginalization, and exclusion; they did have other choices. I view the young men's choices as confined by the structural limitations that they faced. As such, I very much looked at my sample through a Bourdieusian lens, using the concept of symbolic violence to show how the young men internalized these structural limitations (Bourdieu 1998).

The fact that the young men had choices is important for several reasons. Not all second-generation male Muslims in Germany turn to street culture. This group is overrepresented in criminal statistics, but most—regardless of ethnic background—do not partake in street culture, despite facing similar forms of marginalization and exclusion. Equally important, the young men I got to know did not see themselves as victims. They were aware that they faced certain limitations but did not view themselves as having been forced into the drug trade. This allowed them to maintain a degree of agency and dignity, and to dream about changing their lives and their futures.

Adequately balancing structural forces and the agency of individuals is one of the biggest challenges for all urban ethnographers. Because ethnographers become very close to the people they study and observe their day-to-day actions, they may miss the structural-level forces that shape those individuals' actions. As a result, some ethnographers end up putting too much emphasis on individual agency, leaving the reader with the impression that marginalized people only have themselves to blame for their unfortunate situations. At the other extreme, some ethnographers place too much emphasis on the social structure, portraying the study population as helpless, lacking in agency and free will. This depiction ignores the day-to-day decisions and actions that often leave individuals in less than desirable circumstances. By failing to ensure a critical balance of structure and agency, ethnographers have the potential to fail as researchers, incorrectly describing and analyzing their study populations, as well as to fail their study participants, those whose trust they have gained during long-term research projects. Consequently, as I conducted my research, analyzed my data, and wrote this book, I constantly struggled to provide an appropriate balance between structural forces and agency.

When writing this book, I often found myself in a situation opposite to that faced by other urban ethnographers—especially those doing research in the American context. Bourgois and Schonberg (2009), for example, in their study of homeless heroin injectors, had to pull out structural issues from their sample. In the United States, it is very common for respondents to tell ethnographers that they themselves are to blame for their own misfortunes. In my work in Germany, however, I often encountered the opposite. While the young men occasionally put some emphasis on their own behavior and actions, they rarely portrayed their situation as being their own fault—mostly because it often wasn't. Instead, the blame was almost always deflected externally to society, and so I, as the ethnographer, found myself constantly searching to find their agency in everything that they did and had experienced. In other words, the impact of social circumstances in Germany on their lives was painfully obvious to me, and it was their (in)ability to make decisions in a society that limits and excludes them in so many ways that became the more difficult task—again, a situation different from that encountered in most other ethnographies. When writing, my aim was to try to give these young men back their agency—not to blame them (although I don't shy away from this where blame is due) but to show that they do have agency, however limited it may be.

I often wondered why the young men did not blame themselves as others in many North American studies had? Essentially, I found that being excluded within a social welfare system and a socially mixed neighborhood, and constantly being confronted with the wealth of possibilities and opportunities others had, made the young men even more aware of their exclusion and the symbolic violence directed toward them. At the end of the day, they were constantly surrounded by people who were doing much better—they even attended the same schools as Germans, although in a different track in the same building. In addition, Germany is an advanced social welfare state that believes in "society." In other words, it's not individuals who fail; it's the society that does. This backdrop may have amplified the notion of "societal blame" for the young men. Germany is also a society that is easy to blame. Historically, Germany has made tremendous mistakes, which has instilled in the young men the feeling that, as Akin said, "Germany fucked up before." In other words, the young men thought it was somehow universally accepted to say negative things about Germany.

Readers might think, "If nobody forced them to deal drugs, and if they plan to turn their back on street culture eventually, why would they not just quit immediately? Why would they continue to participate in drug dealing, violence, and self-destruction?" I am concerned that by stressing the agency of the young men in Frankfurt and their hopes for a good future free of drug dealing (see chapter 6), I will further stereotype an already-vulnerable population. I am also concerned that by writing about the young men's opinion of women as subordinate to men and the machismo that shapes many of their actions toward women, I will strengthen gender stereotypes about this population. Regardless of ethnic background, street culture has always involved machismo. However, this book risks strengthening the perception of the oppressive male Muslim instead of showing that machismo is one way for an otherwise-powerless population—regardless of ethnic or religious background—to exercise power. To mitigate this potential "blame game" and to understand such phenomena correctly, I have tried hard to demonstrate the interplay between structural forces and individual action in shaping the lives of the young men in this book. They were certainly responsible for their own actions, but the possible choices they could have made were, as will become apparent throughout this book, very different from mine as an upper-middle-class native German. Confined within limited possibilities, they tried to support their lifestyles and earn honor and respect outside of conventional norms and often used unconventional means to do so.

CONDUCTING THE RESEARCH

Almost every community or district in large German cities has a community youth center funded by local government and the state. These youth centers serve as places where local teenagers can get help with homework or job applications, ask for legal advice, or just hang out. I asked staff members in the Department of Social Work at the University of Frankfurt which community youth center in Frankfurt would be most appropriate for my study, and everyone suggested Bockenheim based on word-of-mouth information. I also consulted with two unit commanders at different police divisions in Frankfurt to get their perspectives about the drug trade.[7] Both referred to internal research showing that the district I had selected for my research was the second-largest drug market in the city, and that most drug deals were likely carried out by frequenters of this particular community youth center. Finally, university students pointed to the same community youth center as a place where they could contact dealers. The information from university students was rather vague—they told me that they assumed that their dealers hung out there but that they didn't actually enter the center to buy drugs. As one student told me, "The center is a legend—way back when, you'd walk in and get your stuff there. Nowadays, you need to call your contact, and they meet you somewhere in the neighborhood—they don't want anyone near there—who knows why. But everyone knows that they all hang out there."

The center was run by three male social workers of German background and served between seventy and eighty young men who visited regularly. As is common for most youth centers in Germany, it had a weight-lifting room, a small kitchen, an office for the social workers, and a larger room with several couches, a TV and XBox console, a pool table, a dartboard, a foosball table, and a table tennis set-up. There was another smaller room attached to the large room in which the social workers would unofficially tolerate pot smoking.[8]

Community youth centers in Germany aim to offer various kinds of assistance to youth by providing a place to socialize, get advice, attend classes, and work out. Like many youth centers in Frankfurt at the time, this one did not meet its intended objectives. For example, regulars were composed primarily of youth significantly older than the target age (at 31, the oldest was not even a youth), and their presence at the center discouraged younger teenagers from coming in.[9] The centers are also supposed to serve both male and female youth, but this particular center had no female visitors at all. The space functioned less as an open community institution and more as a personal hangout place for the dealers.

The police seemed to allow drug dealers to socialize freely at the center but kept it under constant surveillance; at least one local police car was parked outside at all times. But over the course of my research, the local police rarely came inside and never entered unannounced. I remember only two occasions on which the police entered the youth center—both times they announced their visits beforehand. This approach can be interpreted as a social control strategy. By allowing the young men to socialize in a safe environment without fear of police raids, the police ensured the likelihood that they would stay in one place rather than loitering all over the district. The assumption was that this confinement made the district safer and police work easier. At the same time, the young men greatly valued "their" community center and prevented police raids by ensuring that no customers came inside the facility. While the young men consumed and sometimes packaged and stored drugs at the center, they never actually sold drugs there.

This youth center was a major research site for the first two and a half years of my study. While establishing rapport over the first few months, I was there every day. After that period, I spent roughly three afternoons per week (for about six hours each day) hanging out with the young men there. Once I had gained their trust, I also participated in their activities two to three nights a week: hanging out in the streets, bars, and cafés, cruising around in cars without a specific destination, and visiting clubs. After the first two and a half years, the center came under pressure from the local police department and the municipal government to meet its intended mandate, and the young men stopped hanging out there. From then onwards, I typically met the young men on certain street corners in the evenings.

This book is based on the many field notes that I collected from conversations and observations during drug transactions, fights among the young men and with outsiders, and family interactions.[10] The information I collected reflects the lives of the fifty-five young men from the youth center who were there the most regularly, which gave me the opportunity to form relationships with each of them. I took detailed daily notes and also conducted more than 100 in-depth interviews during which the young men talked about their social environment, their sense of belonging, and the informal economy in which they participated. Originally, I had developed an interview questionnaire to use as my main source of data collection.

However, after gaining the trust of the young men, I realized that I could collect much richer data using field notes. Whenever I used a tape recorder, the young men became uncomfortable; they tried to sound more formal, and they were obviously nervous. Consequently, instead of using this original interview questionnaire (which I did use to conduct approximately twenty interviews during the first few months), I used interviews only to clarify certain issues that I did not fully understand from observations and interactions. Of these explanatory interviews, approximately twenty-five focused mainly on specifics of the drug trade; thirty focused mainly on relationships with women, marriage, family, and the future; and another thirty focused mainly on the young men's experiences in Germany, including their experiences in the school system and in the job market. Instead of working with a structured interview guide, I used a prompting technique that allowed interviewees to decide what meaning they wanted to attribute to different aspects of their replies. This approach also made interviews more comfortable for participants. I had already built a strong rapport with the young men by the time I started conducting these interviews (two years into my fieldwork), and the use of a more structured and formal interview procedure would have been awkward.[11] I also collected letters from three of the five young men who were incarcerated during the period of my research.

Naturally, I developed different relationships with each of the young men. Some saw me mainly as a ghostwriter for job applications; to others, I was a good table-tennis opponent, a (female) listener and counselor for relationship advice, or a friend. I grew very close to some over the five years, developing relationships that allowed me to gain very detailed and nuanced insights into their lives. With others, I developed formal research relationships that allowed me to conduct interviews or hang out with them, but we never became very close. As is common in multiyear ethnographic studies, a few acted as key study participants, always willing to reflect on topics and provide additional information that I needed for fuller understanding. Three were particularly critical for this research: Akin, Aissa, and Özgur. Each was important at different times and played a different role in my work.

Akin started out as the greatest barrier to my research. As one of the spokespersons among the young men and one of the best-connected dealers in Bockenheim, he considered the group to be "his." Our initial interactions were extremely difficult, and he did everything he could to get rid of me (see also chapter 4). But over time, Akin and I developed a very close relationship, allowing me insight into aspects of the drug market that would otherwise probably have been closed to me. At the same time, I became an important confidant for him. Because I was not actually "one of the young men" and was therefore sufficiently removed, he gave me insights into the context in which he was living and trusted me with personal information about which he did not want the other young men to know.

Aissa and I had a much less rocky relationship at the beginning, but it took about a year to form a close relationship with him. He was one of the very few young men trying to turn their backs on their drug-dealing past and lifestyle, and he was always willing to talk about the difficulties he had encountered and about the *Lebenswelt* (lifeworld) (Habermas 1981) of the young men in general. I met Aissa after he had started turning away from his old lifestyle, but he was previously known as one of the most violent young men in the group—someone no one wanted to mess with. He was exceptionally skilled at reflecting on the young men's position in society and their actions, dreams, and hopes. He often helped me understand their lives and actions more deeply and sparked further questions.

Finally, Özgur, who was one of the younger men, offered insights into the lives of the teenagers who were only marginally involved in dealing when I first started my research. He was the only one among the young men who achieved a high school degree that allowed him to go to college. Our relationship was initially based on his need for tutoring and relationship advice, but over time, we grew to become very close. I conducted my final interviews in 2006, but I am still in regular contact with Aissa and Özgur, as well as with twelve of the other young men in this book.

These three key participants read and critiqued some of my field notes and provided additional information when needed. This technique supports Latour's (2000) idea of objectivity, ensuring that research subjects do not lose the capacity to object to a researcher's observations, but the final word has always been mine. I could never have written this book without the cooperation of all the young men in this study and the rich data they provided, but it was my task to analyze, interpret, and "thickly describe" their lives (see Geertz 1973). As I attempted to produce a thoughtful narrative of their lives—and also of some of their actions that others might find objectionable—I tried to be aware of the postmodern call for self-conscious reflexivity in ethnographic studies. I tried to keep in mind that I—as the researcher—am within the text, and that my ethnographic findings were mutually constructed by the young men and myself.

THEORETICAL BACKGROUND

When starting my fieldwork, I anticipated that I would embed my work in the literature on informal economies and drug markets. While I still draw on this literature when describing the market itself, I employ different theoretical concepts in this book to explain the decision-making processes of the marginalized young men and their actions. I draw most heavily on Bourdieu's concepts of habitus, cultural capital, and symbolic violence, all of which together constitute a theoretical system and none of which act in isolation (Bourdieu and Wacquant 1992, 94). Therefore, even though these concepts may be referred to separately throughout the book, they essentially bind together the larger debate of structure versus agency. In addition to these concepts, I also draw on the concept of social closure as put forth by Max Weber (1972), and I borrow from Michele Lamont's boundary work (2000) and Mary Douglas' concept of purity and impurity (1966). Taken together, these concepts help us to understand the lives and actions of the young men in this book.

The concept of *habitus* refers to the lifestyles, dispositions, values, and expectations of particular social groups acquired through the activities and experiences of everyday life (Bourdieu and Wacquant 1992, 119–21). In other words, the conditions to which individuals are exposed influence the ways they see and understand the world around them. The young men's habitus was significantly conditioned by the fact that they experienced relative deprivation, being constantly surrounded by people who could afford things that were out of reach for them, as well as being excluded from many aspects of life that were naturally extended to their neighbors. They were aware that they had the ability to make their own choices in life, but they perceived these choices as defined and limited by their social context. They internalized their experiences in Germany, and it was within this context of their experienced and lived marginalization in German society, conditioned by their surroundings, that they understood their position in society.

The concept of *symbolic violence* is particularly important for understanding the young men's position in society. Bourdieu argued that symbolic violence is the internalization of humiliations and legitimizations of different types of inequality and hierarchy ranging from sexism and racism to intimate expressions of class power (Bourdieu 2004, 339). He held that symbolic violence is "exercised through cognition and misrecognition, knowledge and sentiment, with the unwitting consent of the dominated" (340). In other words, a host of structural constraints such as the lack of job opportunities in the legal economy, the lack of or constraints limiting access to educational attainment, and discriminatory laws and racism (to list only a few) are all various types of challenges imposed on marginalized populations. The constraints imposed by the larger socio-economic and political forces that comprise the macro-level structure are established and preserved by the higher class in society, that is, the ones "in power." According to Bourdieu, symbolic violence is all the more powerful because it is for the most part exerted invisibly through the everyday interaction of individuals within the symbolically structured physical world (341). The young men in this book were not always aware of the symbolic violence directed toward them—they internalized the limitations they faced to be normal. In other words, they did not wonder, at least initially, why (with one exception) all of them were streamed into schools that would not allow them to earn the degree needed to enter college or university. They simply assumed that "immigrant kids just don't go to college or university."

I refer to the concept of *cultural capital*—both educational credentials and familiarity with bourgeois culture—sporadically throughout the book. Bourdieu (1984) holds that cultural capital is a major determinant of an individual's life chances and that the unequal distribution of such capital helps to conserve social hierarchies. The young men in this study came from families with little cultural capital and hence had a very difficult time navigating both the educational system in Germany and parts of the formal economy. For example, they had not necessarily learned how to write successful cover letters for job applications or how to act in a job interview. This lack of cultural capital—that is, their lack of knowledge about how to navigate those systems successfully—significantly impacted the young men's chances for upward mobility.

Max Weber's (1972) concept of *social closure* is particularly important in trying to understand why the young men in this book experienced exclusion on so many levels. Weber posits that the dominant group in society usually tries to safeguard its own position and privileges it by monopolizing and restricting resources and opportunities to its own group while at the same time denying access to outsiders, such as immigrants. This process happens on many levels in any society, and social closures are particularly salient in keeping immigrants out of the dominant group. Weber holds that the dominant group singles out certain attributes—race or immigrant status, for example—to justify the social closures. Consider the argument that a young man immigrating to Germany cannot ever really be loyal to his new home if he still possesses the citizenship of his country of origin, so German citizenship should not be granted to him.

When talking about *boundary work*, I refer—leaning on Michèle Lamont (2000)—to the need of people to draw distinctions between themselves and the ones they consider above or below them in order to justify their own position in society and create a positive sense of self. The young men's use of boundary work was particularly obvious when they labeled themselves as "good" and "moral" dealers. They may not have made as much money as other dealers, but they were not involved in more serious criminal acts (e.g., trafficking large amounts of drugs internationally) and did not have to stand on a street corner and sell to children. When doing boundary work, the young men often distinguished between "good" dealers (someone who does not sell to children) and "bad" dealers (someone who will sell to anyone), as well as between "pure" drugs (drugs made from natural substances, like cocaine) and "dirty" drugs (chemical drugs), thereby employing Mary Douglas' (1966) concepts of *purity* and *impurity*. By portraying themselves as pure dealers, they distinguished themselves from those who they considered dirty and created a positive sense of self despite engaging in activities that were widely deemed immoral—not only by Germans but also and especially by their own families and religion.

OUTLINE

I expect many readers to be somewhat unfamiliar with the specific social, political, and legal dimensions of Germany today. In chapter 1, I highlight the most important aspects of these features and provide context for the neighborhood in which the study took place.

Chapters 2 to 5 comprise the heart of my analysis. In chapter 2, I describe in detail how the young men tried to make sense of the distinctive forms of exclusion they faced in Germany and how these forms of exclusion not only provided them with rationales for their participation in the drug market but also helped them to form a mutual identity as "Bockenheimers." This strong local identification, I argue, allowed them to find a place of belonging within German society. In chapter 3, I describe the specific drug market in which the young men participated and the business model they employed (the structure and hierarchy of the market, the substances sold, purchase, delivery, storing, turfs, etc.). In many ways, the young men largely conformed to the descriptions of drug markets and drug dealers that exist in the scholarly literature on these topics; however, their particular cultural background differentiated them from other drug dealers in significant ways. These differences are further delineated in chapter 4, in which I examine the young men's distinct notions of purity and impurity and the impact of these ideas on their behavior within the drug market. These concepts influenced, for example, their choice of specific forms of violence, customers, business partners, and the substances they would sell. Finally, in chapter 5, I focus on the young men's future. For most dealers, especially those with lower status in the drug trade, selling drugs is a temporary occupation. The central question I explore in this chapter is how the young men imagined their future and why "marrying" and "religion" became central components of their vision of "life after drug dealing" in Germany.

While this ethnographic study took place in Frankfurt, the general themes of immigration, social exclusion, and the informal economy are particular to Germany. Across borders and for reasons that are still up for debate, it can be observed that the crime levels of most second-generation immigrants are higher than those of their first-generation counterparts. Second-generation immigrants seem to be more cognizant of discrimination, exclusion, and systemic disadvantage than their parents' generation was and are much less likely to interpret these experiences as isolated incidents. The question of whether experiences of exclusion, marginalization, and discrimination have an influence on individuals' involvement in informal markets is one that pertains to all Western countries. Similarly, marginalized populations exist in all Western societies, independent of whether or not they have a history of immigration. In chapter 6, I outline the relevance of this research for other Western countries, especially the United States, and conclude by proposing several policy recommendations for addressing the plight of second-generation Muslim immigrants in Germany and marginalized populations elsewhere.

Furthermore, I have added an appendix for those readers who are interested in how I initially got to know the young men. Reading the work of urban ethnographers ultimately raises the question of how the researcher gained the trust of the people he or she studied. Being a female researcher studying an all-male group, these questions might be even more pressing, especially because it is often assumed in criminology that being female is a research liability. While ethnographers ultimately never know what exactly helped them to gain trust, the appendix provides some background information on how the young men and I formed the mutual understanding necessary for meaningful fieldwork to take place. While building trust and establishing one's role as a researcher is always a highly individualized process, I offer some conclusions that are more broadly relevant for ethnographic research.

CHAPTER 1

Germany's Guest Workers and Their Children

Second-Class Citizens in a First-World Country

They wanted workers, but what they got were human beings who came with their families, their customs, and their culture.

— Otto ily, *former German Federal Minister of the Interior*[1]

Germany is not exactly known for being immigrant friendly. The public debate about the integration of Turks and other immigrants in Germany reached a new level in 2010 when Thilo Sarrazin, a former board member of the Deutsche Bundesbank, fiercely criticized multiculturalism in his book *Deutschland schafft sich ab* (*Germany Abolishes Itself*) (*Economist* 2010). This volume sold out within a few days and after only two months became the best-selling book on German politics by a German author in the past decade. Sarrazin's work (2010a) sparked a nationwide controversy about the costs and benefits of the ideology of multiculturalism, demonstrating the discontent of many Germans with the current integration situation. Sarrazin's main argument is that Germany is becoming biologically and culturally inferior as a result of Muslim immigration. He argues that effective integration requires effort on the part of those being integrated, and that Muslim immigrants are not willing to expend this effort:

I will not show respect for anyone that is not making that effort. I do not have to acknowledge anyone who lives by welfare, denies the legitimacy of the very state that provides that welfare, refuses to care for the education of his children and constantly produces new little headscarf-girls. This holds true for 70 percent of the Turkish and 90 percent of the Arab population in Berlin. (Sarrazin 2010b, 200)

He also remarked that there is "no other religion in Europe" that makes "so many demands" as does Islam: "No immigrant group other than Muslims is so strongly connected with claims on the welfare state and crime. No group emphasizes their differences so strongly in public, especially through women's clothing. In no other religion is the transition to violence, dictatorship and terrorism so fluid" (Sarrazin 2010a, 156). Surveys conducted after the publication of Sarrazin's book found that more than 50 percent of the general German population agreed with the author's political views and that 18 percent would vote for his party if he founded one.

Just two months after the book's release, conservative German chancellor Angela Merkel (a member of the Christian Democratic Union [CDU]) announced that multiculturalism and the idea of "happily living side-by-side has utterly failed" (*Economist* 2010). Her statements supported others made by the CDU's sister party, the Christian Social Union (CSU), which had previously announced that immigrants ought to assimilate into the German *Leitkultur*, the dominant culture rooted in Judeo-Christian, humanist, and Enlightenment principles, and that "multi-kulti is dead!" (*Spiegel Online* 2010).

While social science researchers have pointed to the structural difficulties that Turkish immigrants (and some other immigrant groups) face in German society, some public figures of Turkish origin have recently voiced their opinion in these debates, underlining and strengthening the notion that Turks are isolating themselves and live in "parallel societies" (Ateş 2005; Kelek 2005; Kelek 2006). Not surprisingly, the impact of these public figures speaking out against their own "countrymen" has given new weight and legitimacy to German politicians and policymakers who focus on immigrants' lack of willingness to integrate into German society (often referred to as the immigrants' "incompatibility" with German culture).[2]

While Sarrazin's book appeared after I had finished my research, the debate it sparked in the country and the attitudes toward immigrants it exposed are reflective of the context in which this ethnography took place. The young men that I discuss in this book grew up in Germany in the 1990s as the sons of former guest workers. As children and adolescents, they faced problems stemming from long-standing prejudices against foreigners in Germany, and as young adults their problems were compounded by the severe anti-Muslim sentiment common in many European states in the wake of September 11, 2001 (Open Society Justice Initiative 2009). It is at the intersection of their status as descendants of guest workers and their status as Muslims that the young men have had to create their own place within German society and develop a sense of identity and belonging.

Very often, the young men referred to situations in which they had experienced discrimination based on their ethnic background. Their personal experiences are supported by several studies that demonstrate that compared with other Westerners, Germans are less accepting of their foreign population (see, e.g., Lynch and Simon 2002; Legge 2003; Panayi 2000). Italians[3] and Jews are the most likely immigrant groups to be accepted in Germany, whereas Germans tend to be least accepting of Moroccans, Turks, and individuals from the former Yugoslavia (Legge 2003; Keskin 2002). For a long time, the German government stressed that the former guest workers recruited after World War II should not stay and settle in Germany, and that they were expected to leave the country. As such, the German educational system, formal economy, communities, and government stakeholders were largely unprepared to integrate the children of guest workers, and programs that could have helped such integration were largely non-existent.

Even after it was clear that the families of former guest workers were not leaving, the German government did not change its rhetoric on immigration. Instead, the political rhetoric, reflected in official statements and citizenship law, made it very clear that Germany did not intend to recognize the foreigners living in the country as people who would stay (Geissler 2007; Bommes 2004). The unmistakable message to foreign workers, their children, and their grandchildren was that they were not wanted (Green 2001, 31).

In 1998, German politicians began to acknowledge that Germany finally had to come to terms with the fact that the foreigners who had lived in the country for generations intended to stay and that better strategies were needed for their integration. One significant turning point was the reform of citizenship law, which now allows the children of long-term immigrants to be granted citizenship at birth. However, the official rhetoric toward immigrants is still less inclusive than in traditionally immigration-heavy countries such as the United States or Canada. For example, instead of referring to these people as "immigrants," German newspapers and officials tend to use the term "foreigners." The continuing and derogatory use of this term may have serious effects on the self-identification of immigrants living in the country, as it continuously sends the message that they are seen as belonging elsewhere (even as, ironically, Germany expects them to assimilate). Reflecting this view, official citizenship statistics in Germany compress all individuals into two categories: native Germans and foreigners. Anyone who does not have German citizenship falls into the foreigner category, which even includes third-generation immigrants who were born, raised, and educated in Germany. Another commonly used term for these individuals is "migrants." This term highlights the perception of immigrants as people who are still moving around and have not settled yet, as opposed to people who are in a country to stay. Again, this demonstrates the persistent opinion that former guest workers and other foreigners are not really German, whether or not they hold citizenship.

Has the official shift in political rhetoric at the beginning of the new millennium significantly changed Germany's integration efforts? I argue that Germany remains unsure of how to integrate its large immigrant population. In an effort to highlight the most important aspects of this context, this chapter will provide a brief overview of the social, political, and legal dimensions of immigration in Germany by examining: (a) the history of Germany's recruitment of guest workers, (b) the immigration and integration debates today, (c) immigrants' chances of success in the German school system and formal economy, and (d) crime rates among immigrant populations in Germany. It also provides some context about the neighborhood in which the ethnographic study took place.

GUEST WORKER HISTORY—THE YOUNG MEN'S ROOTS IN GERMANY

Guest-worker systems are not a new phenomenon, nor are they unique to Germany.[4] Economically well-established countries have always acted as "pull countries" for workers from economically less well-established "push countries" (Schönwälder 2006, 13). The German guest-worker system, however, was markedly different than others, because Germany was only interested in developing a workforce and never intended the guest workers to settle permanently (Bade 1996; Brubaker 2001; Heckmann 1981). Germany, unlike other immigration-heavy countries such as the United States and Canada, never conferred the status of immigrants on its guest workers (Brubaker 1992, 33; Gerdes and Faist 2006).

For a long time, Germany's citizenship law was almost exclusively based on the *ius sanguinis* principle, which allowed those with German blood to become citizens but made it nearly impossible for anyone else to obtain citizenship. In effect, German citizenship was defined along ethnic lines as a "community of descent" based on language, cultural values, and cultural norms (Koopmans 1999, 630). In contrast to the status of immigrants in states that adopt the *ius soli* principle, which is prevalent in all major

immigration countries and grants citizenship on the basis of birthright, neither guest workers nor their children, even if born on German soil, were permitted citizenship (Diehm and Radtke 1999, 9). Obtaining citizenship was
merely a theoretical option, and many observers agree that immigrants in
Germany were treated as second-class citizens (Brubaker 1992, 2; Hagedorn
2001, 11–12; Hansen and Weil 2001, 7; Koopmans 1999, 629–31; Panayi
2000, 260; Ostergaard-Nielsen 2003, 109; Schierup, Hansen, and Castles
2006, 154–55). In reality, in the early 1990s fewer foreigners were granted
citizenship in Germany than in any other European country (Koopmans
1999, 631–33). Castles (1985, 529) described German citizenship law
as "institutional discrimination" through which guest workers could be
recruited, controlled, and sent away, as the interests of capital dictated.

The interests of capital were very strong in the mid-1950s, when the
German economy was booming and unemployment was at an all-time
low. Simultaneously, the building of the Berlin Wall stopped the recruitment of workers from the former German Democratic Republic (East
Germany), so West Germany entered into treaties with several countries, including Italy (1955), Greece and Spain (1960), Turkey (1961),
Morocco (1963), Portugal (1964), Tunisia (1965), and the former
Yugoslavia (1968). The recruitment program steadily increased: 85,000
workers came to Germany in 1959, and by 1964, the one-millionth
guest worker had arrived. To guarantee that labor demands were met,
Germany ran 500 to 600 recruitment offices in the treaty countries
listed previously (Cohn-Bendit 1991, 99).

So what did the guest workers on the one hand and Germany on the
other hope to achieve when entering into a mutual agreement? Coming
from economically burdened countries, the guest workers that traveled to
Germany dreamed of earning fast money, which was often impossible in
their own countries of origin. Germany wanted guest workers for several
reasons. Along with enjoying the economic benefits of guest workers and
the fact that they took on jobs in which Germans were generally less interested (Edathy 2000, 17), Germany also used guest workers to boost public confidence and live up to its historic promise of responsibility toward
foreigners (Schönwälder 2006, 115). Evidence indicates that by acting as
a political educator—specifically, by showing guest workers the merits of
the Western system—the German government hoped to take preventive
measures against communism (as discussed by Minister of Labour Theodor
Blank and BDA [Bundesvereinigung deutscher Arbeitgeberverbände,
the nongovernmental German association of labor relations] president
Siegfried Balke in Schönwälder 2006 and Bundesvereinigung deutscher
Arbeitgeberverbände 1962).

While the original idea was for guest workers to accumulate money and return to their country of origin, this did not happen. German politicians tend to act as if the government was oblivious to the fact that many guest workers would stay in the country and settle. However, evidence indicates that the government of the time was well aware that the rapid increase in guest workers would eventually lead to family migration. Numbers released in 1968 revealed that more than 50 percent of all male guest workers had already been in Germany for more than four years—41 percent of these with their wives and children (Bundesanstalt für Arbeit 1969, 48ff.). A 1972 study reported that 21 percent of all guest workers had arrived in Germany more than seven years before, and an additional 12 percent had been in Germany for five to seven years.

The government's awareness of this trend is exemplified by Germany's attempt to strike a treaty with Turkey in 1961, in which it tried to restrict family migration and limit permanent residency to no more than two years. However, before this treaty could ever take effect, the BDA advocated against it. From an employer's perspective, it did not make sense to send skilled workers back home and replace them with new, unskilled workers. In 1964, a revised treaty was signed with Turkey that placed no restrictions on immigrants' length of stay or family migration (Schönwälder 2001, 215–16). After 1964, Germany made several attempts to establish a system of forced rotation among guest workers, but all of these attempts failed for one reason or another (see Triadafilopolous 2006, 9–11.). For example, insisting on a forced rotation system and forcing guest workers to leave after a certain period of time would have significantly harmed Germany's reputation in the Western world, which the country was carefully trying to rebuild after World War II.

Without its guest workers, Germany would have likely never attained its powerful economic position after the war, a fact on which the young men in this book commented quite often. They felt that their parents, who had worked very hard in Germany and contributed to its rebuilding in the postwar era, deserved much better and less discriminating treatment by the country and its population. Indeed, their perception that their parents weren't treated appropriately factored into their decision to deal drugs: they did not want to end up like their parents and work physically challenging jobs that would pay very little and receive no recognition.

Along with helping to rebuild the country, guest workers acted as a significant source of fiscal relief for Germany: as late as 1972, 83 percent of the Turkish population in Germany was legally employed and paying into Germany's elaborate social insurance system (Sen and Goldberg 1994, 27).[5] At no point, however, did Germany's immigration and integration policies reflect the economic importance of the guest workers. As such, the guest-worker system was "purposefully designed to facilitate the exploitation of guest workers while guarding against their social incorporation"; guest workers "served as a cheap and expendable 'reserve army,' used to fuel economic expansion in good times and discarded with impunity during downturns" (Triadafilopolous and Schönwälder 2006, 4; see also Bade 1984; Oltmer 2005). By 1973, Germany had 2.6 million guest workers, and the social–liberal government of Germany issued a "recruitment stop." Officially, this action was justified by the oil crisis and the subsequent recession (Green 2001, 26), but unofficially, the government had become increasingly worried that guest workers would stay in Germany permanently. With no plans in place to handle immigration, the costs associated with educating the second generation of immigrants and expanding the social insurance and health care systems were seen as too great. The German government therefore wanted to halt guest-worker migration (Schönwälder 2006, 254).

The recruitment stop temporarily reduced the number of foreigners living in Germany. Many former guest workers returned to their countries of origin, but around three million chose to stay and brought their families to Germany over the following years (Castles 1985, 520). The stop had some unintended consequences, however, as it completely changed the ethnic composition of the former guest-worker population. Former guest workers of Italian, Spanish, and Greek background were highly likely to return to their countries of origin, whereas a disproportionate number of Turkish and Yugoslavian former guest workers stayed and brought their family members to Germany (Castles and Miller 1998, 189). If they returned to Turkey, former Turkish guest workers faced the risk of not being allowed to reenter Germany. In contrast, as EU members, former guest workers of Italian, Spanish, Greek, and Portuguese background could return to their countries of origin knowing that they could reenter Germany at any time. Consequently, a greater number of former Turkish guest workers decided to stay in Germany than did any other group. In 1970, the Turkish population in Germany was just below 500,000; by 1984, that number had increased to 1.5 million, and a 1984 poll reported that 83 percent of all Turks living in Germany indicated that they would not consider returning to Turkey (Goldberg and Sen 1996, 3).

To reduce the number of foreigners living in the country, Germany also implemented a reward system from October 1983 to September 1984. Every "foreigner willing to return [to his or her country of origin] permanently" was rewarded with 10,500 Deutsche Marks and an additional 1,500 Deutsche Marks for each child he or she had. In return, families had to commit to return to their home country indefinitely, without the option of coming back to Germany. At the same time, they had to forfeit all pension rights (they were reimbursed for their own contributions but were denied any employer contributions). Overall, 250,000 former guest workers returned to their country of origin. Some of the extended family members of the young men in this book made use of this possibility and were subsequently not allowed to reenter the country permanently. Only about 27,800 new foreigners came to Germany in 1983, and only 14,400 came in 1984. Thus, the reward system did reduce the number of foreigners in Germany for a short period of time, but because it was only in place for one year, it had no lasting effect (Sen and Goldberg 1994, 23).

None of the guest workers, or their children, who stayed in the country received citizenship. In the 1970s, only 0.3 to 0.4 percent of the total foreign population residing in Germany was granted citizenship (Green 2001, 31). At that time, 3.9 million guest workers had lived in Germany for longer than ten years (the minimum number of years required for naturalization). Applications were successful only if foreigners could clearly demonstrate that they had assimilated willingly and permanently into German culture ("freiwillige und dauerhafte Hinwendung zum Deutschtum"; see Einbürgerungsrichtlinien 1977). Involvement in any form of ethnic or emigration organization was seen as a criterion for denial of citizenship. Moreover, according to immigration law, citizenship could only be granted for the public interest, not for personal interest. This meant, for example, that it was very easy for top-performing athletes to become German, whereas the average immigrant who could not represent Germany in the World Cup or the Olympics had a much harder time. As such, the entire history of the guest-worker system and the subsequent immigration rules sent an "implicit signal to the immigrant population that they were not wanted as Germans" (Green 2001, 31).[6]

CONTEMPORARY POLICIES OF IMMIGRATION AND INTEGRATION

A 2010 study published by the Friedrich Ebert Foundation—a large German research organization—reported that more than 30 percent of the German population has negative feelings about immigrants living in the country and that about 35 percent of the population believes that most immigrants come to Germany to exploit the social welfare system. Interestingly, Germans identify family members of former guest workers as the individuals most guilty of these activities.

Despite its exclusionary approach and sentiments toward immigrants, Germany has had a large immigrant population since World War II. In 2010, Germany's foreign population was 6.75 million, about 8.8 percent of its total population of 82 million. The foreign population includes anyone residing in Germany without German citizenship, regardless of whether or not he or she was born in Germany.[7] Of these 6.75 million, about one-fifth were born in Germany; among these, Turks comprise the largest group (30.2 percent). The overall percentage of immigrants in Germany has remained relatively unchanged since 1994 (Bundesamt für Migration und Flüchtlinge 2011, 99). Overall, the largest groups of immigrants are those of Turkish background (24.1 percent), followed by Italians (7.7 percent), Poles (6.2 percent), and Greeks (4.1 percent). Moroccans and Kosovo Albanians—both relevant ethnic groups in the context of this book—comprise less than 1 percent of the immigrant population in Germany.

The families of former guest workers are now often viewed as the problem group in German integration debates. Given the absence of early integration plans by the German government, the first generation remains fairly segregated within German society. German politicians and the general public often perceive this segregation as a lack of willingness to assimilate and integrate—often overlooking the history of the guest-worker system or structural forces that keep immigrants confined to the lowest strata of the socio-economic ladder. The children of these guest workers constitute a group that Germany has been largely unprepared to integrate. However, despite not fully adopting German culture and beliefs, the children of the first generation—including the young men in this book—also have not fulfilled the expectations of their parents. Having been socialized in Germany (even if not into the mainstream), they have clearly moved away from their parents' culture. In this respect, many of them do not belong to either culture: they have been born and raised in Germany but lack both citizenship and the ties their parents hold to their home country.[8]

German political parties long debated reforming the citizenship laws to make it easier for former guest workers and their families to acquire citizenship, but reforms did not take place until 2000 (Hagedorn 2001, 204).[9,10] The question of dual citizenship proved problematic and provoked public debate. Polls indicated that more than 70 percent of all former guest workers would apply for German citizenship if they could retain their other citizenship (Bundesministerium für Arbeit und Sozialforschung 1996, 422; Goldberg and Sen 1996, 13; Neumann 1998). These debates were, and still are, framed in the context of loyalty: the conservative CDU and CSU and the liberal Free Democratic Party (FDP) often argue that individuals cannot play for two different teams, have two different religions, or be married to two different spouses. The topic was even the focus of election campaigns (the CDU won the state election in Hessen in 1999 using the slogan "Yes, to integration, no to dual citizenship"). At the same time, in 2000, a petition circulated by the CDU/CSU collected five million signatures from German citizens protesting dual citizenship. The leader of the CSU stated that dual citizenship was more dangerous to Germany than the terrorist organization Red Army Faction had been in the 1970s and 1980s (*Sueddeutsche Zeitung* 1999). Therefore, the 2000 citizenship reforms did not include any changes with regard to dual citizenship, except that children born in Germany who qualified for German citizenship could hold dual citizenship until the age of 23, at which point they would have to choose between citizenships or automatically lose their German citizenship.

The citizenship reforms of 2000 made it much easier for immigrants to become German citizens. Today, the children of immigrants automatically receive German citizenship if one of their parents has resided in Germany for at least eight years and has had an unlimited resident permit for at least three years.[11] Before 2000, immigrants could theoretically become German citizens based on the discretion of a single official; decisions did not have to be justified or explained, making it virtually impossible for anyone to understand why his or her application was denied or accepted (Hagedorn 2001, 24). Obviously, applicants had to fulfill certain requirements, such as having resided in Germany for at least fifteen years (or, for young adults aged 16 to 23, for at least eight years), having no police record, and being willing to give up their current citizenship.[12]

While the citizenship reforms have brought about significant changes for foreigners who were born in Germany, they have not affected the young men discussed in this book. These men were all born before 2000, and the new laws do not apply to them. So despite the changes in political rhetoric and the citizenship laws, the young men are still stuck in a void.

Public discussions on the integration of Turkish immigrants into German society are largely dominated by culturalist ideas, stressing that the Turkish and German cultures are hard to combine and tending to highlight the country's unwillingness to integrate Turkish immigrants. Accordingly, Turkish immigrants (or at least those who *look* Turkish; whether or not they are actually Turkish is a different question) are supposed to adapt to the core principles and beliefs of German society. In the German context, assimilation is often seen as a prerequisite for integration; in other words, immigrants are expected to fully adopt German values, core principles, and beliefs in order to be fully integrated. However, public debates often lead to discussions about how the religious and national identity of Turks tends to "get in the way" of assimilation and thus integration. Debates on immigrants quickly become debates on Turks in Germany, and debates on Turks are almost always associated with debates about Islam.

Islam is the second-largest religion in Germany after Christianity (Federal Statistical Office 2010), and the young men discussed in this book are mostly of Muslim background. In 2009, an estimated 4.3 million Muslims were born in Germany, 45 percent of whom were German nationals. In 2004, about 9 percent of all children born in Germany were born to Muslim parents. The vast majority of Muslims living in Germany are of Turkish ancestry (2.5 million)—in fact, more than 95 percent of all Muslims in Germany are of non-Arabic descent, and most Muslims (98 percent) live in the former West Germany or Berlin.[13] While many Muslims—including the young men in this book—are socially and economically excluded, this has less to do with the fact that they are a minority and more to do with the fact that Germans feel that the Muslim culture is incompatible with the Christian-based German culture.

One aspect that underlines this feeling is the fact that many second- and even third-generation immigrants do not marry German spouses, finding marriage partners among their own ethnic groups who are either living in Germany or brought over from their parents' country of origin. This tendency also applies to the young men in this book, who did not consider marrying outside of their own ethnic and religious group a valid possibility. Sociologically speaking, binational marriage can be seen as a sign of integration and is often considered to be the best indicator of assimilation in the German context (Familienbericht 2000, 201).[14] According to this indicator, even the second generation, being mostly married to Turks or Germans of Turkish origin, is very poorly integrated. Only 43 percent of all Turkish men living in Germany (compared to 63 percent of all Italian men and 72 percent of all Greek men) would view a marriage to a German woman as something positive, and only 50 percent of all Turkish parents living in Germany (compared with 90 percent of all Italian and Greek parents) would give their blessing if their child wanted to marry a German (Mehrländer et al. 1997, 23; Familienbericht 2000, 84). These numbers seem quite low, but it should also be noted that in a survey conducted in the late 1990s, only 15 percent of the West German and 7 percent of the East German population indicated that they would find it "acceptable" to have a Turkish family member (Koch and Wasmer 1997, 465). The few young men in this book who at some point during my research got married fall into this wider trend—they all got married to spouses of the same ethnic background as themselves (as did all the older brothers and friends who were not part of my sample yet were still present in the neighborhood).

In 2000, the Organisation for Economic Co-operation and Development (OECD) published its first international comparisons of students' school performance—the Programme for International Student Assessment (PISA). This report and every subsequent report makes it clear that second- and third-generation migrants and those from disadvantaged socio-economic backgrounds are significantly disadvantaged in the German school system (Organisation for Economic Co-operation and Development [OECD] 2006b, 9–10; OECD 2004, 14–15; Bundesministerium für Bildung und Forschung [BMBF] 2004, 79–80). In no other country is the difference in school performance so great between students from migrant backgrounds and students from non-migrant backgrounds (OECD 2006b, 175). Immigrant students who receive their entire school education in Germany perform even worse than first-generation immigrants who only receive part of their education in Germany. Generally speaking, the reading and writing skills of more than half of Grade 9 students with Turkish heritage do not exceed elementary school levels (Spiwak 2008). Furthermore, students in Germany with Turkish heritage or from a disadvantaged socio-economic background[15] are about one school year behind the same populations in the Swiss school system. Clearly, institutional disadvantages are at play for migrant students in the German system (OECD 2006b, 179).

The release of the first PISA results in 2000 sparked huge debates in the German public, media, and politics about the causes of and potential cures for the educational inequality, and think tanks at universities and other research institutions were asked to come up with solutions. Many factors that work against immigrant students were identified, including (1) Germany has no mandatory kindergarten system, so many students enter Grade 1 without ever being socialized in a German-speaking environment; (2) many immigrant families do not speak German at home, and language support is not available at all German schools; (3) elementary schools (where differences can be addressed and language skills can be improved) are notoriously underfunded, whereas the Gymnasium (the most advanced of all three high school streams) is the best-funded school form in the German system; and (4) Germany still streams children into three separate school forms at the age of 9, based on their grades from their third school year, essentially deciding their educational (and consequently economic) future at a very young age, since only children selected for the Gymnasium leave high school with a degree that will allow them to get a university education[16] Students whose first language is not German and who are only rarely exposed to a German-speaking environment before elementary school are generally unable to acquire the same language skills as their German counterparts by the age of 9. These students usually do not attain the grades needed to qualify for the *Gymnasium* stream. Finally, the German school system is still focused on half-days, with few after-school programs available. Students in elementary schools often finish at noon, putting the children of two working parents at a further disadvantage. Their middle-class German counterparts often enjoy structured afternoon programs (e.g., private music lessons and sports clubs), but children from lower socio-economic backgrounds are often left to themselves. As Rios (2011) points out in his study on marginalized boys in Los Angeles, what happens in between the end of school and bedtime is crucial, because it gives unsupervised children endless possibilities to "get into trouble." In Germany, children are left alone for even longer, because school often ends much earlier. While much money and time has gone into research to address the factors that put immigrant children at an educational disadvantage, the results of subsequent PISA assessments have not demonstrated significant improvements for students with an immigrant background.

In 1998, the German Council for Integration announced that more than 19.5 percent of all students from an immigrant background quit the German school system before earning a diploma. In contrast, only 7.9 percent of native-born students left the school system without earning a high school diploma (Lagebericht der Integrationsbeauftragten 2012, 159–60). While these numbers had improved to 15 percent and 6.2 percent, respectively, by 2008, they still show a stark overrepresentation of students with immigrant backgrounds. More importantly, the young men in this book have not been affected by these statistical improvements, as they all quit high school long before 2008. The official statistics for both 2005–06 and 2009–10 also show that most immigrant students are streamed into, and graduate from, the *Hauptschule*—the least advanced of the three possible school forms, qualifying graduates to learn a practical vocation such as cooking or construction. Forty-four percent of immigrant students were streamed into the Hauptschule in 2005–06 and 40 percent in 2009–10, compared to only 22 percent of German students in 2005–06 and 18 percent in 2009–10 (Lagebericht der Integrationsbeauftragten 2012, 671).

The young men in this study actually fared even worse than the average described here. Twenty-nine out of the 55 left school without a high school diploma, though ten of these managed to get their degree from the Hauptschule at a later point (through external courses or by going to evening school). Thirteen of the 55 graduated from the Hauptschule, and twelve graduated from the Realschule. Only Özgur managed to graduate from the Gymnasium. A degree from the Gymnasium is the prerequisite for attending college and university in Germany, graduating from the other two school forms only allow students to learn practical trade jobs (see chapter 2).

Many researchers have argued that discrimination toward immigrants does not stop in the school system but persists in the formal job market (Boos-Nuenning 2000; Faist 1995). Even immigrant students with good grades and degrees are at a significant disadvantage when trying to land a vocational training position (Boos-Nuenning 2000, 73; BMBF 2004). Male immigrants are disproportionately and increasingly disadvantaged. In 1993, around 82,000 male immigrants were placed in a vocational training position; in 2002, only 48,000 were successfully placed, despite the fact that the number of male immigrants had not decreased. According to the latest "integration report," 54 percent of all 20- to 24-year-olds (and 42 percent of all 25- to 30-year-olds) with immigrant backgrounds are "unqualified," that is, they have not received training in any profession (Spiwak 2008).

High school graduates with immigrant backgrounds seeking jobs and vocational training possibilities in Germany face three main obstacles. First, employers prefer to hire German applicants because they assume that hiring immigrants will bring about various problems. Customers might not accept them, leading business to decline, or they might be less likely to pass the theoretical portions of vocational training. Additionally, high school graduates with immigrant backgrounds lack the cultural capital that companies expect, and employers anticipate that this may interrupt the company climate (Boos-Nuenning 2000, 74). The second main barrier is that jobs and placements for vocational training are often arranged through informal circles, in which graduates with immigrant backgrounds are less likely to be included (Bommes 1996, 4). Finally, certain types of institutional discrimination are also at play. Many jobs are unattainable for graduates with immigrant backgrounds. For example, daycares are often run by churches that expect their employees to be of the same denomination—excluding Muslim applicants from the outset.

The young men in this book experienced these obstacles firsthand. Many of them never got invited to interview for the jobs for which they had applied. I was particularly stunned when Nermin received invitations for two interviews after having claimed that he was Italian as opposed to Moroccan. He had sent the exact same application documents to about 100 positions. On three of those applications, he claimed to be Italian and had a two out of three success rate, whereas he did not receive any invitations to interview for the over ninety jobs he applied to as a Moroccan. While the reader might think that this could have been a coincidence, it very much reflects the general experiences of the young men.

Unemployment numbers among immigrants in Germany are also disheartening. In 2004, the national unemployment rate was around 9 percent, but 20.5 percent of all immigrants were unemployed, with 72.5 percent of all unemployed immigrants (and 82 percent of all Turkish unemployed immigrants) being unskilled (Beauftragte der Bundesregierung für Migration, Flüchtlinge und Integration 2005, 83).[17] In the same year, 41 percent of all unemployed immigrants were younger than 35 (compared with 33 percent of all unemployed Germans).

Overall, these numbers come as no surprise. The streamed school system and the fact that socio-economic background is the single most important factor predicting educational outcome in Germany both work against immigrant students, who often come from lower socio-economic backgrounds, denying them the same starting points that their German counterparts enjoy (OECD 2006b, 9–10; OECD 2004, 14–15; BMBF 2004, 79–80). Prejudice against immigrants (with or without German citizenship) and preferences for hiring "real" Germans tend to do the rest of the damage. However, Germany has now recognized the problems within its school system and has shown a desire for reform. These reforms are complex, because the majority of the German population does not want to change the basic principles of the German educational landscape (i.e., streaming and non-mandatory kindergarten). Changes to these foundational principles would go against core German beliefs that good students will not receive an appropriate education when they must share a classroom with weaker students (despite OECD studies showing that the most successful countries, like Finland and Canada, do not stream students) and that mothers have the right to raise children as long as possible,[18] so kindergarten should not be mandatory. (For the young men in this book, this latter belief meant that only about half had attended a kindergarten program before entering Grade 1.)

Unfortunately, the current system works strongly against the possibility of improving the social integration of immigrants—ironically so, considering that a lack of social integration and assimilation is at the core of public debates like the one sparked by Thilo Sarrazin. Not surprisingly, the lack of social integration has also been linked to crime and violence, a subject that consistently generates great concern in discussions about immigrants in Germany.

The young men discussed in this book are deeply involved in the drug market, an area for which specific data are not readily available. However, research in the general area of immigration and crime has overwhelmingly shown that contrary to public perception, no positive relationships can be found between first-generation[19] immigrants and crime, or between immigration in general and crime. Interestingly, if a relationship appears between immigrants and crime or immigration and crime, it tends to be a negative one (Sampson 2008; Wadsworth 2010; Bucerius 2011). In all countries with available data, first-generation immigrants are less involved in crime than are native-born citizens. This finding also holds true for Germany, but Germany differs from the United States and Canada when it comes to the second generation. In the United States and Canada, second-generation immigrants continue to have lower (or equal) crime levels than native-born citizens (Hagan et al. 2007); in Germany, second-generation crime rates drastically exceed those for non-immigrant Germans. At first glance, however, these generational differences in German crime statistics are not obvious and paint a general picture of immigrant criminality without attending to generational differences and other measurement problems.

German police data show, for example, that non-Germans are suspected of crimes about twice as often as their German counterparts (Bundesministerium des Innern 2005, 13–15) and that foreign young adults are more often suspected of crimes that they did not commit than are native-born young adults (Walter and Trautmann 2003, 73–74). Being registered as a crime suspect in police statistics does not, of course, prove whether or not a crime has actually been committed. Many suspects are registered without ever having committed a crime. It becomes problematic, however, when police statistics based on crime suspects are used to show that foreigners commit more crimes than Germans—a very common practice in the German context.

As with other official statistics on Germany's population, Germany's official crime statistics (*polizeiliche Kriminalitätsstatistiken* [PKS]) only distinguish between Germans (citizens) and foreigners (non-citizens). Non-citizens are lumped together into one category regardless of ethnic background or length of time in the country. Even second- or third-generation immigrants are classified as foreigners if they do not have German citizenship, whereas recent immigrants who successfully obtained citizenship before immigrating are classified as Germans.

The use of German police crime statistics to measure criminal involvement is highly problematic and tends to overstress the criminal involvement of immigrants (Drewniak 2004). Official crime statistics for "crimes by foreigners" include not only crimes committed by non-citizens living in Germany but also crimes committed by tourists or transients (who naturally do not appear in the population census data). Moreover, some criminal offenses, such as immigration offenses, can only be committed by immigrants who lack citizenship. These factors and peculiarities serve to exaggerate the picture of criminal involvement of immigrants in Germany, further strengthening stereotypes and exclusionary rhetoric.

Equally problematic, German research has demonstrated that a victim's willingness to report a crime is significantly higher if the perpetrator is perceived as an immigrant or a group of immigrants (Wilmers et al. 2002; Mansel 2003). German labeling studies suggest that the chances of correctly identifying an actual perpetrator are two to three times higher when the perpetrator is non-German (Mansel and Albrecht 2003). Ethnic profiling and intensified police monitoring in immigrant communities also increase the likelihood of immigrants being overrepresented in the crime statistics of any country. As with findings from the United States, German research has found that convicted immigrants face more severe sanctions than their German counterparts (Pfeiffer, Kleimann, and Petersen 2005, 77–78).

The German public has been led to believe that crime has been rising over the past few decades, and that foreign offending has increased by 50 percent (Pfeiffer, Windizo, and Kleimann 2004). However, official crime statistics tell quite a different story: crimes committed by foreigners comprised 33.6 percent of all crimes committed in 1993, 22.5 percent of all crimes in 2005, and 21.9 percent of all crimes in 2010 (Pfeiffer, Windizo, and Kleimann 2004; Polizeiliche Kriminalstatistik 2010, 5). Additionally, the number of crimes committed by foreign children under the age of 13 and youths aged 14 to 18 and 18 to 21 has been declining steadily since 1993 (Bundesministerium des Innern 2006, 16). The only crimes for which rates have been increasing among foreign 14- to 18-year-olds are violence (for which rates also increased among their German counterparts) and property damage (17).

When distinguishing between immigrant generations in self-report studies, second- and third-generation immigrants indicate, on average, that they have been more involved in crime than first-generation immigrants and German natives. First-generation immigrants, on the other hand, indicate, on average, lower involvement in crime than both the second and third generations and the native-born population (Walter and Trautmann 2003). Self-report questionnaires of high school students generally indicate that some ethnic groups, including Turks, are disproportionately engaged in crime.[20]

German scholars have offered various explanations of why more violence is seen among young adults of foreign background, ranging from friendship networks, disadvantaged neighborhood settings, media consumption, racism, and discrimination to increased exposure to violence in the family setting.[21] Certainly, many of these factors can be seen at play when reading about the lives of the young men in this book and trying to understand why they started to deal drugs as opposed to staying in school and learning a profession or, for those who did stay in school and did learn a profession, why they didn't continue to work in their trade. Some of the explanations German scholars have offered for the increased prevalence of violence seemed less important among these young men. For example, their media consumption was astonishingly low—the community youth center had a TV that was almost never on, and the young men rarely talked about TV shows or video games. The Internet was not yet prevalent during the time of my research. Also, the neighborhood in which these young men grew up was not disadvantaged, although the young men were certainly part of a disadvantaged social environment *within* a mixed-income neighborhood. Their social capital did not allow them to forge links to mainstream society, leaving them confined to their disadvantaged situation. Other factors, such as having friends who engage in violence or experiences of discrimination and racism, played a tremendous role in the lives and life choices of the young men in this study.

DRUG LAWS IN GERMANY

If the annual press conference held by Germany's drug commissioner Mechthild Dyckman in November 2012 was any indication of how much the press and public cares about Germany's war on drugs, it would be safe to say that there seems to be very little interest. The thirty-minute press conference was attended by no more than twenty or thirty largely unenthusiastic journalists, who learned that cannabis is still the most consumed drug in Germany and that the country spends an estimated US\$4.8 to \$6 billion per year to fight for a drug-free country, a task involving law enforcement officers, prosecutors, and judges (Hardinghaus 2013). In comparison, estimates of what the US spends on its war on drugs every year range from US\$40 billion on the low end to well over US\$100 billion.

As in most Western countries, harder drugs like cocaine and heroin are illegal in Germany. The possession, sale, transport, and cultivation of cannabis products—the substance that most of the young men in this study sold—are also illegal (and have been since the country's first narcotic law was enacted in 1972). However, consumption itself is legal and falls under the category of "self-harm." This distinction is quite ironic: obviously, it is hard to legally smoke marijuana if possessing and cultivating marijuana are illegal. After all, how can an individual obtain the marijuana that he or she can legally smoke? Essentially, these laws mean that an individual is complying with the legal framework if he smokes a joint that someone else is holding for him.

In the 1990s, the laws around cannabis possession were relaxed, and Section 31a of the Narcotics Act (Betäubungsmittelgesetz) allowed prosecutors to drop charges in cases that deal with "small amounts." The question of what constitutes a small amount in Germany depends on the *Bundesland* (state). In the most liberal states, like Berlin, the threshold is 15 grams (0.5 ounces); in the most conservative ones, like Bavaria, it is 6 grams (0.2 ounces). In Hessen, the state in which the young men of this study lived and did their business, the possession of amounts up to 6 grams is generally not prosecuted. Prosecutors have the option to drop charges for the possession of 6 to 15 grams of cannabis and for the possession of even larger amounts of marijuana. Similarly, the laws allow prosecutors to drop charges for the possession of small amounts of cocaine and heroin, the other two substances that the young men dealt. In Hessen, charges are usually dropped for crimes involving the possession of 0.15 grams of pure cocaine or heroin (which is equivalent to about 1 gram of cocaine or heroin cut for selling purposes).[22]

Even when charges are dropped, the police still have to write a report (which takes time), and the prosecutor is still required to initiate the proceeding, read the file, and eventually drop the charges. The offender is still required to appear before the court even if the charges are being dropped, thus leaving a paper trail and essentially being criminalized, though not charged. For the young men in this study, who have had to appear in court several times for the possession of small amounts of drugs, this practice underscores their impression that "nothing ever happens." Despite not facing charges, however, the young men are still registered in the system every time they are caught with small amounts.

FRANKFURT, BOCKENHEIM

Frankfurt is one of the most multicultural cities in Germany. It is known internationally as Germany's financial hub and as having one of the largest airports in the world; however, the city is not that large compared to other German cities. In 2009, Frankfurt had a population of just under

700,000, and 24 percent of the population were foreign nationals (i.e., living in Germany yet not having German citizenship—a label that could be applied to first-, second-, or third-generation immigrants), about one-quarter of whom were younger than 25 (Bürgeramt, Statistik und Wahlen 2011, 20, 30). Of Frankfurt's German nationals, 13.1 percent had a history of immigration (i.e., they have an immigrant background but have acquired German citizenship).[23] Demographics in Frankfurt differ somewhat from those of other German cities in general. Turks comprise the largest group of foreigners (18.4 percent), followed by Croatians (7.1 percent), Serbians (5.9 percent), Moroccans (3.5 percent), Russians (1.4 percent), and Albanians (0.1 percent) (Bürgeramt, Statistik, and Wahlen 2011, 40).

Bockenheim's population is approximately 35,000 residents and has a slightly higher than average percentage of immigrants compared to Frankfurt overall. As described in the introduction, it is a mixed-income neighborhood and, for many, one of the most desirable neighborhoods in the city. Its centrality (it is just 1.9 miles away from the downtown core), its many cafés, restaurants, and bars, and the fact that it is home to one of Germany's biggest universities make it a very vibrant neighborhood. Bockenheim has several sport fields and park areas, and because the neighborhood is popular among university students and faculty, it has a very active street life, with many people sitting out on café and restaurant patios in the summer until late at night. Outdoor life is especially characteristic of the neighborhood—I was always astonished by how much was happening on the streets and in public places, even in the colder winter months. I believe that both the proximity of the university and the walkability of the neighborhood play a huge role in encouraging this activity, making the neighborhood feel like an extended campus whose students frequent its many businesses.

Because it is a popular place to live, Bockenheim has a very established infrastructure in terms of transportation, shopping, and health care. A very elaborate subway, tram, and bus system connects it to the rest of the city, and it contains several big grocery stores, bakeries, and specialty food stores, as well as pharmacies and drug stores, a few corner stores, gift shops, bookstores, and copy centers. There are two hospitals and several clinics, doctors' offices, daycares, and preschools, as well as three primary and four secondary schools. The housing mainly consists of three-, four-, and five-story apartment buildings and a few residential family homes. There are no high rises in the neighborhood.

Crime statistics in Frankfurt are not broken down by neighborhood; however, as a city, crime rates are very high. Although several studies have reported that Frankfurt has the highest crime rate of any German city, it should be noted that visa crimes committed at the Frankfurt airport—the biggest airport not only in Germany but in all of Europe—are included in the city's crime rates. In other words, many of the crimes committed in Frankfurt are committed by people who never actually enter the country, let alone the city. Because many credit card companies and banks are located in Frankfurt, the financial hub of Germany, financial crime rates are also particularly high.

No specific data about drug-dealing crimes in the city are available, but Frankfurt, along with Hamburg, has a well-known drug scene, with city-funded safe injection sites and needle exchange programs. Many studies of drug consumers have reported that addicts, particularly heavy users of heroin and crack, will travel great distances to purchase drugs in Frankfurt, which is known as the "go-to" place for drugs. Like any large city, Frankfurt has local drug markets in most neighborhoods, which are mostly serviced by immigrant youth such as the young men discussed in this book.

As in many American cities, the influx of crack in the early 1990s changed the drug scene in Frankfurt in significant ways. Research shows that violence increased significantly (Dörrlamm 2004), and stakeholders, as well as users, working in the open drug market at the main train station claimed that the overall atmosphere changed from a very "communal" feeling to more of an "individualistic" one that was often infused with violence (Langer, Behr, and Hess 2004). The scene before the 1990s was dominated by heroin users, who could last several hours or even days before looking for their next hit. Crack users, on the other hand, more or less look for the next "stone" immediately, a tendency that transformed the drug market into a space where transactions are much more rushed, chaotic, and potentially dangerous.

During this period of change in the 1990s, the older brothers and cousins of the young men in this study dominated the local drug market in Bockenheim. Significant changes in the drug trade began not only with the influx of crack, but also with the formation of immigrant youth gangs in response to the emergence of neo-Nazi groups after Germany's reunification in 1990. The very slow responses to these developments by law enforcement did not help halt either of these shifts. The "older generation," as the young men in this book refer to their older brothers and cousins, essentially took greater risks in the drug market for a few years before law enforcement started to seriously clamp down on them. Many of the members of the older generation were incarcerated or deported, which is one reason why the young men in this book have seriously changed the way they conduct their business.

CONCLUSION: THE IMPACT OF MACRO-LEVEL POLICIES ON MICRO-LEVEL ACTIVITIES

Permanently labeled as "foreigners," "migrants," and "Turks," the young men in this study unsurprisingly feel excluded from opportunities to receive a good education, find good jobs, and participate in political life. They feel that Germany has denied them an "official sense of belonging" through the restrictive citizenship laws that were in place when they were growing up. They repeatedly told stories about Germans treating their families like "dirt" and about mainstream German society discriminating against them and their loved ones. These experiences are probably not unique to the young men in this book—yet not all immigrants exposed to discrimination choose to commit crimes. In fact, most do not (Bucerius 2011). It is fair to say, then, that the young men actively chose to participate in the drug trade, even though such an activity not only conflicted with the law but also went against many of their religious and cultural beliefs and backgrounds. In the following chapters, I will describe in detail how the larger social forces described in this chapter shape the everyday lives of these young men.

CHAPTER 2

"I Am a Bockenheimer"

Social Exclusion and Local Identification

I know this district better than the pockets of my pants. I know every fucking street, every corner, every bar, every waiter, every cop, I know which dog shits at which corner—there is just nobody who knows Bockenheim as well as we do, believe me.

—Erol

For eight months, I had worked to build a trusting relationship with Akin, often believing that we would never get there. I was therefore somewhat surprised when he called me one morning to come out and meet with him. The phone conversation had been brief. "Bullock,[1] you want to know how I do shit, right? Come and meet me at two at the subway station." So here I was.

I was in for an emotional rollercoaster ride. I was standing at the Bockenheimer Warte (a public place in the neighborhood with a café and a farmers' market), waiting for Akin, who had promised to take me along to a drug deal. This was the first such opportunity for me, and I flip-flopped between being happy about the chance to finally observe Akin's business firsthand and being nervous because I had no clue what to expect. What if the police paid closer attention to Akin today?

Akin showed up a few minutes late and greeted me with: "Bullock, you're not going to chicken out, are you?"

I replied: "No, of course not. So . . . what are we doing?"

I learned that Akin was about to deliver 100 grams (about 3.6 ounces) of marijuana to two of his regular customers. Noticing that Akin had no backpack on him, I wondered where he was keeping the stash. Clearly, the amount was too large to be carried in the pockets of his jeans. Noticing my confusion, he looked at me, half-amused, half-serious, and said, "Wait and learn."

Akin and I walked over to a newspaper kiosk where the young men often bought cigarettes. We entered the little store and, as expected, Akin bought cigarettes and a Turkish newspaper. He made small talk with the kiosk owner, chatting about their days, the weather, and the brand-new bakery in Bockenheim that no one seemed to like. After a few minutes of chatting, we left the kiosk and Akin suggested that we have a drink on the patio of a café close by.

I agreed, though I was beginning to get a little impatient. I did not know what exactly we were going to do, and Akin seemed to have all the time in the world, running errands and having drinks. As we sat down, I asked him, "So, you gotta tell me what the procedure is here . . .. Are we meeting this guy on the patio?"

Akin laughed. "Bullock, I am taking you along for the first time, and you are already missing what's happening. You gotta pay closer attention!"

I was perplexed. I had literally been next to Akin for the past ten minutes and had not seen anything closely resembling a drug transaction between him and a customer.

Akin now picked up his phone, typing a quick text message to someone. He turned to me, saying, "In a few minutes, you will see a cab. Watch that cab."

Sure enough, a cab came, and two young guys got in. The cab drove off.

I said to Akin, "You have to explain. . . . I really am too dumb to get this."

He laughed and said, "Deal done, Bullock, deal done. You have lots to learn."

I learned that Akin's regular customers had delivered their money for the purchase to the lady at the newspaper kiosk. The great weather she had talked about was an agreed-upon code for "Everything is paid for." Akin had then texted Haldun, a young man from the older generation who had become a cab driver. Haldun had the 100 grams of marijuana in the trunk of his cab and would pass it to the two customers after their ride.

While I had completely missed that the kiosk owner had hidden an envelope of money in the newspaper he had handed to Akin and did not understand how the two young men knew which cab to get into, I quickly learned just how closely connected young men in Bockenheim are. Their often-repeated statement "We *are* Bockenheim" made much more sense to me when I reflected on how different business owners seemed to work in close accord with the young men through a series of highly choreographed interactions. It took me some time to fully understand how the business owners benefited (obviously, they got a cut from the deals and the young men's continued business), but even this early on in my research, I gained the impression that part of the young men's success in the drug market was dependent on the strong relationships and connections they had established in Bockenheim. These relationships and the sense of belonging they fostered in young people like Akin and Aissa also made Bockenheim, in many respects, a place of refuge within what was commonly perceived to be a xenophobic nation (Panayi 2000; Hagedorn 2001).

While the young men held their neighborhood in high regard and constantly stressed that identifying with their locale was not the same as identifying with Germany, they also encountered negative experiences in Bockenheim. Many of their experiences of discrimination (e.g., encounters with the police or experiences while attending local schools) happened in the neighborhood. Because their life in Bockenheim was not just rosy and the young men experienced the world outside of Bockenheim as excluding and negative, it would be tempting to assume that the young men in this book took up their place in the informal economy because of weak social integration. However, the story isn't that simple: while some disadvantaged immigrants engage in crime, other similarly disadvantaged immigrants do not.[2]

While the young men turned to the drug trade, most of their immigrant parents were employed in the formal economy, trying to advance while doing everything in their power to avoid conflict with the law. This scenario is part of a more common generational phenomenon among immigrants in all Western countries. For reasons that are still up for debate, the crime rates of second-generation immigrants are higher than those of first-generation immigrants (Tonry 1997).[3] The increase in crime rates of second-generation immigrants suggests that not only weak social integration but also assimilation may enhance criminal involvement. This is commonly known as the *paradox of assimilation*—the more immigrants assimilate, the worse they do on many levels, especially those related to health and crime.[4] Even so, these factors alone cannot capture the complexity of the experiences described by the young men in this book.

Another way to explain the increase in crime rates among second-generation immigrants more generally is these individuals' lack of a consciously decided immigration experience. Second-generation immigrants may not be as determined to obey the laws of the new country as members of the first generation, who do not want to risk their status in the new country. Also, the first generation may interpret experiences of discrimination and exclusion in the host country as the actions of a few rude individuals and not as systemic prejudice (Viruell-Fuentes 2007). In sharp contrast, second-generation immigrants are more aware of systemic disadvantages and less likely to interpret them as isolated incidents; they tend to understand these experiences as processes of discrimination, marginalization, disempowerment, and social exclusion (Waldinger and Feliciano 2004; Viruell-Fuentes 2007; Bucerius 2008).

The reader may ask how, within this context of social exclusion and marginalization, second- or third-generation immigrants form the sense of social identity and belonging that are important prerequisites for integration.[5] This question is a topic of great political, academic, and popular debate in Germany (Heckmann and Schnapper 2003; Wolf and Tudose 2005; Reich and Gezer 2009; Vermeulen 2010). Why do some attempt to assimilate into German society (as politicians urge them to do) whereas others form subcultures or live in so-called parallel societies? It's also not clear why some immigrants choose to live in diasporic communities or immerse themselves in transnational networks when others do not, or why still others simply form their own culture within German society.

To understand the various paths that second-generation immigrants may choose, and keeping in mind the prominent role that the host country's reception plays in social integration, it is revealing to examine the young men's narratives about German society. What did they think about Germany and their own chances in the country? Did they feel any sort of belonging in the country? And what was the relationship between their feelings and their involvement in the drug trade?

This chapter will address these questions and, in particular, describe how the individuals in this book formed a sense of social identity through their strong identification at a local, not national, level. For the most part, the young men rejected the idea that they were German, instead identifying with their neighborhood of Bockenheim. This identification served to create a positive sense of self as they struggled with two challenges: (1) a socially exclusionary and xenophobic German society that permanently labeled them as foreigners even though they were born and raised in Germany; and (2) their parents' fear that they were becoming Germanized. Although the young men's sense of place within German society factored heavily into their ongoing participation in the informal economy, their strong local identification and sense of belonging to their group helped them solve these often-contradictory dilemmas.

These findings are particularly interesting in light of marginalized populations more generally. While law enforcement strategies are typically geared toward destroying criminal youth groups or gangs like the group of young men in this book, the social function of such groups should not be underestimated. While Akin, Aissa, and the others felt that they were treated unfairly on many levels, the friendship networks that connected them to one another and to their neighborhood instilled strong feelings of belonging and inclusion. I argue that despite being criminally active, the young men's identification with their neighborhood fulfilled an important social function—one typically overlooked by gang enforcement teams— and enabled social identification within German society.

SOCIAL EXCLUSION

To understand how these young men struggled with their social identity, it is necessary to examine their perspectives about the various forms of exclusion they experienced. As Muslims, the young men have been globally defined as "the Other" and were subject to public fears linking Islam with terrorism. While the young men were aware of the inferior position Muslims hold on a global level because of these concerns, in Germany and as sons of former guest workers, they were not so much seen as potential terrorists as unproductive and non-assimilated members of society who were exploiting the welfare system. Their exclusion should be understood within this national context, as it is distinct from the global context of general fear of Islam. Instead of expanding in detail on each of the forms of exclusion that the young men faced, my analysis focuses on two exclusionary factors to which the young men repeatedly referred during the course of my research and that they found to be the most pressing issues: discrimination within the educational system and citizenship status.

The School System

It has been widely documented that children from an immigrant background, particularly second-generation immigrants and boys, experience significant disadvantages within the German education system (Blossfeld, Paulus, and Kleine 2009). The three basic streams to which students are assigned in this system are the Hauptschule (the lowest stream), Realschule (the middle stream), and Gymnasium (the highest stream). A fourth stream, *Sonderschule* (special school), caters to students with special needs. Elementary school teachers recommend students for a particular stream based on criteria including academic achievement, self-confidence, and ability to work independently. However, in most states, parents have the final say as to which school their child attends following the fourth grade.[6]

Compared with their German counterparts, students with immigrant backgrounds are more likely to be recommended for lower streams, even if they have a similar or better record of academic achievement than native-born youth. Aissa's experiences serve as a good example of how certain forms of institutional discrimination expressed through educational streaming can make students from immigrant backgrounds feel that their academic achievements and attempts to integrate into mainstream society are not being recognized. In determining educational outcomes, the actions of individuals are often less significant than the actions of various institutions (Gomolla and Radtke 2009):

AISSA: Well, in elementary school I only had six A's, two B's, and one C on my report card. But the C was in music. In music! I mean, who cares, right? I mean, shit on music . . . as if that counts [for] anything! Everybody else in my class who had these sorts of grades was sent to the Gymnasium. But the teacher told my mom that I should go to the Realschule. I asked my teacher why I wasn't supposed to go to the Gymnasium and she said that the German will get more and more difficult and that you have to be perfect at German. That was just crap—I had an A– in German. I mean, I don't even speak anything but German. That's the only language I speak. Tell me that's not bullshit! Well, my teacher told my mom that she could bring me to the Gymnasium if she thinks that she can help me with my homework later on. So my mom got scared because she never went to school in Germany and German is not her mother tongue. But, we only speak German at home . . . but somehow the teacher scared the shit out of my Mom. . . .

SANDRA: So, what do you think about all this now?

AISSA: At the time, I did not give a shit because all the foreigners were sent to the Real- and Hauptschule, and I wanted to be with my friends, of course. I mean, that's all you care about at that age. But when I think about it now, it really annoys me! I mean, you know how the social workers are always saying that I should have done social work? But you need the *Abitur* [the Gymnasium diploma] for that. Well . . . I am honest, I don't know what I would have thought when being like 20 years old or so, but now . . . if I had an Abitur now, I would definitely go to college in a second. I was even thinking about going to school again, to get the Abitur, but I am working shifts now,[7] so that's not working out with school and stuff . . . .. I need the money . . . and then three years of high school and then another five years of college. . . . That's really tough! And just because of this racist whore of a teacher. I mean, really, there is just nothing else to say about her.

Aissa was not the only good student in the group—his experiences in the German educational system were similar to those of many of the other young men. Although many started off quite well in elementary school, more than half did not obtain a high school diploma. The great majority of those who did receive a degree only managed to graduate from the Hauptschule, the lowest of the three basic school forms in Germany. Graduates from this form can realistically only pursue practical vocations such as hairdressing, plumbing, and baking.[8]

Max Weber's (1972) concept of "social closure" and Bourdieu's (2004) notion of "symbolic violence" can help us understand why Aissa (and the others) were so frustrated with the German educational system. Weber describes how the dominant group in society—in this case, German mainstream society in general and the teachers in the German school system more specifically—safeguards and privileges its own position by monopolizing and restricting resources and opportunities for its own group (German students) while denying access to outsiders (students with immigrant backgrounds like Aissa), independent of their educational achievements. In this sense, the educational system severely limits upward mobility (Portes, Fernandez-Kelly, and Haller 2009) and structurally blocks people from creating new forms of social or cultural capital that enable social mobility (Bourdieu and Passeron 1977). This process has become so normal that Aissa did not fight to be sent to the Gymnasium as he claimed, he did not "give a shit because all the foreigners were sent to the Real- and Hauptschule." As Bourdieu's concept of symbolic violence describes, the young men internalized the structural limitations that they had faced from a very young age and were not always aware of them. In other words, initially, when they were young, they didn't realize the exclusion and marginalization that they encountered and the impact they would have on their life chances.

Weber (1968) explains that the dominant group singles out certain social or physical attributes (e.g., immigrant or foreigner status) as a basis to justify various forms of exclusion. It's clear from Aissa's narrative that his teacher only based her recommendation on the fact that he was not of German background—neither his grades nor his enthusiasm about going to the Gymnasium would have justified her recommendation. Weber argues that members of the dominant group consciously or unconsciously deprive outsiders of social and economic opportunities to secure privileges like a good education for themselves. His teacher's claim that Aissa might encounter difficulties in the future because he was not a native German may have allowed her to rationalize her decision on the ground that she was just trying to look out for him. But as Aissa's case illustrates, social closure happens at the expense of the outsiders through a process leading to their subordination. Bourdieu, building on Weber, explains that by initially being unaware of structural limitations and perceiving the social order as just, marginalized people perpetuate the social structure favored by and serving the interests of those agents who are already dominant—in this case, Germany's mainstream society.

In retrospect, Aissa recognized the irony and injustice of the events by stating that his teacher's rationale was "bullshit." I spent countless hours listening to Aissa talk about his inability to obtain a university degree because he did not have the required high school degree (Abitur). Although he recognized that personal and institutional discrimination had hindered his ability to advance into a higher educational stream, he also expressed a strong degree of self-blame: "I just did not care enough back then. I mean— I did . . . but I did not fight enough. I can't only blame her, I also need to blame myself. I should have fought more."

This wasn't the only instance in which one of the young men perceived the effects of systemic discrimination and structural limitations as a personal failure. Bourdieu (2004) explains that the injustice and structural limitations marginalized people face can become so mundane, so commonplace, that these individuals become not only oblivious to but also complicit with their own exclusion and marginalization. In fact, a number of the young men insisted on recognizing their culpability when trying to explain a negative outcome and would not immediately blame structural forces. Despite knowing that not all second-generation immigrants who faced the same limitations dropped out of school or engaged in crime, this was something that always troubled me, but at one point Aissa explained the obvious: "Sandra, of course, it is my fault, too. If you're saying this is not my fault, you're saying that whatever I do or whatever I don't do, I'd always end up in the same spot. But that's bullshit. There are still good people out there. I can still change things myself. You just have to be really strong and want to change." Without knowing it, Aissa was contributing to one of the key dilemmas ethnographers face when researching marginalized populations—the structure versus agency debate (Giddens 1984; Bourdieu 1990). Briefly, this debate hinges on whether the behavior of actors can best be explained by pointing to the structural limitations and opportunities he or she faces or whether individuals have the capacity and responsibility to make their own free choices in life, independent of structural circumstances. Simply put, the debate centers on socialization versus autonomy.

By insisting on his agency, Aissa made it clear that I should not take away his hope for change. Believing that he "would always end up in the same spot" would not leave any room for him to make a different life for himself.

As a German academic, I have naturally been exposed to the ample documentation of the systemic discrimination that immigrant students in Germany face (Becker and Biedinger 2006; Bos et al. 2004; Geissler 2004; Ditton 2004). Being aware of this research, my personal feelings of indignation about these findings, had, perhaps, made it hard for me to accept the young men's self-blame as assertions of agency. But it was clearly important for Aissa to point out to me that even when facing systemic disadvantages and structural limitations that may severely limit his or her options, a person is not completely deprived of the capacity to choose. In this sense, it is important to understand the circumstances in which the young men grew up as important factors pushing them toward the conclusion that the drug trade was a viable option, even if they were not aware of those factors at the time. When these young men were little, being streamed away from the Gymnasium was accepted as a normal process by most of the young men and their parents, just as drug dealing was seen as a normal choice for foreigners like them (chapter 3).

The normalization of the streaming process for Germany's immigrants rests heavily on variables outside the control of any student or family. Whether a child ends up in the Gymnasium stream is strongly predicted by parental socio-economic status. Only 38 percent of all lower-class[9] parents with children who have high grades and are recommended for the Gymnasium actually consider sending their child to the Gymnasium, whereas more than 90 percent of all middle- and upper-class parents of children with the same grades consider choosing the Gymnasium for their children (Ditton 1992).[10] The influence of social class on streaming, irrespective of other systemic disadvantages, was captured by Akin:

> Well, in the beginning, my mom was very relieved when I was told that I should no longer go to the Gymnasium. Well, at that point, no one knew that I would not stay at the Realschule either [laughing]. I think she thought it was somewhat strange that I was the only kid going to the Gymnasium, whereas the children of her girlfriends would all go to Haupt- or Realschule. So, she was relieved when she heard that I was now going to a school with other foreigners [laughing]. But you can't blame her; she just doesn't know anything about the school system!

As Akin noted, not all of the young men were streamed into the two lower school forms; some of their elementary teachers actually recommended them for inclusion in the Gymnasium stream. However, children from an immigrant background in the Gymnasium stream are far more likely to repeat a year or be "streamed down." My ethnographic material revealed that none of the young men who enrolled in the Gymnasium stream actually stayed there for very long. In fact, most of the young men who had originally been recommended for the Gymnasium were streamed down to the stream below within the first year of secondary school (Grade 5). As Ferdi said:

> I was once at the Gymnasium . . . can you fucking believe that? Yeah . . . I beat the shit out of someone in Grade 5 and they put me in the Realschule right away. They said I wasn't mature enough for the Gymnasium. But I wanted back, you know . . . desperately. I don't know why, actually, but I just wanted back. So, my teacher said that I just have to give my best and get good grades, you know, and then they would send me back to the Gymnasium at the end of the school year. So, that's what I did, but at the end of the school year, the cunt tells me that they don't have space and that I have to wait. So, I freaked out and yelled at her and called her a liar and a fucking slut.

So why did Ferdi not question his school's decision to drop him down a stream when he got involved in a physical fight? As the various narratives of the young men in this book revealed, they saw the restriction of educational opportunities as the normal response to behavioral problems. Conformity to the norms of social behavior and a good education seem to go hand-in-hand in Germany, and so Ferdi automatically tried to comply with all the rules and perform at his best level in order to return to the Gymnasium. When he realized that his teacher had made empty promises ("She was just radically lying to me for an entire year") and that—despite his performance ("I got really good grades, not a single C!")—and he would not get a spot in the Gymansium stream, he openly showed his frustration through a verbal attack. The teacher responded by moving Ferdi into a different class:

> FERDI: When she moved me to the other class, I really couldn't care less anymore . . . so I just stopped doing anything . . . you know . . . stopped participating. . . . They can't fuck around with me like that. And then I got a D on a German exam. Then the teacher said that if I were to spend less time with my Turkish friends and if I stopped hanging out at the Bockenheimer Warte [a public space in the district], I would get better grades again. So I called her a Nazi. I mean, why does she care what I do? And why does she care about my friends? So they put me in *the Hauptschule*. Right away.

Because I wasn't bearable at the Realschule because I said Nazi. So, I stopped going. Grade 6. School was over. End of story.

SANDRA: Well, did anyone ever ask you what had happened and why you were so mad?

FERDI: No . . . not a single dick was interested in that. I actually wanted to talk to the principal because of that slut who had lied to me about going back to the Gymnasium—but they did not give me an appointment. She was too busy—the entire week. They always told me tomorrow, tomorrow, well, and tomorrow she had something better to do as well. They were just radically interested in not having foreigners at the Gymnasium. They all had to go down a stream. Just ask around, a lot of them started out at the Gymnasium.

Ferdi had wanted to explain himself to the school authorities, but after being denied access to the school's principal several days in a row, he decided—as did many of the other young men in this book—that trying to make it in the formal school system was not worth it. Thus, at the age of 12, he quit. Interestingly though, he did not reject formal education or stop thinking about the school system altogether. Years later, he was still trying to understand the poor performance of immigrant students:

> [It's] as if all foreigners are dumber. Don't you think it is a bit weird that there was not a single foreigner in the Gymnasium stream any more in Grade 7? I am just saying: Can really *all* foreigners be worse than Germans? I mean, biologically speaking? And the Germans in my class, they also got the occasional D or E, and they did graduate. I mean, there is just no logic here. Do you know what I mean?

Was Ferdi's experience typical? Research shows that yes, it was: the most common reasons given for the decision to move students down a stream or have them repeat a school year in Germany are language difficulties, cultural differences (Gomolla 2000, 55), a lack of support (or false support) from parents or guardians (Gomolla and Radtke 2009, 177–78), a lack of willingness to integrate, and a lack of conformity in social behavior (Gomolla 2000, 57).

Though the young men did not comment on this fact, it should be noted that institutional discrimination does not start in school; it often begins earlier. Children from an immigrant background are more than twice as likely as German children to have their elementary school enrollment delayed by one year (Gomolla and Radtke 2009, 135).[11] They are also disproportionately represented within the "special school system," which was originally designed for children with special needs arising from severe learning difficulties or physical disabilities but now also caters to students with "behavioral difficulties."[12] In fact, more than twice as many children with immigrant backgrounds attend special schools compared with students with a German background.[13] Unless one assumes that children from immigrant backgrounds collectively have more learning disabilities and behavioral problems than German children, it appears that institutional discrimination is at work. As Metin noted, his story was a "classic" example of those young men who were down-streamed within the regular school system and were eventually expelled into a special school:

> Well, my case was classic, I would say. I did a lot of bullshit at school—like little boy's stuff, you know? I talked a lot during classes and built paper airplanes . . . and just stuff like that—nothing radical, only like little bullshit . . . but they immediately put me one stream down, from Gymnasium to the Realschule in Grade 5. Even though I did not have bad grades or anything, I was average . . . always. There were many Germans in my class who were much worse than me . . . academically speaking. . . . I was just average . . . you know, one A, one B, one D . . . some C's—I had an A in physical education and in maths.

While at the time, the young men did not seem to significantly protest being down-streamed, nor did they mobilize their families to complain, they clearly came to understand that they had been treated unfairly, especially in comparison with German students. The young men came to perceive the special education label as something that should be reserved for students with serious physical disabilities; this led them to resent German society in general and the school system in particular. As chapters 3 and 4 demonstrate in greater detail, because they came to understand these early experiences of marginalization and the severe limitations of their educational and thus occupational futures as discrimination, the young men factored these experiences in important ways into their ongoing decision to participate in the drug trade.

Metin explained that he and two friends from his class at the Realschule were streamed down to the Hauptschule at the end of Grade 5. According to him, "the teacher was radically racist" and "ensured that all the foreigners in her class were streamed down to the Hauptschule."

SANDRA: Why was that?
METIN: Well, once, we locked the slut [teacher] into the classroom. It was just little boys' stuff, you know. Just having fun, in my eyes. After that, we were told that we're now going to the Hauptschule.

So Gymnasium to Hauptschule within one year. And there, it was just unbelievable . . . only foreigners in my class . . . really *only* foreigners . . . totally ridiculous. I stopped participating . . . it was basically just like kindergarten. . . . I mean, academically speaking . . . I was totally bored. The only one of the three of us who still graduated was Georgio—and he was the worst of the three of us, academically speaking.

Metin's experience at school clearly taught him that fitting in took precedence over academic achievements—despite the students' good academic standing, they could always be down-streamed because of their immigrant status. "Fitting in" was a challenge, however, as all the accounts of the young men showed that they lacked the specific cultural capital required to fulfill institutional expectations—fitting into the mainstream was just not possible (Bourdieu 1990). Instead, their behavior and membership in a certain ethnic group restricted them to a form of education that seemed about as challenging as kindergarten. Given this scenario, it's not hard to understand why so many of them dropped out of school.

SANDRA: So why did you quit school?

METIN: One day, there was this beef after school. One of them had to go to the hospital, broke a couple of ribs, and his nose was fucked up. I did not have anything to do with it. I wasn't even there when it happened, but because the teacher knew that I did not like the guy, she blamed me and wanted to send me to the principal. The slut just did not believe me! So I pulled a knife and told her to keep it quiet. Well . . . same story: they expelled me from school, and I got sent to the special school because I was characterized as unbearable. So I went for one week. There were only, like, handicapped people in my class. I mean, I am not retarded, you know. . . . I did not want to sit among all these kids who constantly drool out of their mouths. So . . . I haven't been to school since Grade 7. I ran into my old elementary school teacher the other day. She was totally shocked. . . . I was one of her best students in elementary school. I was better than most Germans in my class. But she was also a good person—not a Nazi or something like that.

What impact did Metin's placement in the same class as handicapped people have on him? Germany's segregation of students with any form of disability into a separate school system sends a clear message that these students are not valuable members of mainstream society, and it hugely affected Metin. Being treated like a "retard," as Metin put it, signaled to him that he had been dismissed as incapable of contributing meaningfully to society, and it also increased his general frustration with Germany. Metin's awareness that he had been treated unfairly ("I am not retarded") made him feel fewer constraints concerning Germany's legal and moral order when he eventually entered the drug-dealing world: "I honestly don't give a shit what people think about this. This is what I do now."

Metin's experience of quitting school and becoming cut off from mainstream society was common among the young men. Frustrated with the German school system and perceiving discrimination from teachers and the school more generally, many of them made a conscious decision at some point to drop out of school (an outcome common among children from an immigrant background more broadly). While the great majority of the group had already quit school by the time I met them, many of the younger men (those who were between 16 and 18 years of age at the time) were still in high school, where they planned to stay in order to graduate and subsequently learn a trade. But by the time I finished my research in 2006, all but one had quit school.

The young men often recounted that they stopped caring or "giving a shit" early in their school experience. As Georgio told me:

> Well, in the beginning, you're really motivated and you want to be good at school and earn a degree and just do it right—not like everyone else around here. But honestly, if you're always treated like shit, you'll stop caring at some point. In the end, I was the only one left and the only one who got a degree. They all quit . . . and honestly, I would have done the same, but back then, I was too afraid of my parents. And I wasn't that close with the others yet, with Akin and those guys. I mean, I had some connections, but I was just a little chicken. But I can totally understand that they all quit. You really get a lot of shit . . . I mean racist shit. It's just absolutely ridiculous!

As I listened to the young men recount their stories about school, I wondered at what point they became aware that what they were experiencing reflected the broader discrimination apparent in German society. In many of their narratives about why they quit school, they often retold the sequence of events by placing blame on specific individuals: the "Nazi" teacher, the "racist whore." It was in their present-day analysis of the situation that they expressed awareness of the connections between these individuals and the systemic discrimination they themselves faced. It was also only in retrospect that some wondered what they could have done with their lives had they had the chance to graduate from a higher educational stream. Even so, the majority of the young men did not focus on what could have been; when they told their stories, they were merely stating the facts, taking the disadvantages and discrimination they experienced almost for granted. That is to say, they called these experiences "ridiculous" and "racist," but they were not surprised to encounter this treatment in the educational system. From the very beginning of their school careers, these young men were treated differently from German children by official actors such as teachers. Thus, they talked about their experiences in a matter-of-fact way as stories about things that "just happen to immigrants." As Bourdieu (2004) has explained, this form of symbolic violence becomes ingrained and commonplace in an individual's everyday life.

This goes a long way toward explaining why the young men perceived themselves as different from Germans. They saw Germans being treated favorably within the educational system,[14] and many of them noted that the schools and classes they attended were mainly composed of students from an immigrant background. Given this, it's not surprising that the young men, despite their specific ethnic backgrounds, perceived their experiences of exclusion as part of a universal immigrant experience in Germany. Interestingly, it is this perception of exclusion and otherness that generated a feeling of solidarity among them and that played a key role in the formation of their identity as "Bockenheimers," ultimately helping them to justify their actions within the informal economy.

Citizenship

The school system is not the only area in which the young men reported discrimination and exclusion. Germany's citizenship law also made them feel excluded. When examining how second-generation immigrants form their identity in Germany, it is especially important to consider the way in which these individuals think about citizenship and conceptualize a sense of belonging to the country. For many years, the young men experienced Germany as a country that would not grant them citizenship, despite the fact that they had been born and raised there. Only six of the group members had German citizenship, but of these, four had at least one parent who was a German citizen, which granted them automatic citizenship at birth. German citizenship law was reformed in 2000, but since this reform was not retroactive, it did not affect the nationality status of the young men, nor did it change the way they thought about Germany.

Earlier German citizenship law, which established a clear border between outside and inside and built solidarity from the inside (Bös 1993, 623), thus making it almost impossible for non-Germans to obtain citizenship, was undoubtedly perceived by the young men as a means of excluding them from mainstream German society. By upholding the law for so many years, they felt that Germany had repeatedly reinforced the state's interest in maintaining closed relationships (Weber 1972, 23) that excluded a significant proportion of Germany's residents.

The young men were not always aware of the current political debates on various topics (as Metin said, "I can't even vote. . . . Why would I read the newspaper every day?"), but they kept each other informed about the current citizenship rules. In fact, the great majority of the men were aware of the main aspects of German citizenship reform and had a general idea and opinion of the various aspects of the political debate leading up to the reform. The young men were clearly aware of the consequences of the reform and how it could potentially affect their own lives.

In 2000, when the law changed (one year before the start of this project), the young men had reached a mean age of 22. At that point, they largely perceived themselves as having been socialized into a country that did not grant them the same rights as Germans and, subsequently, did not accept them as full members of society. The new law did not drastically change their opinions. Rather, they saw it as a change that came much too late.

> AISSA: You know, that's very nice, that the Germans finally get that the children here should also get a passport. But honestly, that's like . . . like . . . very, very last minute, and it's not like they would become real Germans, they only become Germans on probation.[15] And when you're honest, that's just fucking bullshit.
>
> SANDRA: So, that's your opinion? Aren't you a bit happy about the change?
>
> AISSA: Well, what do you expect? That we all dance and be happy? Do you think the Jews loved the Germans when Hitler was dead? They did not forget, they will never forget! OK . . . I don't want to say it's the same thing, like that the Germans treated us like they treated the Jews, but . . . you know . . . it's not like you forget these things easily. You can't always say: These fucking foreigners should just return, we don't want you here . . . and then they suddenly say: Yes, that was all a mistake . . . so sorry . . . you can become German now. As if Turks have become nice people overnight and everyone will now forget that they are really just fucking foreigners. That's just what they did with the blacks. I mean, really . . . that's just bullshit . . . so that they can feel better about themselves.

Aissa's statement exemplifies how the young men found it difficult to understand the changed law. They had experienced the exclusionary German rhetoric for so long that they simply did not know what to make of the change (as Mesut said, "I am not sure what this is all about now. It just seems very weird to me"). They tended to be irritated by the official modification of the German rhetoric and consistently commented that the reform would not automatically help immigrants *to forget*. Their emphasis on this point revealed how strongly they had been affected by the fact that they could never obtain citizenship. They also perceived the reform as only affecting future generations and having little to do with themselves.[16] Because of their criminal records (and the fact that they were born before 2000), German citizenship was still out of reach for most of them. On a very practical level, citizenship reform did not change their situation. In contrast to their narratives about school, when talking about citizenship, the young men were more likely to point to systemic problems that they had encountered, rather than expressing self-blame for not qualifying for citizenship (i.e., by taking responsibility for their criminal record).

> TALAT: Well . . . I get that they don't want to have criminals become Germans. Who would want that? No country. But . . . you know . . . they fuck us up at school . . . like they put us in the Hauptschulen and then they give you like the most racist teachers and so on . . . and then . . . you know . . . even the guys who did graduate and who did do vocational training [e.g., Lehre] . . . nobody gets a job! They don't hire Muslims. Look at Nermin—he sent out over a hundred applications and he was only invited when he lied and said he was Italian. That's screwed up.
>
> SANDRA: But what does this have to do with your criminal record and citizenship?
>
> TALAT: Well . . . if you're fucked at school and don't get a job, you need to make some money somewhere. And then they fuck you for making that money and you don't get citizenship. That's screwed up. If they treated all the same, like everyone was treated the same from the start . . . like in school and stuff . . . then that's OK. But like this . . . they fuck with you and then they say: "Ha, ha . . . you did not make it . . . so you can't be a German."

This interaction shows that not only were the young men frustrated with not having German citizenship and with facing other limitations in life, but they actually contextualized their involvement in drug-dealing activities based on these experiences. Essentially, when the young men started out, they viewed drug dealing as normal for them; everyone in their circle of friends was doing it (chapter 3). When asked for an explanation for their drug-dealing behavior in retrospect, they portrayed their participation as a response to the social, economic, and political exclusion that they experienced (yet they also understood that their actions and activities strengthened and reinforced the stereotypes that caused them to be excluded). Why didn't they decide against a criminal lifestyle despite these problems? Since not everyone who is faced with these sorts of disadvantages becomes a drug dealer or criminal, was this decision an "easy way out" for the young men I was studying? And why were they so quick to blame "the system"? As we got deeper into these conversations, the reactions of the young men when agitated suggested that they did not absolve themselves from all responsibility. Instead (and as Aissa had pointed out earlier when talking about school and teachers), they did appear to be aware that they had the ability to make their own choices, but they perceived these choices as being defined by their social context. In other words, within the context of their experienced and lived marginalization in German society, they internalized this situation to be their position in society (see Bourdieu's [1977] concept of habitus). As Rahim, a 21-year-old of Turkish background, told me:

> Sandra, did you hear about this PISA[17] shit? It's black and white . . . that you don't have a chance here as a foreigner! From the minute you're born they treat you differently . . . but then you're supposed to go to university and not do any shit. I know some people make it anyways . . . but that's not for me. . . . I have to stand up for myself. . . . I just can't take so much racist shit day by day. I guess that's my own fault . . . but I just get very mad.

The young men legitimized their criminal involvement by claiming that they had a very limited framework in which to operate, so to them it was natural to find innovative ways to attain their goals. However, they did not argue that they were forced into dealing, but rather, that it was merely the best of the choices that were at hand. As Rahim indicated, they felt that by quitting the formal system and "not taking all that racist shit," they were standing up for themselves as much as they could within their social roles (Bourdieu 1990). Although being denied citizenship was only one of many forms of exclusion they faced, it seems especially ironic that group members were once again denied full membership status (this time on the basis of their criminal records) after Germany changed its citizenship laws. While we will learn in chapter 3 that the young men more or less drifted into dealing, they also liked to portray themselves, in retrospect, as active agents. Upon reflection, instead of being active agents in their exclusion, they perceived themselves as having resorted to criminal lifestyles because they were denied many of the opportunities open to German citizens and refused to be complacent with the exclusion that they faced. And now, when they otherwise would qualify for citizenship, they were denied it because they had taken the most obvious opportunity open to them "to make money somewhere." As Nermin explained:

> So, that's a joke. They change the law but nothing changes! That just makes me mad. It's a total joke. They just pretend, just pretend. . . . "Yeah, we did something great" . . . but then they tell you: "Well, this is not for you because you fucked up." You know, I want all of these fuckheads to just spend one day in one of these Hauptschulen and see for themselves how fucked up that is . . . so that they know why people here fuck up . . . so that they understand what's going on. I don't want to say that all people fuck up . . . but you know . . . how many guys come to the community center? How many . . . like 60? And there is only one single person who has an Abitur? Don't you think that's a bit strange? So are we all dumb? I want one of these politicians to come here and explain that to me! And to explain why I can't have a fucking passport.

Whether or not one empathizes with the young men's negative opinion of Germany, the ethnographic material helps show how their rage was an attempt to cope with their real and perceived exclusion from the society to which they desperately wanted to belong (Weber 1972). This, and the particular significance of citizenship, becomes especially clear when deportation enters the analysis. The possibility of being deported to their parents' country of origin was a looming and realistic threat to these young men. Even though they continuously justified their involvement in the drug market by claiming that Germany was an exclusionary and racist country that "does not deserve any better," they clearly favored incarceration in Germany over deportation. As Akin described it: "Sandra, you know, getting deported would really be the worst. There's nothing I fear more. I'd rather go to jail for a couple of years. I just don't know anybody back in Turkey." The other young men in the group shared Akin's pressing fear. This fear seems ironic at times, considering that the young men did not comply with the law, degraded Germany at every opportunity, and tended to glorify their parents' countries of origin in other contexts and conversations. Nevertheless, they clearly favored long-term incarceration over deportation to a country with which they did not identify and about which they knew little (as Inanc said, "Well . . . in jail . . . you know . . . you're maybe lucky and at least have the chance of running into someone you know").

The limited promises made by the German government under the new law had serious implications.

When the young men envisioned what their lives would be like after "having been a drug dealer," they all imagined themselves to be living in Germany. Not having German citizenship put them at risk for deportation, but more importantly, it also endangered their plans for the future. If deported, their plans to retire from drug dealing, marry, and have children in Germany would be seriously threatened. And so, despite their negative views of Germany, the young men strongly wanted to become German citizens. Possessing German citizenship was seen not only as a way to prevent deportation but also as an important factor of identification and, equally importantly, as a sign of officially belonging to the country in which they were born and raised.

In light of supranational citizenship norms and the discourse of citizenship rights as human rights, some scholars have argued that national citizenship is becoming increasingly unimportant as new forms of postnational citizenship gradually emerge (Jacobson 1996). Although the young men actively constructed and practiced citizenship on the local level by claiming their own neighborhood as their space (and thereby creating a form of social identification), they still stressed the importance of national citizenship (see also Koopmans et al. 2005; Faist 2000; Hansen 2008). Not being granted citizenship was clearly considered a sign of discrimination against them. Consider Ülker's comment:

> I can't speak for everybody here, but a passport would really mean something to me. I mean, I would still be a foreigner, but at least I would officially belong to this country. . . . I mean, I would never be a German, but you know, I was born here and I have always lived here . . . ! I just want that passport, I just want to officially belong here, you know? I'm more of a German than all these fucking East Germans, am I not?? C'mon, Sandra, be honest! What do they have to do with Germany? Definitely less than us!

This has never been addressed in any previous studies of immigration in Germany, but the young men invariably spoke about the reunification in a negative way. The fact that East Germans were suddenly considered Germans again and received full citizenship rights was perceived as a great injustice. Moreover, the young men sensed the tension between East and West Germans and felt even more devalued by the fact that East Germans—who were not particularly liked by West Germans—were still more accepted by society than they were.

TALAT: I can understand that Germany wants to protect itself from too many foreigners and that they don't want them to become Germans. Or let's say I would have understood that if they hadn't fucking accepted all these idiots who have done nothing for this country. Nothing. This country would be nothing without our parents but I swear, these people come along and our parents feed them with their tax money. Let's face it: nobody likes those East Germans anyways. I always read in the newspaper how much they cost us and what kind of trouble they make. But you know, the Germans are too stupid to defend themselves against these fucking idiots. . . .

SANDRA: But you know, it used to be one country, so the Germans were actually quite happy to be reunited again.

TALAT: Sandra, don't give me that crap! I know you don't believe that.

SANDRA: Well, I do believe that most Germans were initially happy about the reunification.

TALAT: Come on! Everyone makes fun of them! Don't tell me you're not making fun of East Germans. You know, the way they talk? That's just ridiculous [imitating East Germans]. . . . See, you're laughing! You don't like them either!

Talat had a point, and interestingly, by arguing against East Germans, the young men were actually adopting a very West German standpoint. Provocatively put, arguing against East Germans using the vocabulary of many West Germans can actually be seen as a sign of integration. Researchers have tended to focus on injustice in the educational system, injustice in the labor market, and political exclusion, but the young men in this study felt especially excluded when they compared themselves and their citizenship rights to East Germans and the rights they enjoyed.

Racism

In addition to their opinions about the inclusion of East Germans as valued members of German society, the group members felt even more betrayed by the constantly increasing number of hate crimes against foreigners committed by East Germans. Although none of the group members had actually ever been a victim of a hate crime, they could not understand why Germans allowed the hate crimes to be committed. They perceived attacks that they read or heard about as personal offenses and as additional indicators that Germany was unwilling to take care of its immigrants.

> RAHIM: That is like a twofold kick in the butt!! They already treat you like the last shit in this country, and suddenly all these fucking East Germans come along and just get everything that you don't get. And as if that wasn't enough, they are all fucking Nazis. I would never go to East Germany, never. You really have to be careful there as a foreigner.
>
> SANDRA: Is that really the case? I mean . . . if you never went, how do you know that's true?
>
> RAFET: Didn't I tell you the story with my cousins? That was ridiculous! They came from Turkey and traveled all over the place, also to the East. Well . . . and then there were these asshole Nazis that beat my cousin up big time. Welcome to Germany. They will not come back, I swear!
>
> REMZI: The same happened to my cousin, too. They wanted to visit friends in Magdeburg—and boom. They're crazy! I've never heard of anyone that got beaten up by a Nazi in Frankfurt. Here, the Nazis run away from you. They know they can't do anything but walk around in their stupid Nazi look. But they know they could never come to Bockenheim. We would just turn them into hamburgers.

Although the young men talked a lot about German racism, they had never actually experienced a physical race-motivated attack. However, the prior conversation shows that they experienced vicariously a lot of racism that could be violent and physical at times. In addition, their daily life was shaped by nonviolent racist experiences.

Racism and social exclusion are very delicate topics in Germany. International scholars have long labeled Germany as the most exclusionary of the Western countries and have not shied away from talking about deep-seated racism within the German population (Green 2001; Legge 2003; Panayi 2000). Some authors have even referred to the country's xenophobic environment and the discrimination and disadvantages that immigrants tend to face in the educational system and the formal economy as violations of human rights (Ostergaard-Nielsen 2003). Interestingly, German scholars appear to be much less comfortable making such claims. German politicians tend to shift the focus of the conversation to immigrants' inability to assimilate and/or integrate, portraying them as suffering from cultural conflicts and/or being deeply committed to religious fundamentalism (Heitmeyer, Müller, and Schröder 1997).

During my fieldwork, I encountered many situations in which the young men experienced discrimination or symbolic violence in one way or another. Interestingly, they often did not pay much attention to these experiences; they had become so ingrained into their daily lives that they were nothing out of the ordinary. One of the first incidents that I observed occurred when Akin asked me to accompany him to the local branch of his bank. By that point, he and I had established a good relationship, and he would often ask me to come along when he was running errands. On that day, he had an American $100 bill that he wanted to exchange for euros and was anticipating problems. He asked me to wait in the foyer of the bank while he talked to the clerk at the counter. As he had expected, the woman refused to exchange the currency, stating that she had "no idea where you [Akin] got the money from." From what I could tell standing in the foyer, Akin was very polite, trying to convince her that she would probably not ask other customers where their money came from and arguing that he was a customer at this branch, but she would not change her mind. Akin returned to me, handed me the bill, and asked me to exchange it on his behalf. I went back to the same counter and asked the bank clerk politely to exchange my bill. She did so without hesitation. I was too shocked to ask why she had not exchanged the bill for Akin or whether she knew that this was exactly the same bill that she had refused to exchange two minutes earlier. Akin was not surprised at all; on the contrary, he seemed to gain great satisfaction from the fact that I was so puzzled: "Why are you so upset? That's normal business. If I had not known that this would happen, I would not have asked you to come along. Things like these happen every day! I know, I know, everything is different in your student world."

Akin's insistence that this incident was part of everyday life made me very curious, so I started to accompany the young men on their daily chores (e.g., shopping, going to the post office and bank, etc.). I was forced to rethink my own hypothesis that, in addition to a certain degree of racism, the explanation for the young men's negative treatment was that they generally came across as rude. While I had believed that they would probably receive the same treatment that I did if only they were polite enough to the people with whom they were dealing, this assumption proved to be very naive. Over time, I came to understand that the arbitrariness with which Akin was treated was commonplace within mainstream society.

Obviously, this kind of day-to-day discrimination shaped the young men's perception of Germany and German mainstream society. The kinds of disadvantages that they experienced in the educational system, job market, criminal justice system, citizenship policies, and so on can provide us with an understanding of the context in which the young men formed their negative opinions of Germany. The discrimination they encountered kept them from feeling as if they belonged to Germany and thus from "feeling German." More importantly, it kept them from fulfilling Germany's main expectation of immigrants: full assimilation and, crucially, acceptance of German mainstream values and norms. Consider the following comment by Özgur, a 19-year-old of Turkish background:

> When I was younger, I really wanted to be German. I hated it in the village [that his parents are from and where his family spent their summer vacations], and I really could not understand why my parents liked it so much in Turkey. I was very little and did not get anything. And I thought the Germans [we]re super cool. . . . I never understood why my parents don't like them. But everything is different today. Today, I'd rather cut my dick off before being German. I've seen things and . . . you know . . . I get that they treat us like shit. It's like, now I don't want to anymore. I mean, I want to live here, but that's all. They would never accept me as German anyways. . . . I would always be a Turk for Germans.

Özgur clearly understood that he would never be accepted as German by Germans no matter how much he might try to fit in, a statement that was echoed by the vast majority of the young men. And while they accepted this fate by claiming that they "d[id]n't want to [become German] anymore," they were also firm about wanting to spend their lives in Germany. This naturally created major difficulties for their sense of self and sense of belonging.

CREATING A SENSE OF BELONGING

When analyzing the experiences and stories of the young men, it is important to keep in mind that social exclusion always works in an interactive, dialectical way. Max Weber (1972) noted that group action by mainstream society provokes a corresponding reaction on the part of those against whom it is directed. As such, the young men tended to respond with outrage to personal situations in the school system; these situations were soon interpreted as discrimination against foreigners as a whole and no longer as one individual's personal failure. As a consequence, the other people involved quickly got labeled "Nazis" or "fucking Germans." These responses consequently amplified the reactions of the other people, who then became even more convinced that the existing social closures are justified. As a result, the young men in this study felt even more rejected and unable to identify with German mainstream society. At the same time, they feared nothing more than getting deported—a justified fear, considering their involvement in the informal economy and their status as foreigners.

So how did the young men cope with their situation in Germany? Their legal choices for economic success were extremely limited, so they sought other ways to achieve their financial goals and search for respect. Their participation in the informal economy presented opportunities that the formal economy could not. They were able to establish strong connections to others within the informal economy and, as Sutherland (1939) would say, had established various differential associations, so this seemed to be a way to cope with the fairly closed formal economy. Furthermore, by considering their ongoing involvement in the informal economy to be a *response* to their social exclusion, they were able to maintain their view of themselves as active agents, and not simply as victims of racism or discrimination. From their perspective, they were actively choosing not to comply with the expectations that mainstream society seemed to have, and they used their perceptions of social exclusion and their negative opinions about Germany as defense mechanisms to neutralize their involvement in the informal economy. In other words, their assessment of German society and its treatment of them released them from the constraints associated with the moral order. As Gezim pointed out:

> The Germans just want you to do the lowest of the lowest jobs. I mean, that's what they needed our parents for, and that's what our parents did. Basically, to do the jobs that they did not want to do themselves. Well, that's done. They can't play the same games with us, we already know the game.[18] I am not going to work in a fucked-up company for, like, six euros an hour and let a Nazi German tell me what to do. They could do that with my dad, but not with us anymore. We know how to make good money.

In addition to helping the young men cope with their limited economic possibilities, the informal economy allowed them to demonstrate their masculinity and gain respect on the streets (see chapter 3). Considering the various forms of social exclusion experienced by the young men, it is important not to underestimate the importance of gaining respect and establishing status. In contrast to the formal economy, the street allowed them to prove that they were "someone" and that they could help form the laws of the street and climb the ladder, an experience often denied to them in the formal economy, as pointed out by Yakut:

> Well, you have a chance here, you know. For one, you make so much more money in comparison to one of these idiot jobs at the airport . . . but people also respect

you for what you are. I mean, you can earn respect, you can really become really important if you have the right connections and know how to turn yourself into someone. That's not possible in any of these ass-licking jobs. When you have one of those, you just lick ass . . . year after year.

Participating in the informal economy did not, however, solve the problem of belonging. The young men saw their involvement in the drug market as a response to their experienced social exclusion and not as their preferred occupation and clearly did not want to portray themselves as dealers (or gang members) per se. Nonetheless, by engaging in this illegal behavior, they fed into the stereotypes and preconceptions of German society and were consequently even more socially excluded. Faced with labels that included "foreigners," "drug dealers," and "gang members," they needed to create a new identity independent of these categorizations.

It is important to mention that marginalized populations like these young men exist in all Western societies and face different kinds of structural limitations. What makes these young men's situation particularly salient is that their marginalized position is magnified because their drug-dealing customs reify long-standing Western antipathy toward drugs (Aas 2007a, 206) and their religious and ethnic backgrounds often define them as Hudson's "monstrous other" (Aas 2007b, 289) in European society, whereby "the red menace [communism] is now replaced by the green peril [Islam]" (Mohammad 1999, 308). While the young men may not have been consciously aware of the fact that they held an inferior position not only within Germany but also within the broader global context as Muslims and drug dealers, their position in society made creating a positive sense of self particularly difficult.

Developing a sense of belonging and identity was a much different process for this generation of young men than it was for the previous generation. Their parents, faced with legal barriers that denied them political participation, and the German insistence about Ausländerstatus (the practice of labeling and treating all immigrants, regardless of their generational status, as foreigners and non-citizens), were forced to organize collectively along ethnic lines. They had no representation in their new country, so they directed their hopes and political activities back toward their home countries and dreamed of a future there. In contrast, the young men in this study were irritated by their parents' orientation toward their home country; they felt no strong sense of belonging to their parents' countries of origin and did not visit ethnically exclusive cafés or bars, as Inanc described: "When my Dad is off, he's hanging out with all these other men at the Turkish Café all day long, drinking one Turkish coffee after the next. They all sit there and talk about Turkey. For the entire day. All day. Men only. It's pathetic!"

This does not mean that the young men never spoke about their parents' country of origin; in fact, they often glorified it. However, the only ties that they really seemed to have with these countries were their own nationality, support for one of the country's soccer teams (e.g., Fenerbahçe or Galatasaray), attendance at Turkish, Moroccan, or Albanian dances, and memories of summer holidays when they were young. The great majority had never spent an extended period of time in these countries, and most had not visited their parents' home country for several years. When asked whether they planned on ever moving to their parents' country of origin, they clearly stated that they had no intention to do so. As Nermin said, "No, this is my home. I mean, I will always be a foreigner here, always. But I was born here, I was raised here, this is my district. I will never really feel at home, because they always treat me as a foreigner, and I will always be a Moroccan at heart, but I want to live here."

Nermin was quite clear about wanting to live in Germany, but the young men's daily dialogue and experiences within German society made them feel that they were not recognized as full members of that society. In contrast to their parents, who accepted the stigma associated with being outsiders and foreigners and constructed their lives around this stigma (Goffman 1975), the young men turned the logic of stigmatization upside down, creating a niche within German society and trying to make themselves visible. This approach seems to have been made possible by the young men's strong identification with their local district, which allowed them to feel a sense of social inclusion despite their otherness (see Tietze 2001, 205). This was most evident when they were asked what they considered to be their home: the most common answer given by the Turkish young men was neither Turkey nor Germany, neither Ankara nor Frankfurt, but Bockenheim—the district of Frankfurt in which they grew up. Only two out of the fifty-five young men could imagine moving away from that district.

Because they did not feel at home in either their parents' country of origin or Germany, they were constantly creating their own niche within their neighborhood district. The Turkish young men, for example, were labeled and stigmatized as "Turkish" in Germany, and called *"Almancilar"* (Germans) in Turkey, exemplifying their in-between status and showing their need to create a form of bricolage. In this sense, they were acting as social agents who were capable of making decisions with whatever was at hand (Lévi-Strauss 1966).

MESUT: Of course, it would be great if things were different here. I mean, if the Germans were different.

SANDRA: What do you mean by that?

MESUT: Well, more hospitable. Simply not as cold. Not like they were all robots . . . if they were just a little bit more cheerful, you know? Nobody is smiling here, everyone is dead serious. Well . . . that would be cool. But, you know, no country is perfect, and this is not my country, but the country in which I am living.

SANDRA: Did you ever think about leaving Germany? I mean, for longer?

MESUT: You mean, going to Turkey? No . . . I would not do that. I mean, it's my blood and everything, but, you know . . . honestly, I am also a foreigner over there. They think that I am German. And if I am a foreigner over there and here, I'd rather stay here. My family is here, and my friends, you know.

As Mesut noted, the young men felt like "foreigners" in both Germany and their parents' respective countries of origin. They felt that the influence of German society had made it impossible for them to identify clearly with their parents' country of origin, so they always felt like twofold members—or, rather, two-fold non-members (Mecheril 2003, 21). When asked to which nationality they felt a stronger sense of belonging, they could not decide. The official German discourse on *Ausländer* (foreigners) had a strong effect on their self-identity. As Aissa described it, "How I feel? Well, I think a foreigner who lives in Germany probably comes closest. I have everything in me, but I guess Germany's had the strongest influence on me. But I am not German, so I am a foreigner."

In their position as second-class citizens in both countries, the young men recognized their commonality with other immigrant youths in the same situation as they struggled to define their identity. The common experience of segregation and structured social exclusion led the young men to realize that they all shared a mutual experience as members of marginalized populations in Germany. This common experience became more important than ethnicity, binding them together and allowing for the creation of a distinct identity within German society. As outlined in chapter 4, other similarities (such as Muslim affiliation) became increasingly important and gave them a way to distinguish themselves from Germans. Cafer described it this way:

Everybody just calls you foreigner in Germany, or, even better, Turk. No matter whether you're Moroccan, Albanian, Iranian—he has black hair, oh, he has to be a Turk. You know, I was born here. I live here. I went to school in this fucking country. My kids will grow up here. But they will also be Turks and foreigners. And you know—when you visit your family back in Morocco or wherever—they don't call you Moroccan . . . they just call you German. You don't belong there. Fine, these are my cousins . . . but honestly, what do I have in common with them besides my blood? Of course, I would do everything for my family—but, you know, honestly . . . I probably have more in common with my friends from Turkey or Albania here in Bockenheim than with my own cousins. My dad would kill me if he could hear me now. But, you know, I am a Bockenheimer.

When emphasizing the fact that he was a Bockenheimer, Cafer also talked about his relatives and his father, who he imagined might disapprove of his way of thinking. By stating, "I am a Bockenheimer," the young men accomplished two goals. First, they were able to express clearly that they belonged to the neighborhood (which they viewed as distinct from the German state), that they were part of it, that they did not see themselves as foreigners, and that they would not move to their parents' country of origin. This close local identification with Bockenheim without necessarily identifying with Germany was possible because the young men felt as if they owned and represented Bockenheim, thereby actively contributing to and shaping its identity. This feeling was confirmed and amplified each time they met people outside of Bockenheim who emphasized the area's reputation as a tough neighborhood and well-functioning drug market, thus closely associating it with the young men or their older brothers and cousins. Needless to say, these interactions resulted in a belief that I heard many times over my research: "We *are* Bockenheim." Erol also emphasized this belief by stressing that nobody knew the neighborhood as well as him and his group of friends:

I swear, there is nobody who knows Bockenheim as well as we do. I know this district better than the pockets of my pants. I know every fucking street, every corner, every bar, every waiter, every cop, I know which dog shits at which corner—there is just nobody who knows Bockenheim as well as we do, believe me. Also the air—this is the Bockenheimer air—you can even breathe it. It has its own rhythm, its own beat. You can feel it. This is where I am at home.

Second, the association with Bockenheim allowed the young men to counter their parents' fears that they were becoming increasingly Germanized. The young men explained that their parents worried about becoming alienated from them in the foreign environment if their children became Germanized. By stating, "I am a Bockenheimer," they countered this fear by effectively rejecting a German identity while adopting a local one.

Needless to say, each of the two worldviews (German and immigrant) involved only stereotypical knowledge about the other, making it even more difficult for the young men to live in between these two worlds and find their own space. At any given time, one aspect of their existence was devalued, as each group tended to depict the other as problematic. For example, the young men's families tended to associate Germany with broken homes, sexual freedom, alcohol, drugs, and Nazism, as Tarki's parents did:

> My parents just don't know anything about Germans. But the worst thing that my dad can say to us, the worst accusation, I mean . . . I mean, when he is really, really mad and upset . . . he would say, "You are like a German." That's the worst thing that he can say. It's not that I like Germans, not at all, actually, but I think my parents don't even know much about them. It's even worse for my dad than saying that you are like a Jew. And that means a lot. . . . I mean, you know what I mean, don't you?!

In contrast, Germans tended to view the foreigners' families as backward, authoritarian, oppressive, violent, and hostile to women. Being seen as Germanized by their parents and as foreigners by Germans created a complex problem of acknowledgment for these young men, and the statement "I am a Bockenheimer" addressed both these issues simultaneously.

In addition to creating their identities as Bockenheimer, the young men used their own language when speaking to one another: a dialect typical of some groups of adolescents and, in particular, second-generation immigrants in Germany known as *Kanakisch* (Wiese 2006). *Kanakisch* speakers do not use any pronouns or participles, so they sound as though they do not speak German fluently. The young men were perfectly fluent in German, and so their use of *Kanakisch* could be seen as another way of demonstrating to their parents that they were far from becoming real Germans. It also fed certain stereotypes but openly demonstrated that "these foreigners who can't even speak German still belong to Bockenheim."

Identification with their own neighborhood was made possible by the distinct cultures that have developed in particular districts of Frankfurt. As discussed previously, one of the young men said that Bockenheim has a distinct air that one can breathe and a distinct rhythm and beat that one can feel. This character, or personality, made it possible for the young men to identify with the district without having to identify with the entire nation, and this identification did not come into contradiction with their experienced social exclusion. It is important to note that this form of belonging is only possible in large global metropolises that are complex, heterogeneous, and diversified. Some cities and their districts have a distinct character that makes it possible for individuals to develop very strong emotional ties to the neighborhood and/or city, regardless of how they are treated by the mainstream society. One example is how many individuals develop very strong emotional ties to New York City without approving of American politics in general.

There is great potential in this local identification. For young immigrants, it can allow them to develop loyalty and experience integration and solidarity without conforming to the mainstream. The young men's love for their neighborhood acted as a positive symbol at times when they felt torn or rejected. Their strong ties to Bockenheim allowed them to create an identity as Bockenheimers and find a place *within* German society. They transformed Bockenheim, a public space, into a private space for their own purposes. In this sense, the streets became essential to the production of space (Lefébvre 1991). After all, Bockenheim was inseparably connected to the young men's individual biographies—they all grew up in Bockenheim. As children of guest workers, they spent their days outside in the streets and at community centers, getting to know each corner of the neighborhood well and spending much time together. They stood out from the get-go—growing up within a mixed-income neighborhood, they were the only ones who were, as Erol said, "hanging out unsupervised, loitering at public places, and invading the community centers" (first the center for children and then the one for youth, where I met all of the young men). In contrast, German children were not as visible in the neighborhood (as Akin said, "The Germans don't play outside, they go to piano lessons. It's just the dirty foreigner children that hang at the street corners").

Another factor that contributed to the young men's close identification with Bockenheim was their connection to many of the businesses in the neighborhood. When the young men went out at night, they would usually spend larger sums of money than other customers in Bockenheim, because they were dependent on cafés, restaurants, and bars as hangout spaces for the evening. Whereas many of the middle-class residents had spacious-enough apartments or houses to welcome their friends after having gone out for a meal or a drink, this was not common or even feasible in the small and crowded apartments in which the young men lived in their parents and siblings. In addition, the young men ate out very frequently; it was rather rare that they shared a meal with their family at home. Most of the local restaurant and bar owners knew the young men very well and appreciated their business. Moreover, many of the business owners also cooperated with them with respect to the police. For example, they would inform the men if they saw undercover police in the area. The first time I noticed this type of mutual arrangement, I was playing darts with

Akin at the community center when his cell phone rang four times in a row. Four different local businesses—two restaurants, one café, and one corner store—called him to let him know that they had noticed several undercover cops at the Bockenheimer Warte, a large public space where drugs were often exchanged. Akin explained to me that such communication happened frequently.[19] In return for this information, he and his friends would make sure to visit these businesses regularly for food and drinks. This close cooperation with local businesses not only helped the young men's drug-dealing activities but also fostered their identification with the neighborhood. For these reasons, and because they spent most of their time outside, the young men were probably the best-known "faces" in the community. Every time I entered a local business (be it a corner store, a restaurant, a bar, or a vegetable store) with one or a few of the young men, the people working there knew them by name and greeted them in a very friendly way. The young men also put great emphasis on building good relationships with business owners in the neighborhood: they were great networkers who knew that maintaining such connections was important for being successful at what they were doing. This again likely instilled a feeling of "owning the neighborhood" within the young men, something on which they commented quite often.

This close identification clearly disproves the common German opinion that integration and assimilation are prerequisites for loyalty and solidarity. These young men show that strong ties to a local area can allow individuals to love a city or district, to boast about it, and to be proud of it without having to share the values and norms of most other citizens. For the young men, local identification was necessary to cope with the exclusion and discrimination they experienced and to demonstrate to their parents that they might be Bockenheimers, a neighborhood they actively shaped and in which they had found a place, but were far from being German.

The fact that the young men found their identification locally is, however, also reflective of the current state of the world. As Bauman (2000) argues, in the globalized world, we can see a new form of postmodern penology whereby punishment may no longer be equated with rehabilitation, retribution, or deterrence, but instead with exclusionary social immobility. Today's world is divided into people whose home is the world and who constantly move to achieve upward mobility and success and those who are locked into one locale. In light of this shift, "one does not need prisons to be, or feel, incarcerated in the locality" (Aas 2007a, 93). While the young men did not consciously perceive themselves as being "imprisoned" in Bockenheim, they certainly lacked the mobility to participate in the world of global movements. This restriction of movement in today's globalized world is in itself yet another form of exclusion that "guards the natural selectivity of the globalizing effects" (Aas 2007b, 293). However, within these restricted possibilities on the national *and* global levels, the young men actively created their own niche as Bockenheimers.

CONCLUSION: BOCKENHEIM AS A SOURCE OF IDENTITY

In conclusion, the young men appear to have used local identification to cope with the two different worlds they inhabited. By creating their identity as Bockenheimers and recognizing their commonalities as second-generation immigrants, they rejected identification along ethnic lines and formed their own niche in the district. Similar developments have occurred in Paris, where immigrants from differing backgrounds have created a common identity based on their experiences in their respective *villes nouvelles*. Similarly, in various cities in the United States and elsewhere, immigrant groups have formed neighborhood gangs independent of ethnic affiliation.

To the young men in Bockenheim, the district became important not only as a physical space but also as a place where they could produce their own language and culture. Furthermore, their strong local identification with, and extensive knowledge of, the place was a key factor in ensuring their success in the informal economy. My experience observing Akin's drug dealing for the first time (though I missed out on the details) was a great illustration of how the young men's connections within the neighborhood helped them to become successful at their business. In addition to their connections, their deep knowledge of the physical layout of the neighborhood, the tram and train schedule (both of which proved helpful when trying to escape the police), and individual policemen also all contributed to their success.

Strong local identification can give hope to those who claim that certain groups of second-generation immigrants in Europe, like the young men in this book, are a "lost generation." Despite their extensive complaints about German society, the young men's connection to this neighborhood group revealed that they did, in fact, feel a strong sense of belonging that was independent of ethnic differences among themselves. At the same time, we have to acknowledge that local identification is also one of the few possibilities open for marginalized people, as more global identities are restricted for those with greater cultural and economic capital. In an otherwise-globalized world, the young men are fixed in the local.

The local identification exhibited by the young men also suggests that the typical law enforcement approach to disrupting such youth groups may be misguided. Recent research on Muslims in New York City shows that those who feel a sense of belonging and inclusion are more willing to engage in cooperative actions if asked to do so by the police (Tyler, Schulhofer, and Huq 2010). In contrast, those who feel discriminated against and excluded are less likely to cooperate with law enforcement (e.g., in terrorist matters). While Akin, Aissa, and the others felt no sense of inclusion with German society, belonging to their group and developing such a strong local identification allowed them to form a social identity *within* Germany, which in return made them more likely to choose Germany as their home. Their sense of belonging to "their" neighborhood instilled a great feeling of responsibility toward it in them (illustrated, for example, by their attempts to rid the neighborhood of crackheads and junkies), which opened up possibilities for constructive social action, as Akin pointed out: "We really cleaned up here in Bockenheim. We got rid of all these disgusting junkies. . . . We really don't want them to be hanging out here, there are also kids around here, and the cops don't do anything. Bockenheim is now a junkie-free zone. They know that they have nothing to do here anymore." Despite their perceived exclusion from mainstream society and the fact that their efforts were often met with disregard, Metin described how the young men were open to taking up more formal forms of involvement within the district:

> Well, I'd be really up for telling these politicians here in Bockenheim what is really going on. I mean, they have no clue whatsoever. And when they do something involving the guys, it's just crap, because they have no clue. Like bringing Bifis to the soccer tournament, how retarded is that? But no one is asking us about anything anyways. We're just *Kanaken*.

Bifi is a snack consisting of pork meat. Given their Muslim background, most of the young men did not eat pork. Thus, providing them with Bifi at a citywide youth soccer tournament was seen as ironic and underscores the mainstream disregard for the culture of the young men. Such experiences opened up many ways for the young men to justify their participation in the drug trade. Many of these justifications became even more important in retrospect when the young men tried to reflect on their life choices. This does not mean, however, that they were unaware of their marginalization during the experiences themselves. Rather, their rather negative experiences with, and their relationship to, mainstream Germany were so ingrained in their everyday lives that they were not always fully cognizant of them (Bourdieu 2004). This social context will serve as a backdrop when we look at the structure of the drug trade and their day-to-day life as drug dealers.

We should keep in mind that the young men's involvement in crime is not unique to their group of friends but a greater phenomenon among second-generation immigrants in general and among second-generation immigrants of guest-worker and Muslim background in Western Europe in particular. As in the United States and Canada, the crime rates of second-generation immigrants in most Western European countries are typically higher than those of their parents. However, unlike the crime rates in the United States and Canada, "the crime rates of *some* second-generation immigrant groups in the European context drastically *exceed* the crime rates of the native-born population" (Bucerius 2011, 387, emphasis added). While this shows that these patterns do not hold true for all immigrant groups, studies from Germany and the Netherlands suggest that the children of former guest workers with Muslim backgrounds, like the young men in this study, are disproportionately involved in crime compared with other second-generation immigrants (Engbersen, van der Leun, and de Boom 2007; Baier et al. 2009; Albrecht 2011). As Berardi and Bucerius (2013) have argued elsewhere, the second-generation immigrant status puts individuals generally at a higher risk for criminal involvement in Germany and the Netherlands, but the second-generation immigrant of Muslim origin status, like that of the young men, multiplies that risk. The young men's drug-dealing behavior, which I will describe in the next chapter, is part of this larger phenomenon in Western European countries.

CHAPTER 3

"As Long As You Don't Get Carried Away"

Choosing Lifestyle and Gaining Respect

You know, it's fast money and you basically grow up with it. If all of your friends were dealing, you'd think it to be normal, too! Of course, it's still illegal, I mean, independent of the fact that everyone you know is doing shit. . . . It's still illegal, but it's somehow normal, so you start doing it, too.

—Ayan

The third winter into my research, there was a shortage of marijuana in Frankfurt. The young men were very annoyed by this, as they feared missing out on a lot of good business. Customers tended to buy more before the holidays. Akin, Aissa, and the others simply did not have enough product to meet the customers' needs, and a week before Christmas, there seemed to be no marijuana left in the city. The young men had to deal with a lot of complaints from their regular customers who were banking on the young men's supply for their respective holiday parties. At the same time, those of the young men who regularly smoked weed themselves became quite agitated about the shortage.

One December morning, Aissa and I had breakfast at our usual spot and started talking about the supply crisis. Feeling pressured by customers and concerned over lost profits (as in any other business, when supply goes down, prices go up), Aissa and three others had traveled to the Netherlands to buy marijuana. He had just come back from his trip the night before and started reflecting on the drive back.

AISSA: We were so paranoid last night. There was this BMW following us for 200 K. That's not really unusual on the Autobahn, but he always kept close by . . . even stopped at the same gas station. We thought for sure, it must be cops.

SANDRA: Did anything happen?

AISSA: No, it was two guys, and they kept close by for another hour after the gas station. Eventually, they just disappeared. I am still convinced that they were cops. Maybe something more important came up for them. I tell you, we were panicking. . . .

He went into great detail, explaining that this trip had been a huge mistake and that he couldn't believe he "got carried away." Knowing Aissa, I was surprised that he had gone on the trip in the first place. I had gotten to know him as a very risk-averse young man who would never carry drugs on him unless he had a prearranged deal to complete. Over the years, Aissa had been very successful as a dealer, in part because of his skill at diverting police attention. Because he was one of the few young men who had steady employment and led an otherwise-quiet and unsuspicious lifestyle, he did not seem to be at the center of law enforcement's attention. He saw dealing as a way to supplement his income and not as his primary occupation. In an effort to avoid the negative consequences that a criminal record would have on his more "legitimate' pursuits," he was usually very careful about how he conducted his business.

> You know what bugs me the most? It's that I *know* it's dumb. I *know* the risk. I *know* that you should not do it. And I did it *anyways*. I am an idiot. I can't believe I have been such an idiot. You know who warned me before? Akin, of all people. He said: "Man, I would be really careful. It's too hot right now. The cops must know we're out of luck here." And I did not listen because I thought he's just annoyed that we will make the business and not him.

The young men were generally very risk averse. Much of their success was built on the fact that they tried not to engage in any risky moves and deals. Going to the Netherlands and smuggling large quantities of drugs into Germany was generally viewed as risky. Despite the fact that official borders do not exist in the European landscape today, there is a lot of anecdotal evidence that the previous Dutch/German borders are still controlled heavily by undercover police trying to stop drug tourists from buying drugs in the Netherlands and smuggling them into Germany. As Akin had pointed out to Aissa, these patrols are usually intensified during times of shortages in Germany.

Aissa was generally very well aware of the risks and—under normal circumstances—would have declined to make the trip. However, given the current shortage and the lure of a potentially higher financial gain because no one in Bockenheim could sell at the time, he did not heed his usual safety measures and went anyways. The young men referred to the process of dropping the carefully established safety measures and—against all odds—engaging in something known to be risky as "getting carried away". Their business success was built on *not* getting carried away—indeed, they claimed that adhering to their safety measures would guarantee that law enforcement would not pay any serious attention to them. Aissa and I ended our conversation that morning with him demanding that I make him a promise: "This hasn't happened to me in years. I don't know what is wrong with my head. Sandra, you need to promise me to stop me next time. Promise that you will tell me if I ever want to do something that stupid again."

While I did promise to do so, it was not necessary. During the remainder of my research, Aissa did not let himself get carried away again, and, in fact, I rarely observed the young men engaging in deals that could fall into this category. In many ways, I would agree with the young men's assessment that the chances of facing charges were pretty low as long as they adhered to a set of rules that served to avoid detection by the police.

Faced with limited options, the young men all eventually started making money outside of the formal economy. Just as Murphy, Waldorf, and Reinarman (1990) described in the 1990s, most of the young men discussed in this book more or less drifted into dealing. Growing up in Bockenheim during the 1980s and 1990s, the young men were exposed as children to the drug trade by their older peers. At the end of the day, in their situations, dealing was the norm. Most of their peers were involved in drug dealing, so "differential associations" (Sutherland 1939) were a given, and making important connections was easy for them. The idea of differential associations holds that through interactions with others, individuals learn the necessary skills, values, and attitudes for criminal behavior, as well as make important connections to key people in the underground world. The young men had the best teachers available to acquire such skills, and, as in any other trade, becoming a successful drug dealer is facilitated by, and somewhat dependent on, having access to good mentors.

> VELI: You just learn from the older ones. You just observe what they're doing and they tell you, you know. They'd say: "Hey, this is shit, you have to do it this way." I mean, that's the way it works once they've accepted that you also do business. . . . In my case,

Jo taught me a lot. Tricking cops and so on. He really showed me a lot. . . .

SANDRA: How did you know this guy [a customer]?

EROL: Through Yildirim. I learned everything from him. Selling, getting customers, buying, everything. He showed me everything. He loaned me 12,000 [Deutsche] Marks [approximately US$8,700], just like that, so that I could build up something when I was not doing so well. He also referred customers, like this one judge.

SANDRA: And how did he know these people?

EROL: Well, he's just been around forever. He basically built up everyone, like the older generation, back in the day.

The reader might wonder how many of the young men discussed in this book made an income as drug dealers. When I started my fieldwork in 2001, thirty-eight of the fifty-five young men were involved in drug dealing, specifically of cannabis products (marijuana and hashish), cocaine, and heroin. The younger ones among them were set on graduating from high school and learning a trade. "Not making the same mistake" that the older ones had was a common theme among these young men, who had seen how dropping out of school further restricted opportunities in the formal economy for individuals like Akin and Inanc. They hoped that they could increase their chances in the formal economy by obtaining a good high school degree and vocational training. Despite these hopes, when I conducted my last formal interviews in 2006, all but three were involved in dealing.[1]

In the beginning, most of the young men's activities in the drug market were still coupled with "making it" in the formal economy; drug dealing, as Georgio pointed out, was seen as a way to make some money on the side for a while:

You know, it's kind of a slippery slope. At some point, you get that you can make so much more money when you're just doing drugs, and you start doing more and more, and at some point, you're just not up for school or vocational training or work anymore. You either have to force yourself, like blatantly force yourself, to stay in school, or bye-bye. But when you start off . . . like, I'd say that everyone here thought that they'd just do something on the side for a while. Except maybe Akin. . . . But then, there is also no chance for life if you stay in school. It's not like *your* life.

Georgio's reference to *"your* life" seemed to suggest that I had had a wider range of possibilities to choose from when finishing school. Many of the young men began their careers in the drug market after encountering the frustrations described in previous chapters. For them, the formal economy offered few possibilities, whereas the informal economy opened up many. Because they lived in the heart of Frankfurt, the banking capital of Europe, and because they constantly saw people who made a lot of money, relative deprivation was ever-present in the minds of these young men (who, despite leading an excessive lifestyle with their friends, often lived in cramped two- or three-bedroom apartments with their families and many siblings). When I asked about bankers, Akin once told me: "These suit fuckers, they got money big time. . . . They have everything: convertible *and* the BMW 7, the wife *and* the mistress, mansion, vacation and so on. Crazy life." Given their limited options, these young men saw dealing drugs as the only way to rise up through the social and economic strata of society.

In this chapter, I will describe my own introduction to the Bockenheim drug market, Bockenheim as the setting of the drug-dealing business, and the business model used by the young men, particularly with respect to partnerships, ethnicity, hierarchy, and the influence of previous generations. The reader will also gain a deeper understanding of the day-to-day business of the young men, including the buying, cutting, storing, and selling of drugs. Last, I will examine the connections between the formal and the informal economies and provide the reader with a better sense of the underlying theme of this chapter's opening story about Aissa: the importance of not getting carried away.

LEARNING ABOUT DRUG DEALING

When I started my fieldwork, I did not know much about drug dealing. Naturally, I was very interested in learning everything I could possibly learn from the young men. I was excited to learn how they purchased drugs, how they got customers, how they cut the drugs, how they kept customers and got rid of those they did not like, and how they stored the drugs and paraphernalia. However, my access to this kind of information was initially blocked because I wasn't able to establish a good rapport with Akin—arguably one of the key people in the group and an influential player in the drug-dealing world. When I initially started my research, the social workers at the youth center pointed him and Inanc out as the "leaders" of the group, whose approval I would have to gain. While I soon discovered that Inanc did not have the high standing in the group that the social workers assumed (for details, see Bucerius 2013), they were right about Akin, and our relationship was initially rocky at best.

Because Akin had announced publicly that he wanted me out of the youth center, many young men paid close attention to my relationship with Akin. At some point, I began to see gaining his trust as a personal challenge: ultimately, that task took me seven and a half months, because he initially had an intense and profound personal dislike for me. Establishing a rapport with Akin was much harder than with anyone else. In contrast to the others, Akin saw no positive side to or "practical value" in my presence. He had never aspired to graduate from school and dropped out at age 12. He earned his living exclusively by dealing drugs and did not seek any form of employment in the formal economy. I couldn't help him with homework or writing job applications. Akin was surprisingly non-athletic and did not seem at all interested in playing pool, which was clearly the favorite activity at the youth center.[2] He did not have a girlfriend, which removed the possibility for conversations about his relationships (although it is highly questionable whether he would have shared any information about that subject with me anyway). Berk and Adams (1970, 103) have noted, "The greater the social distance between the participant observer and the subjects, the greater difficulty in establishing and maintaining rapport." This proved to be especially true in my relationship with Akin. Akin saw me as a person with nothing in common with him and as a woman who totally contradicted his views on gender: "I just expect my girlfriend not to ask any questions. It's none of her business how I make my money or things like that. If I want to tell her at some point, OK, if not, fine as well. It's just a matter of respect that she should not be nosy. That's why nobody around here would ever date somebody like you."

Furthermore, he was involved in many of the discussions that occurred within the group about the "female duties" that I supposedly had and did not fulfill at the youth center, like cleaning and making coffee (see Appendix). Although he didn't always initiate these conversations, he routinely used them to rally everyone present behind these very traditional and patriarchal gender roles and, thus, against me. He also continually reiterated his incomprehension of why I would go through the hassle of gaining the trust of the young men, especially because I was so different from them.

> Sandra, you're a student. You're intelligent. . . . I get that. . . . You might have rich parents, but no matter what you're doing, no matter what you try, you will never know what our life is like, never. You will not have a clue! There is no way that you could ever completely understand! So, tell me, what exactly are you still doing here?

Akin was extremely creative in planning little schemes to make my research difficult. These actions started out as fairly harmless tricks, such as locking me into the bathroom and expecting me to scream for help or cry. The young men had decided not to test me the same way they would test a masculine "intruder" (physical violence, beatings, etc.), so gender difference (enacted in the form of "gendered violence") played a significant role in those interactions. Most often, these tests (usually initiated by Akin but executed by everyone) involved some sexual aspect: provocative questions, presenting me with porn and waiting for my reaction, cornering me as a group and asking me about my sex life, verbally threatening me with rape, or locking me in a room with Akin (who started masturbating but stopped thirty seconds later). The last two "tests" occurred only once and ended when I did not react as expected (screaming, crying, trying to escape, etc.).

Akin went to extreme measures to test my patience and my sincerity about my research. To me, his threats, even those of rape, never seemed very serious. My reactions to his attempts to scare me or test me were of great importance to him and eventually helped me gain his trust.

> I honestly don't know any woman who would have stood this. If I just think about that . . . if I had to face thirty guys in bomber jackets with knives in their pockets and what not who tell me that they are going to rape me . . . I would panic. Everybody would. I can't even believe that you didn't run off crying for help. . . . I don't know anybody who would not have fled. . . . Respect, Bullock, respect. Honestly!

None of the other young men "tested" me to the same extent or attributed so much importance to my ability to endure highly sexualized situations. When Akin eventually accepted me, he talked about how much it impressed him that I—as a woman—put up with "this bunch of crazy guys."[3] This turn in our relationship, after close to seven and a half months, was unexpected. Erol gave me a stuffed panther on behalf of Akin; Akin and I never discussed this "peace offering," but we both knew what it meant. After Akin sent me the gift, he never initiated another discussion about my role at the youth center or took any action against me. My presence there was never questioned again.

Akin ended up taking on a very special role in my research and became one of my key informants. He always let me know about upcoming events, especially within the drug business, in which I might be interested. He also shared his knowledge and experiences, trying to convey his subjective truth about his lifeworld. Having gained his trust, I was guaranteed access to other dealers, especially older ones. This good rapport was certainly very helpful when trying to get access to the drug-dealing world in which the young men participated and about which I knew little.

One of my very first encounters with cocaine occurred when I entered the small TV room at the community youth center and found four young men sitting around the table with a huge pile of powder cocaine and some scales; they were weighing it, cutting it, and putting it into little bags for selling. While they did this, a little dog belonging to one of the young men ran in between their legs, acting absolutely crazy. While I was stunned by the amount of cocaine lying on the table—it reminded me of a scene from a movie about dealers—I was more shocked by the little dog, which looked like it had been stung by a bee. He sprinted from one side of the room to the other, stopped sharply, shook his head, and started to move in a way that almost looked like a dance, only to sprint to the other side of the room, jump up and down on one spot, and then suddenly make a giant jump to the couch and back to the floor, where he once again started "dancing." I had never seen anything like it. No one seemed to pay attention to the dog, which worried me, and so I focused much more on the dog than on the drugs. I asked whether something was wrong with it. The four young men had not even really acknowledged me when I had entered the room and just continued what they were doing, but now they all looked at me and started laughing.

> GEZIM: Sandra, don't tell me you've never seen a dog on drugs?
> SANDRA: What do you mean . . . are you out of your mind? You're not giving this poor dog cocaine, are you?
> GEZIM: I always thought you had a brain, Sandra! Think . . . ! What do dogs do?
> SANDRA: I don't know what you're talking about [still shocked to realize that the dog was on drugs].
> LEMIR: Sandra, dogs sniff around . . . all day long . . . that's what dogs do. They sniff, sniff, sniff. So guess how much cocaine that dog has sniffed in his life? There's no way to avoid that. Drugs are everywhere . . .

I was shocked to learn that the young men's dogs (of which there were many) were all exposed to drugs, and that all acted similar to Gezim's dog, but the young men continued to package the cocaine, ignoring the animal. His behavior was absolutely normal to them, just as drug dealing seemed to be the most practical way for them to make a living.

During the early weeks when I was granted access to their dealing (a number of months into my fieldwork), everything was very new and exciting to me. While my gender was always salient in my interactions with the young men, it was probably *most* salient when I was present during drug deals. Normally, their drug deals only took place among men, so I was particularly glad that they allowed me access. I was also happy to finally be allowed into a room when drugs were on the table, and I soaked up all the information I could get about the drug trade. But later, I started to realize that the drug trade about which I was so excited to learn was just another type of work and not so different from any other job. At the end of the day, drug deals were just transactions, and decisions about pricing, choosing business partners and wholesalers, and assessing risk did not differ greatly from similar decisions made in the formal economy. About one and a half years into my research, I realized that I had stopped asking questions about the drug trade and had become much more interested in other aspects of the young men's lives. After a long period of being constantly surrounded by people who dealt drugs and witnessing many kinds of drug transactions, I lost my fascination with the drug trade and saw it as just another business, a perspective shared by Selim: "Well, I'd say it works like any other business, too. You meet, you exchange goods and money, you part again. It's no different from buying a TV; it's the same procedure. You just don't get a receipt [laughing]."

BOCKENHEIM AS A SETTING FOR THE DRUG TRADE

The young men all agreed that the drug market was the most practical and fastest way for them to make a living. In addition, their neighborhood provided an ideal setting for drug dealing. As noted in chapter 1, Bockenheim has built up a reputation as a hotspot for drugs over the years, which has attracted many customers. Despite its middle-class character during the time of my research, Bockenheim maintained a reputation as a rough neighborhood. This image was less influenced by the drug scene that characterized Bockenheim than by the history of gang fights that took place in the neighborhood in the early 1990s. During that time, young men in many neighborhoods in Frankfurt formed together into gangs, used gang names, symbols, and slogans, and engaged in regular fights with rival gangs from other neighborhoods.[4] The young men involved in these gangs were mainly regulars at community youth centers in their respective neighborhoods, and most had similar ethnic backgrounds to those of the young men described in this book. The fights were less about drug turf and more about "honor" and "power."

AKIN: I was, like, really little back then . . . like a child. But I made it into the newspaper. . . . On the day this journalist came to interview the guys, I was there, and she took a picture of all of the gangsters. I was in the picture. That was a big deal, because it was about all the old ones [previous generation], but they allowed me to be in the picture. I still have it. . . . I'll show it to you!

SANDRA: What was that all about?

AKIN: It was just about honor. It was about showing that we're stronger than others. That Bockenheim is the power, that Bockenheim has the real men, you know. You know, they wrote that sentence on anything . . . every fucking wall we could find. "Bockenheim is the power." It was lots of bullshit, meeting other groups with baseball bats and then just beating each other up. The cops were terrified . . . totally shitting in their pants. There was even a guy who wrote this book about all these fights [Herman Tertilt]. It was a power game—taking jackets away from rich German schoolkids, showing them that we're in power. Everyone did that. In every neighborhood . . . you know, like, showing them that we're in power. It's not that we needed the clothes. We just wanted to beat up other groups to show that we're the strongest. . . .

SANDRA: How did this all start?

AKIN: It all started because of the Nazis. You know, in the nineties, there were suddenly all these Nazis. . . . They started beating foreigners, [and] we wanted to be "ready" for the Nazis, just in case. It was a power game. Really, I think we also watched too much TV. Like American gang shit. Suddenly, we also thought we're a gang. . . . Everyone suddenly said: We're a gang. Club 77 and then the Bockenheim Bomber Boys for us, the young ones. There were Turkish Power Boys in Bornheim and Croatia Boys and so on, and so on.

SANDRA: How did that stop?

AKIN: Well, the cops cleaned up big time. Lots of people got busted. And it was just stupid. It was this thing that we did for, like, two years, and then it got stupid. And we got more careful—especially when you do shit [dealing drugs], you don't want to get in trouble because you're beating someone up with a baseball bat. That's just stupid. But, you know, we were the power—Bockenheim *was* the power, we won every fucking fight. That's even in the book! And this guy did not write about us, but about Bornheim—they were number two.

Although I started my research approximately ten years after these gang fights, they still influenced the perception of Bockenheim, at least in the minds of the young men.[5] For many, Bockenheim remained the rough "hood" where they could purchase drugs and needed to be careful.

> VELI: It does not matter whom you run into, everyone always says that Bockenheim still has this reputation of being tough . . . you know, all the bad guys and the drugs and so on. I'm sure that's just because of the reputation back in the day . . . because today, no one is getting beat up just for the sake of it. . . . But you know . . . the drugs and stuff . . . that's also because of the university. It's just that because of the university, there's just more people around who buy drugs than in the other 'hoods.
> AISSA: When I met my girlfriend, she was really unsure about us, just because I was from Bockenheim. . . . Especially when I met her brother, he was totally suspicious . . . so I basically had to tell him that things have changed and that these gang wars and everything that was going on in the nineties, that that is basically over. But he basically said that Bockenheim still has that kind of reputation and that everyone he knows still buys their shit [drugs] here. Bockenheim is still the number-one drug market after the main train station. But really, if you ask me, that's because of the students and the university and not because of its reputation. Or maybe it's both.

According to the young men, Bockenheim's reputation as a drug hotspot and the ready market provided by the university (as Ükler said, "In other neighborhoods, you have to go to clubs or hang out at street corners, et cetera. But here, you've got thousands of students coming in and going out every day—it's just a lot easier that way") made it an ideal neighborhood for drug trafficking.[6] At the same time, the young men's extensive networks in the neighborhood and positive relationships with many of the business owners contributed to their success as drug dealers in Bockenheim.

THE BUSINESS MODEL

Researchers often differentiate between open markets that feature street-level drug sales between anonymous participants and closed markets that are characterized by close ties between buyers and sellers (see Sampson 2001). Frankfurt has both open and closed markets—the main train station is a good example of an open market, but the young men discussed in this book were involved in a range of open and closed markets. They had regular customers, who constituted their main clientele, but they also sold to strangers on campus or in the park when they were starting out, short of money, or reentering the drug scene.

Bockenheim had several public spaces in which dealers and customers had the opportunity to exchange drugs, including a huge park and the public space at the entrance to the university campus. This space was called Bockenheimer Warte and included several cafés, two subway station entrances, some book vendors, and a small weekly farmer's market; it was also well known as a drug-purchasing spot. Most of the young men did not use these public spaces for drug deals, but if one of them was just getting into the business or reentering it after a prolonged absence (e.g., after imprisonment), he might linger near the park or the Warte, hoping to be approached by potential clients (actively approaching potential buyers considered a "no-go," as discussed in chapter 4). As soon as he had (re)built a clientele, he would withdraw from these public places and would only enter them again if he needed more money, as Aissa had done:

> When I first wanted to get into the business, I started hanging out at the park. Everyone goes there to buy: *Kanaken*, students, bankers, junkies, grandfathers— just everyone. It's the easiest way to build up connections. I mean, especially in the summer,[7] there are tons of students around, and they buy lots. I guess they're sitting in a circle at night, listening to Bob Marley, and rolling four joints out of one bag, debating about children in Ethiopia—but what do I care? At any rate, they buy a lot.

The park at Bockenheim differed from the open drug market of the central train station, which had needle exchange programs and city-run safe injection sites. That area was mainly used by heavy heroin and crack users, and the dealers there tended not to operate in networks. The young men, conversely, were organized in what could best be described as "socially bonded businesses" in which sellers were linked through both the desire to make money *and* the bonds of kinship, ethnicity, and neighborhood (Curtis and Wendel 2000). They shared more with each other than just their identity as dealers. While they were not all necessarily involved in the same deals, they were willing to assist one another when required, as Akin explained:

> Well, for example, if someone tells me about a very good deal, but I just don't have the time to take it on . . . or just don't feel like it . . . then I think about

whether I want to do it . . . and when I know that it's not for me, then I'll say, "No, thanks" or something like that, and then I'll go to the guys and ask around if someone is interested in the deal. Maybe someone can benefit from my connections, you know.

Business Partners and Networks

Akin was often the first to know about "good deals," as he would say, and was very generous in passing this information on to others if he or his direct business partners were not interested in them. The overwhelming majority of the young men were committed to a single business partner with whom they worked together closely on the same deals (see also Adler 1993). These business partners usually handled the main transaction of a deal together (transporting drugs from the wholesaler to storage), but other tasks were divided up (e.g., one was involved in initial negotiations with the wholesaler, while the other organized acceptable storage). The transportation was handled together to avoid legal risks. Ümit described this business relationship as follows: "You do that together, you and your partner, because . . . not because you can't trust him—he's your partner, you can trust him, no . . . but because it's a lower risk for both of you. Let's say it's like 100 grams of cocaine, then both of you are only charged with 50 if the cops bust you."

The first choice for a partner was often a best friend or a relative (as Aissa said, "I only do business with my brother. He's the only one I really trust. Who can you trust if not your own brother?"), but most young men had three or four additional partners with whom they could potentially form these kinds of business relationships, depending on the circumstances (see also Coomber and Maher 2006). Obviously, business partners had to have a certain level of trust in and sympathy for each other. While the group of young men portrayed itself as a closed unit to outsiders (e.g., the police, social workers, me as a new researcher, etc.), there was great variance among individuals in terms of friendships and sympathies for one another. As such, the young men only had a very small pool of people with whom they'd potentially form business partnerships.

Alliances involving three or more people rarely survived the test of time. The young men told me that they were afraid of somebody snitching and not knowing which of the three or four people had talked to the police. Working with only one business partner gave them a certain level of security, but it also highlighted the reality that the level of loyalty and trust within the group was not as high as was commonly claimed.[8]

Working by oneself was rare. Again, a certain degree of risk assessment was part of the calculation—as explained by Ümit previously, having a business partner also meant sharing a certain amount of responsibility and guilt or even being released from any feelings of guilt. As Aissa pointed out, sharing helped to normalize the act of dealing: "You probably think I am totally stupid, but it's just a different feeling if you share the business with someone. The only times that I really thought that it's not OK what I am doing was when I was doing shit by myself. All of a sudden, you really feel guilty."

While the young men were not all directly tied together as business partners, they still profited from many of the same connections and the same network. Many of the young men did business with the same wholesaler, often even buying and transporting drugs together to get a better deal. After completing that common transaction, however, they would all take separate paths.

The group of young men also worked together in other ways. They saw themselves as "brothers," so they made sure that the individual good was never placed above the common good—at least as long as the stakes were not too high. One night, for example, the police stopped a car with five of the young men and found a very small amount of marijuana (10 grams) that belonged to Mesut, the driver. The young men in the car, however, claimed that the marijuana was common property, belonging to all of the co-passengers for their own consumption. As such, each of the four co-passengers was held responsible for 2.5 grams, while Mesut himself came away clean. Saadettin, one of the passengers, confirmed this sense of loyalty:

> Of course, the cops are fucking with your head because they want to know who the fuck is the owner. But they can't do anything, they can only say: 2 grams for you, 2 grams for you, and they have to let you go. Nothing happens. That's just normal. And no one would ever say: "Well, but it's Mesut's stuff." This way, nothing happens to anyone, but if 10 grams are put on just one person, they have to do an hour of community service. And if you're driving, it's even worse.

As Saadettin pointed out, driver's licenses would be withdrawn if drivers were found to be in the possession of drugs. Not many of the young men had licenses, so it was crucial for the overall business that those who did have licenses kept them. The entire network of young men depended on their drivers,[9] who not only made it easier for them to get around in the evenings, but, more importantly, also enabled them to buy and transport drugs from wholesalers and deliver to steady customers, a task mostly done by car.

The young men also profited from sharing knowledge. While they did not all work as business partners nor deal the same drugs, they all shared an interest in the business of dealing drugs. Each had substantial knowledge about drugs, the police, wholesalers, and customers, and it was common practice to share that knowledge within their network. Additionally, if one young man was short on money, others often stepped in and loaned him funds so that he could get back into business (as Tarik said, "This could happen to anyone sometime, so it's not a big deal, we just help each other out"). Furthermore, their network served a security function: by knowing one another, having grown up together, and being friends with each other (though with different levels of closeness), the young men knew that others would support them if need be and that they could generally trust them not to provide police with information (even though there were very rare instances of snitching, discussed in more detail later). The network itself also did not really fluctuate much—while the younger men became closer over time and the older ones eventually left, membership in the network was dependent on an individual having grown up in Bockenheim. Outsiders were only integrated if they were related to or a long-time friend of one of the young men in Bockenheim.

Ethnic Aspects

While ethnicity played an important role in the drug trade for previous generations, especially in terms of forming business partnerships and working with a wholesaler, this was not the case at the time of my research. "Back in the day," as the young men would say, specific drugs were sold by young men of specific ethnic backgrounds: cannabis products were mainly dealt by young men of Turkish background, cocaine by those of Moroccan background, and heroin by those of Albanian background. Although all the young men agreed that this was once how the drug trade was divided, none could explain the reasons for such a division, as Mahir confirmed: "That was just the way it was. No one ever questioned that; it was just the way it was. Other places may have been totally different than Bockenheim. I mean, we did not only buy from Turks, for example, so it must have been different in other places."

As noted by other researchers (Ruggiero and Khan 2006), differences between ethnicities have become more blurred over the past few years. When I conducted my research, substances were no longer bound to a particular ethnic background, with the exception of the young men of Albanian background, who continued to deal primarily cocaine and heroin.

Unlike the other young men, those of Albanian origin did not live with their families and had to make their own living. Additionally, the formal economy was not even a theoretical option for these young men, because they did not have legal status and thus could not obtain a permit to work in Germany. This made them more dependent on their income from drug trafficking than the other young men. According to the group members, money was best in the cocaine trade, which explains why the young men with Albanian backgrounds focused on that drug.[10] Gezim, who was him-self of Albanian background, noted: "If you ask me, doing this marijuana shit is just not worth it. People have different opinions on that, but I think you're making way more money with cocaine."

Dealing heroin was a way to carve out a niche; the young men of Albanian heritage did not share the other young men's moral hesitations about deal-ing heroin, and, as such, they were able to fill the gap in Bockenheim's drug market by offering a substance that no one else would sell. Dealing cocaine and heroin was a simple choice for these young men, because they were generally granted immediate access to this market when they arrived in Germany, as Gezim experienced:

> When I got here, Jetmir referred some customers to me right away . . . so I got the customers and I could make a little bit of money. That was most important, more important than papers and so on, just to have some money. You just do what everyone else does. And because they all do heroin and cocaine, that's what you do. If they had sold cars, that's what you'd do. You don't have any connections.

With the exception of these young men of Albanian heritage, ethnic-ity did not seem to predict what drug a young man would sell. At the same time, contrary to previous assumptions (e.g., Dorn et al. 2003, 353; Natarajan and Belanger 1998), ethnicity and nationality did not play a role for these young men in terms of finding business partners or wholesal-ers. Other newer qualitative studies have come to the same conclusion; as Murji wrote (2007, 796), "In a world of increasing sources of supply and product destinations, a great many drug transactions are simply that—transactions." Nermin confirmed this finding:

> What good would it do if I were to only do business with Moroccans, and they are only idiots . . . I'd be stupid, you know. We've known each other for such a long time, and there's this brotherhood, and I am not thinking, "Ah, he's a Turk, so that's not on. . . . I only do shit with Moroccans." You know, he may just as well be more skilled, or I may have actually known him for much longer than a Moroccan.

Nermin's comment shows that long-term friendship and a rational assessment of a partner's skills were more relevant to the young men than an individual's ethnic background when deciding on business partners. Still, the young men said that when it came to wholesalers, initial trust was higher among people with the same ethnic background.[11] As Ibor noted: "I know it's irrational, but it's just that you simply trust a fellow countryman a bit more. But if you've known someone for a long time, it does not matter where he's from."

Again, the young men with Albanian background were an exception to this rule. They all said that they really wanted their business partners to speak the same language that they themselves did, whereas the other young men said that they would not choose an Albanian business partner. Interestingly, the other young men were afraid of becoming the targets of ethnic profiling if they engaged in business partnerships with young men of Albanian background. Lemir expressed this hesitation: "They are constantly being fucked [with] by the cops and put into jail, deportation and so on. It's just too dangerous to do business with them, because then you're part of that, and, in the end, you're fucked." Essentially, doing business with Albanians posed a higher risk for the young men and lead to increased wariness.

Hierarchies

Despite the popular opinion that drug markets usually have a very rigid hierarchical structure and organization, research has consistently shown this to be a myth (see, e.g., Bucerius 2007; Hess 2008b; Murji 2007; Zaitch 2002). At first glance, the drug market in which the young men were involved seemed very unorganized; one could get the impression that there were no hierarchical structures whatsoever, especially because the young men dealt different drugs at different times, with few constants. The young men themselves claimed that their group was utterly egalitarian in terms of drug dealing. They actually actively resisted a formal "pecking order" with respect to dealing in an attempt to conduct business differently than older generations of Bockenheim dealers.

How, then, did the young men conduct business, and did they have any form of structure in which some had more decision-making power than others? Very quickly, I learned that the young men did have a social structure that functioned both at the youth center and among them more generally. Identifying and learning to navigate this social structure was particularly crucial for me at the beginning of my research, when I was trying to gain the trust of the young men while hanging out at the youth center. Socially, there were young men who had higher standing, particularly those who made up the core group. This "core" group consisted of fourteen young men who dominated the day-to-day interactions at the center. They constantly hung around the center and were heavily involved in drug dealing. Because of their constant presence, they also received the most attention from the social workers and continuously tried to negotiate new rules for themselves (e.g., pushing for longer opening hours or for use of the center outside regular hours). The core group was highly respected among all the young men I met for their abilities as drug dealers, their physical strength in fights, their friendship networks and relatives, and their beliefs, leading others to often consult them on controversial topics (e.g., whether Kaner should be allowed to store his drugs at the youth center, or whether that would risk too much police attention).

It took me a long time to gain the trust of these core group members, and they established clear boundaries about how I ought to be treated. However, while these core members had more influence among the young men than did others, there was no clear top-down leadership. In other words, when a group of young men wanted to go to a certain bar at night, but Akin preferred to go to another, the majority still got its way (even if that meant that Akin chose not to come along). Furthermore, besides the core group, there were various "subgroups" reflecting the various degrees of friendship among the young men—that is, smaller networks of young men who were close friends and often spent their time together. Some of these subgroups were aligned according to age, while others came together as a result of shared interests (e.g., four of the older young men trained together at the same gym). Because these young men were not just part of one group with a simple hierarchical order, I had to gain the trust of each subgroup and did so in very different ways and at a different pace.

I had the hardest time establishing rapport with or gaining the trust of the core group. I often thought that I would never actually be able to build a relationship with many of the core group members that would allow me to dig deeper into my research questions, but I seemed to have very unexpected "turnaround" moments with many of them. One such moment happened about twelve weeks into my research. On that day, a young man named Acun (at 16, he was the youngest man at the youth center but was twice my size and very aggressive) tried to push me into the storage room at the youth center and was just about to close the door behind me, locking us both together into the room. Mesut was watching, which did not make me feel any safer. Up until that point, Mesut had either completely ignored me or stared at me; he was the only young man who had never said anything to me, and frankly, I was afraid of him. He was one of the oldest young men at the center and belonged to the core group. To my surprise, he grabbed Acun, pushed him away from me, slapped him in the face several times, and said, "I'm not going to see you again for the rest of the week." Acun said nothing and left—I did not see him again until the following week. I thanked Mesut, who only said, "Shit, Sandra, there are boundaries. Who does this asshole think he is?" From that point on, Mesut and I had a positive relationship; he never glared at me again. Essentially, Acun had tried to cross an established moral boundary—it was acceptable to challenge me verbally, even on sexual topics, but trying to actually touch me was a completely different situation. As such, Mesut stepped in, reestablishing "moral order" and sending a clear message that although the core group could challenge me and give me a hard time in many ways, there were certain limits.

The young men also operated within a business structure that applied in the drug-dealing world. Essentially, those with a higher standing usually had more connections, and thus more possibilities (in other words, being well liked and respected usually meant that one had higher social capital within the drug-dealing business). However, bigger dealers, like Akin, would not actively keep others from dealing more. In fact, there were—at times—young men who would deal larger quantities and make greater profits than Akin, despite the fact that Akin was certainly more popular within the group. In other words, the social hierarchy among the young men did not necessarily reflect involvement in drug dealing. The young men agreed that there was a social hierarchy among them but rejected the idea of being hierarchically structured in their business world.

> SANDRA: Would you say there is a certain hierarchy among you?
> ÖZGUR: No, that's not the case anymore. You know, back in the day, there were people who had more to say than others and of whom everyone was afraid, but that is not the case anymore today. We're all equal.

On the second day of my fieldwork, the youth center had arranged a canoe trip on a nearby river.[12] I shared a canoe with Gezim, who had a fairly high standing among the young men. Before we started paddling, he gave his personal stash of pot to Ayan, a much younger man, who was in another canoe. I don't know why he didn't keep it, but the whole trip came to center on him not having his pot. At some point, he decided that it was time to smoke a joint. Unfortunately, Ayan's canoe, containing Gezim's pot, was out of sight. Gezim and I started paddling madly to catch up, until we realized that Ayan's canoe was actually behind us. Gezim wanted to turn around and paddle upstream. I said that was crazy, if not impossible, so he and I got into an argument and finally decided to stay where we were and wait for Ayan. When Ayan's canoe got closer, we found that he had used up his own stash and had smoked Gezim's as well. Gezim was infuriated and started screaming that he would kill Ayan and the other two young men in his canoe. He started gesturing wildly, throwing his arms up and down, and actually tried to jump into Ayan's canoe. As a result, our canoe tipped over, and we both fell into the water.[13]

Despite Gezim being older and having a much higher standing than Ayan, this did not prevent Ayan from smoking Gezim's personal stash. Gezim did punish Ayan with a slap, which Ayan seemed to expect and did not fight. This little incident was very reflective of the social hierarchy among the young men more broadly: the powerful young men might punish those with lower standing, but the weaker young men were not always obedient or servile. Ayan smoked all of Gezim's marijuana without fearing severe consequences, and he did so in front of me—the new person—in a public test of Gezim's power.

With respect to hierarchies in the drug market, the young men constantly compared their current situation with how it was "back in the day" among "the previous generation." While all of the young men and the social workers at the community youth center agreed that the previous generation was much more violent and hierarchically structured, it would be incorrect to claim that the current generation lacked *any* hierarchical structure.[14] While the young men generally claimed that there were no leaders among them, this certainly did not mean that they were all equal. The core group, for example, had a better reputation among the young men than did others.

Reputation was very much based on being a successful drug dealer, measured by an individual's ability to deal drugs over a long period of time without getting into trouble with law enforcement. However, one did not have to be the biggest dealer at all times (on the contrary, it was seen as smart to disengage from dealing for a while if that kept one from conflict with the police). Obviously, other factors influenced reputation as well, such as physical strength, the willingness to vouch for friends unconditionally, financial resources, and age.

Young men with a better reputation did not seem to use their position to order around younger dealers or to have them perform certain services (like delivering drugs). Apparently, this was the case among the previous generation, as Akin recalled:

We all worked for them. They gave us money and we had to run. Sometimes we also had to buy food, and they did not give us enough money, and we had to pay ourselves. Or they thought that we had not given them enough change back, and we got beat up all the time. It was very different. There were lots of beatings, lots. Today, we're giving them money, they buy food for us *and* for themselves, *and* they get to keep the change! It's very different. But we'd never use them for transporting shit. No one has to know your shit.

As Akin noted, the young men wanted to have as few people as possible involved in their business. Therefore, the great majority of the young men actually carried out each step of the deal themselves (with their business partner) and avoided involving the younger members; in this sense, they saw themselves as having "become much smarter than the old ones," as Aissa said. Jawad explained why he would not involve younger members in his transactions:

For one, to involve younger ones is just a shitty thing to do . . . but also, how would I know whether they keep their mouth shut when push comes to shove. I mean, the cops will do everything to make you talk—they threaten you, they beat you . . . whatever you can think of! That's the reality. If you have a little guy, like Jeton, he might pee in his pants, and I'll be the one who suffers. It's stupid to involve younger ones.

At the time of my research, a better reputation within the group did not mean that an individual had other people working for him directly, but a good reputation certainly had an indirect influence on the drug market. For example, a good reputation generally made it easier to establish connections within the drug market and to make use of existing networks; it also meant getting first dibs at the best places to store drugs and the ability to negotiate for lower prices. To some extent, the young men with better reputations (such as Inanc, Aissa, and Akin) controlled the drug market in Bockenheim, because younger members had not yet established their own networks and were completely dependent on buying drugs from those who had access to bigger wholesale dealers. Younger members who wanted to get into the business were discouraged by Aissa, Akin, and others (a form of social control) and thus had a very difficult time getting started. Aissa explained his thinking about this:

They should just stay in school. You know, they can do things on the side, maybe . . . but they have to finish school. So I turn them down, just out of principle. But there is always one idiot who lets them into the business. . . . Once you're in, there's no way back. There is always one person who does not care, and then it's too late. Like Veli. . . . He could only get started because Jo, the retard, needed help with his fucking deal. So he let Veli quit school. He had begged for so long, and everyone always said, "Just finish off . . . you're so close" . . . but of course, Jo is a fucking idiot—he does not care.

While several of the young men had better reputations than others, one particular man had a unique role in the drug scene during the first few years of my research—Ulun. The young men claimed that no hierarchy existed among them, yet everyone agreed that Ulun stood out and was somehow better than the others. Ulun belonged to the previous generation at a time when not many members of that generation were around anymore. Some of them had been incarcerated, some had been deported, and some had started families and separated themselves from the drug scene. When I initially met Ulun, he was in his late twenties, older than most of the other young men. He was the neighborhood's wholesale dealer and brought in huge quantities of drugs, mostly in collaboration with Akin. Many of the young men bought drugs from him and then packaged and resold them in direct or indirect sales, so Ulun did business with almost all of the young men in one way or another.

Ulun was incarcerated in February 2004. Against all expectations of a normal market structure, no one stepped in to fill his shoes after his incarceration. Akin picked up most of his business and continued to act as one of the wholesalers from whom the young men would buy, but he was never interested in taking on the same kind of power that Ulun had wielded, proving again that the young men were striving for a system that was less hierarchical. Akin explained:

You know, he was one of the old ones [previous generation]. I'll continue the business because we were partners . . . but that anyone of us would be like him, someone that everyone has so much respect for, I don't believe that. The guys respect me, but it's not the same thing. He was just the last person of the old ones. . . . It has something to do with that—nowadays, that just doesn't exist anymore. No one wants that. . . . If you want to be someone like him, you first got to stab a couple of people to get that kind of reputation, and everyone is afraid. No one is interested in that—people just want to do their business.

Thus, many of the young men could coexist without arguing about each other's position and could choose to be involved in large or small deals. There were certainly young men who dealt on a larger or smaller scale, but these structures were not at all fixed, and the young men could easily move between them, that is, dealing more or less at different times (see also Murji 2007, 783). Ulun's incarceration also had no influence on the stability of the market—his absence did not seem to matter, even a few weeks after his incarceration. This shows that drug markets and the actors within them are not static structures but are instead dynamic and able to adapt to new situations (see also Valdez and Kaplan 2007, 896).

Influences of the Previous Generation

Ulun was regarded as being somewhat outside the core network, yet before his incarceration in 2004, he had a very strong influence on all of the young men. In many respects, everything stopped when he appeared. Personally, I was always somewhat afraid of Ulun. I never knew what he really thought of me, but he respected me enough to not start discussions about my role. Akin, the only one of the young men with whom he worked closely, was responsible for clearing my way with Ulun. On several occasions, Ulun inquired about me and whether or not I could be trusted. Even in the first couple of months, when Akin and I had not yet established a positive rapport, Akin told Ulun that I was "cool" (i.e., that I was not an undercover police officer). Later, he often referred to me as "princess," which Ulun and the others who did not know me very well took as a sign not only that I was "cool" but also that I was respected and accepted among the young men and that no one should question my status in the group.[15]

Over the years, Ulun and I never had very personal conversations, and I heard most of the things I learned about him through the other young men. I only hung out with him on one single night, three years into my fieldwork, as he did not usually spend his evenings with the young men. Akin once told me that Ulun liked socializing with him but had no interest in spending time with anyone else from the network. As such, Akin never brought him along in the evenings, except for one night when I ended up hanging out with Ulun, a girl he brought along (it was not clear to me whether she was a sex worker or a random girl he had just met), and Akin. It was Akin's birthday, and we celebrated the occasion in different bars until early in the morning. Even then, I did not get to know Ulun any better. For most of the night, he was on cocaine, which made conversations difficult, because everything seemed to make him paranoid. He yelled at me numerous times when I was driving because he thought I was going too fast, when in fact, and as a consequence of his paranoia, I was already the slowest car on the autobahn and was worried police might pull us over because of it. Ulun was athletic, muscular, and short. He did not have the same kind of people skills that Akin did, making me wonder how he rose to the top position in the drug trade of Bockenheim. The other young men reaffirmed my impression, telling me that Ulun had not been a high-ranking drug dealer in his generation but had been more of a follower. Essentially, he had only risen to the top because others had left the playing field involuntarily in the mid-1990s when the police conducted a massive drug bust and he was one of the few who did not get incarcerated or deported. His close relationships with the big players who were taken out of the field suddenly put him in the position to take over much of the business.

This is not to say that Ulun was an angel, or that anyone doubted his position among the young men when I met them.

EROL: Yeah . . . he was not one of the big guys back then, but he is now. Trust me, you don't want to get into trouble with him. Stay far away from him. He's got a bad reputation.

SANDRA: Should I stay away from him because I am a woman?

EROL: No, no [laughs]. All I am saying is: be careful. I'd say that to anyone. It's a different generation. You think we're bad. Well . . . they were much worse.

Erol's warning supported the other information about Ulun I had gathered from the social workers and the other young men. Ulun had a big scar on his face and a few others on his upper body (the young men used to play soccer shirtless, leaving their scars exposed), reminding me, and others, that he had been in a few fights involving weapons. Ulun's little brother Nurbay (who was 17 when I met him) was a regular visitor at the community youth center and was strongly protected by everyone. Akin once told me that Ulun essentially expected him to take care of Nurbay. When Akin was not around, he asked others to fulfill that role and report back to him. Nurbay did not enjoy the same freedom as most of the young men his age—he always had to stay on the right track regarding school and was not allowed to drink alcohol or consume any drugs, because every action would be reported back to his brother. One day, Nurbay came to the youth center with the worst black eye I had ever seen. When I asked about it, he said that his brother had punished him for failing a test at school. As was common among the young men when talking about punishments from relatives, Nurbay did not think that there was anything wrong with the beating: "Sandra, I deserved it. I should have studied a lot more."

Except for Nurbay's black eye, I never directly observed Ulun being violent. Clearly, however, I was not the only one who was warned about Ulun.

On the very few occasions that he would stop by the community youth center, many of the young men left.

> DARIO: Well . . . it's just like, when he's in the room, you're definitely a bit nervous. I mean, you're not totally paranoid, but there's a lot of respect. You've got a lot of respect for him, and you just pay really good attention to what you're saying and what you're doing, and, you know . . . I just prefer to leave then. It's just that when it's just us, especially the younger ones, when it's just us, we're different and are behaving differently than when Akin and the other older ones are around. . . . You just have even more respect for him. . . . It's a way of showing respect that he's just a number too big for me, so I basically just leave.
>
> SANDRA: What kind of respect is that? I mean, why is that such a great respect?
>
> DARIO: Well, it's respect because of age. . . . You know, just the normal respect because he's so much older [he was ten years older than Dario]. But of course, also because he's one of the old ones. . . . They were just so much tougher. And he's the one . . . you know . . . the one who's not been in jail, *even though* he's one of them. And of course, one knows what he's done. You know, what he's capable of.

Dario's feelings toward Ulun were similar to those of many of the young men. The question of what Ulun "was capable of" always loomed in the background. I tried on several occasions to get an answer from the young men about what that might be, but I was unsuccessful. However, several young men talked about Ulun's "capabilities" in relation to other topics. Erol, for example, spoke very clearly about Ulun's violence when talking about the cocaine trade:

> I was part of so much shit. So much shit. One time, we took someone along in the car, to the Taunus [an area near Frankfurt]. He owed [Ulun] 50,000 marks [approximately US$34,000] and claimed to not have it and so on and so forth. We stabbed him badly, and we just let him lie there, on the street. Just like that. I think I dreamed about it for at least one year, if not longer. Today, I sometimes wake up and hear his voice. . . . And I had a bad conscience—whose side do you take? But if I had stopped them, who knows what would have happened to me. I did not have a choice. He survived—thank God.

Essentially, Ulun was capable of exercising power over the young men just by being present. His status as being "one of the older generation" was of major importance; the young men deeply respected him for being one of the "previous ones." After Ulun had been incarcerated and finally released, I asked why he had been so highly respected for such a long time and why he did not seem to have any influence after his release. Özgur explained how the young men had been able to build up their own structure, independent of the previous power relationships:

> I would say this was only the case because he was one of the old ones, so you just had to show respect. You also don't go to your dad and say: "Now, I am an adult, now I don't need you anymore." Well . . . Germans may do that . . . [laughing]. But usually you'd never do that! But that does not mean that you can't live without your dad, right, Sandra? You respect your dad, and if, someday, he is not around anymore, life goes on and it works . . . and you don't need a new dad for your life to work. You know what I mean? I don't want to say that Ulun was the dad here . . . but in terms of respect, he was something similar. As long as he was here, everyone respected him, even though no one wanted to have anything to do with all that bullshit from back then [referring to the previous generations].

For the time being, Ulun had psychological power over the young men, but in terms of drug dealing, he did not act as a "Godfather." In collaboration with Akin, Ulun brought large quantities of drugs into the neighborhood, but the young men were not bound to purchase their stock from them. I was surprised that the young men did not seem to revert back to the old drug dealing structure after Ulun's release from prison. The younger ones in particular appeared to hold their breath for a couple of days to see whether the older ones (like Akin and Aissa) would form close bonds with Ulun again, but everyone seemed very relieved when the routine was not disturbed by Ulun's sudden reappearance. Essentially, Ulun's incarceration was just what the network of young men needed to free themselves of the previous generation's influence. By the time Ulun returned, enough time had passed for the network to evolve and come to terms with its own beliefs, especially its strong feelings against leadership, making it impossible for Ulun to claim any such role (Popitz 1969).[16] Additionally, Ulun's reputation had suffered a serious blow as a result of being incarcerated. The young men believed that his incarceration was a consequence of him getting "carried away," that is, he had broken the number-one rule of being a successful dealer, making it impossible for him to reclaim power over others. Similarly, other young men who were released from prison struggled with their new roles and were forced to re-create themselves upon their return.

Speculations, Snitching, and Life after Incarceration

When Ulun was incarcerated in 2004, everyone thought he would be deported back to Turkey. To everyone's surprise, he was released after just two years. The young men speculated about his release just as much as they had about his incarceration.[17] No one really believed that Ulun had gotten out without having snitched, including Ümit, who said: "Well, to be frank: this is impossible. I bet you anything you want, he snitched. There's no other way. . . . Why would they keep him here [in Germany] and let him walk around after just two years, no electronic bracelet, nothing. No way, no way!"

Speculations about snitching were typical and occurred every time someone was incarcerated, deported, or released. Anyone who had just been released from prison had to face mistrust and skepticism, which naturally led to feelings of abandonment among those who had just regained their freedom. Ferdi recalled his experience upon being released from prison: "You think everything will be just like it's always been . . . party on, you'll see your friends again—yay! That's bullshit. In the beginning, no one wanted to do business with me. 'No, sorry, I have enough on my plate' and bullshit like that. Really bad! But you know . . . brother, brother, brotherhood. It's all bullshit!" The young men did not want to risk anything when it came to those who had just been released. Obviously there was never a guarantee of safety, and the young men were even somewhat understanding of those who had snitched to cut a better deal. Having spent time in prison, Matthias understood the possibility of doing something drastic to get out:

> Theoretically, I'd say no one around here would ever do that. But it's a question of character. I mean, I trust everyone around here, but if you think about it, you're sitting in this small cell, and no one comes to visit and no one writes letters. . . . I mean, it's possible that you become weak. Even though you know beforehand. I mean, I know that no one would ever write . . . maybe just the very closest friends. I mean, you know that![18]

Apart from the question of character, the young men stressed that one's willingness to live outside of Bockenheim also factored into an individual's decision about whether or not to snitch. When talking about Reza, who had snitched and greatly incriminated Jo and Inanc to cut himself a better deal, Inanc explained why Reza was the real loser in this scenario and why he himself would never cut a deal:

> INANC: But you know, he just can't set a foot in Bockenheim anymore. If he did that, there's no mercy—I swear! But you know,

if he stays away, that's basically already punishment: he doesn't have any friends anymore and can't come back to Bockenheim. And he can't really go anywhere else in Frankfurt—these things get around. Well, at least everyone will be very, very suspicious. . . . You know, if someone from Gallus [a different neighborhood] would suddenly only hang out in Bockenheim, I'd ask a few questions. . . .

SANDRA: Did anyone ever try to cut a deal with you? The cops or a lawyer?

INANC: Sandra, my lawyer told me just last week that I should just talk a little and that something could be done then. She thinks if I just talk a little, she could get me on probation, but if not, I'll go in for at least six months . . . maybe more . . . and probation on top of that. You know, she's really cool . . . she's young and just really cool.

SANDRA: So . . . what do you do?

INANC: Yeah, I don't know. . . . What should I do? You know, you really start thinking. But I told her . . . I said, "Look, I am not an asshole, I'll go in." She said that I should think about my life and my future and that Reza also snitched. So I told her that this is exactly the reason why I would not talk. She did not get it even though she's pretty cool. But, you know, I just want to keep my honor and be able to show my face in Bockenheim. Well . . . what are six months, Sandra, really?! I can do that, right? You know, you also have to think about what comes after . . . and not just about the six months. I want to continue to live my life here. You know, I don't want to sit in a hole under the earth like Saddam.

The young men were aware that snitching would have a serious effect on their lives after incarceration. Given that their group of friends was such a central part of their lives and that Bockenheim was the one place in the world to which they felt closely attached, many could not imagine life without the other young men or in a different area (at least until they were married). During the five years of my research, I was aware of only two proven occasions when any of the young men snitched on others.

After being released from prison, it took some time for individuals to earn back the trust of the rest of the young men, but they almost never regained their original status within the network. Incarceration significantly tarnished their reputation among the group, who believed that the German police were stupid and that it was your own fault if you got busted. At the same time, the young men's network was constantly evolving and adapting to new situations; power relations shifted with every incarceration or decision to become more or less involved in the drug trade. As mentioned previously, Ulun was unable to regain his original position after being released from prison, and today he plays only a minor role in the drug market. Akin explained that life always goes on, stressing the importance of being present and the focus on the "here and now":

> I can tell you how it works: out of sight, out of mind! With everything. If someone moves, fine, but we don't write letters. If he comes back, fine, but life went on. Nice to see him again, you're always happy to see good friends again, but no one was waiting for XY to come back and try to play boss. If that's what he wanted, he should not have gone in the first place [alluding to Ulun]. Life always goes on and on and on, you know.

DAY-TO-DAY BUSINESS

As mentioned previously, the young men mainly sold three drugs: cannabis, cocaine, and heroin. Only a few subjects restricted themselves to selling a single drug, and most showed considerable flexibility in that regard. Cannabis products were by far the most commonly dealt drugs, and fifty-one of the fifty-five young men sold some form of it. More than half (twenty-eight) of the young men also sold other drugs, primarily cocaine. An additional six, most of whom were of Albanian heritage, also sold heroin. Varying the supply was actually a very common practice among the young men, since they believed that it made good business sense, as Nermin confirmed:

> It's this thing, you know. If you're making good money for a while, let's say with coke, the cops start looking for you more intensely at some point. They want to know where you're going, what you're doing, and so forth. So if you stop doing coke and just take a break or you're starting with shit [hashish], then they might think: "Hmm, he's not around the same places anymore, he's got a different lifestyle, so he quit." And then they just let you get away with it. But sometimes a connection is fucked up, maybe because the other one quit his business or got arrested or whatever, who knows, and then the whole business is just too hot, because the cops are around or you don't have anybody else to buy from. So a friend would say: "I have a very good pot connection." So, of course, you'll go for that one, because you want to have your money, right?! Well, or sometimes, you just have really bad clients who are standing in front of your door in the middle of the night, begging for a line, and everybody takes notice because it's so damn

obvious. . . . Then you just have to get rid of them, and you change your number and tell them: "No more." So when everything is a little quieter, you can start again.

The young men typically offered one drug for a certain period of time and then switched to another. This was done for many reasons: to get rid of annoying customers, to divert police attention, to overcome supply difficulties, and to profit by filling a gap in the market. Generally, they tended to accept any "very good deals" that promised fast and easy money, even if they had been mainly or exclusively dealing a different drug. This flexibility again shows how the drug-dealing business does not differ greatly from other businesses: many of the considerations in a transaction involve a cost-benefit analysis (though, as will be explained in chapter 4, the considerations of the young men moved way beyond normal cost-benefit calculations). Kash noted, "Actually, you know, I mainly do pot, but if it is a really good coke deal, why not, I'd go for it. It's just fast money and boom, boom; everybody has to look out for himself."

Risk assessments were also part of the young men's calculations. Some, for example, refrained from selling harder drugs because of possible legal repercussions (as Fadil said, "There's just much more on the line with H [heroin] or coke"). Most generally preferred to sell larger quantities of drugs, primarily because this approach involved fewer transactions and therefore less risk of attracting the police (and also because they could avoid the cumbersome job of packaging the drug into smaller units). Aissa offered the following argument in favor of selling larger quantities:

> That's always better, even if you get less. It's annoying to pack these little bags and hassle down customers and so on. All of that just doesn't exist in this world. You give them 100 grams, bang, bang, and you say bye-bye. Done. It's much more likely that someone pays attention to you if you do this a couple of times a day.

Weighing and portioning the drugs into the little bags not only was an annoying task, but also had to be done very carefully. Some customers weighed the drug after they got home, and if they had been shorted, they might try to find a new dealer. For most of the young men, like Georgio, this was understandable:

> Well, I mean, it's natural. . . . No one likes to be fooled. But it also depends on whether they know others who deal. If not, out of luck. . . . They complain, but that's it. But if they know others, they're gone. Naturally . . . I'd do the same

thing. But you know who's weighing and who's not. Most of them are students who really need to calculate their costs and who want to know exactly what they're paying, et cetera. They also don't care as much about quality—for them, it's all about the price. Germans. . . .

The risk assessment concerning the volume of drugs that a young man would deal on a daily basis was also heavily influenced by the individual's police record and immediate financial situation. Young men who were currently involved with the police tended to restrain their involvement in the market unless they urgently needed money. My systematic observations and interviews over the course of the five years revealed that on average, eight of the fifty-five young men trafficked more than one kilo of cannabis products a week, three sold more than 500 grams of cannabis products a week, thirteen sold more than 50 grams of cocaine a week, and two sold more than 50 grams of heroin a week. The remaining young men sold smaller amounts. Thus, the young men I observed could mostly be classified as belonging to the upper tier of low-level dealers, with the remainder generally being classified as mid-level dealers.

Getting Drugs

Those young men who sold smaller amounts of drugs (i.e., less than 100 grams of cannabis or less than 20 grams of cocaine or heroin per week) tended to purchase their supplies from other members of the group (see also Adler 1993). Because they shared a common identity as Bockenheimers and the same experiences as other marginalized immigrants in Germany, the young men often felt compelled to help each other. Exceptions to this rule arose when dealers from other neighborhoods offered substantially lower prices or when larger dealers within the group refused to sell their substances to smaller dealers. As Aissa described previously, these refusals sometimes occurred when the person wanting to buy drugs was a younger brother or cousin of a close friend who, from the bigger dealer's perspective, should not be permitted to enter the business (see also Tertilt 1996). Interpersonal conflict with another group member and the desire to prevent him from being successful was another reason for refusing to sell. For example, for a very long time, Aissa refused to share a very good pot connection with Erol. During that time, both of them were dealing marijuana on a large scale, acting as wholesalers by providing drugs to many of the other young men in the network to sell. In addition to being competitors, Aissa and Erol had many personal differences, and Aissa enjoyed being a step ahead of Erol: "I just don't like him. Never have. I like this. I am not helping him, unless he begs."

Large amounts of drugs were generally purchased from Ulun and Akin, others like Aissa or Erol who sometimes acted as wholesalers, or wholesalers from outside the group who were generally met at parties, bars, or clubs. Many such connections were established by coincidence and by word of mouth. Interestingly, the young men did not think of these connections with strangers as particularly risky. Essentially, the drug market relied on a referral system, similar to that found in the formal economy or in the academic world. Instead of writing reference letters, dealers were referred to others verbally, a practice they found commonplace:

> UMIT: What do you mean, dangerous? These are always people that you somehow know. Because they're the friend of a friend or a cousin of a friend. You know, we all know each other.
>
> AISSA: Yeah, it's like you also know that the other one is doing business with that particular guy. So it's not just a random person. It's not like going to the Netherlands and randomly making business with someone you've never heard of before.

As Aissa noted, it was uncommon for the young men to purchase drugs, especially cannabis products, in the Netherlands. During the five years of my research, the young men only drove to the Netherlands a handful of times.[19] One winter, the marijuana supply in Frankfurt was particularly low, and a few young men drove to the Dutch border several times to purchase drugs in order to meet demand. I had been present during many other transactions, but I was never able to go with them on one of these trips. The trips were never really planned: usually the young men would drive off in the middle of the night after spending an evening talking about their frustration with the market situation in Frankfurt. Nermin described one such occasion: "We just had to go that night. There is just nothing going on here, it's crazy. All these customers and no pot, no nothing to sell."

Most of the young men knew more than one wholesaler and typically conducted business with the one who offered the best cost-quality ratio (they always placed a lot of emphasis on the purity and overall quality of the substance, preferring to pay a slightly higher price for a better product). This approach was in contrast to the enduring connection between wholesalers and customers that had characterized the market in an earlier era. Ibor disputed the idea that dealers were restricted to a single wholesaler to find supplies: "That's bullshit! That was back in the day, but nowadays . . . business is business, the client is the king, you know. There are *soooo* many. . . . Everybody knows that, and nobody can be mad. That's just not the same anymore. You can buy wherever you want to."

Before beginning my research, I naively assumed that there would always be one wholesaler on whom everyone could rely. However, the young men very quickly disabused me of this belief; even when Ulun was still around, he was not the only wholesaler with whom the young men worked. As Ümit pointed out, it was necessary to have different dealers, because no one knew when things would change: "Things change quickly. The cops are also faster than they used to be. You're doing business with someone today and that person is gone by tomorrow, or he quit, or he is suddenly too expensive, or you hear from someone who's cheaper and better and you buy there. . . . That's just life.

The young men worked with more than one wholesaler for various reasons. Price calculations were certainly an important consideration; by doing business with more than one person, they could get the lowest possible price. Also, wholesalers sometimes had supply difficulties or had to lie low for a while to avoid police. Inevitably, it was necessary to have connections to more than one wholesaler.

Clearly, the drug market was very flexible, both at the retail and the wholesale levels. Relationships to wholesalers were rarely long lasting because of arrests, deportation, entries and exits from the illicit market, and a variety of other factors. Evidence has consistently refuted the popular idea that organized crime dominates illegal drug markets (see Adler 1993; Arlacchi and Lewis 1990; Curtis, Wendel, and Spunt 2001; Genterczewsky 2008; Hess 1992; Hess 2008a; Jansen 2002; Reuter 1983; Reuter 2004; Reuter and Haaga 1988; Reuter, MacCoun, and Murphy 1990; Warner 1986; Williams 1989; Zaitch 2002).

Meetings with wholesalers were usually arranged outside Frankfurt at highway service areas. The young men felt that meeting wholesalers in the city would attract too much police attention; highway service areas were considered safe places to meet, and the young men had a very good sense of whether or not they were being followed.

I vividly remember one night shortly after Ulun was incarcerated. Akin and Erol wanted to pick up a large amount of cocaine, and I was in the car with them when they received a phone call from the wholesaler about when and where to meet. As Akin drove down the highway, he said he thought we were being followed. Erol and Akin agreed that they should stop at the next gas station to see whether the car would also pull in. It did and left relatively soon after we did. (Akin said: "I know this bastard, it's the same car that was outside the Panama Bar—remember, Bullock, when I told you the undercover was there?"). I was trying to figure out what to do in case the young men decided to go through with the transaction, but Akin and Erol very quickly decided to turn around. The evening ended up being a four-hour car trip, back and forth along various highways in and around Frankfurt. Erol and Akin seemed to get high on the fact that the police were wasting their time following us for so long. (Akin said: "They are so stupid. They cannot seriously believe that anything is happening here. So stupid.") We drove around in circles all night but were never stopped by the police. To be on the safe side, Akin called off the transaction.

Selling Drugs

Cell phones were essential for selling drugs. Each of the young men typically had several phones and numbers and changed them frequently. Whether this was really necessary is unclear, but they strongly felt that these precautions were warranted in order to prevent the phones from being tapped by the police. When the young men prearranged a transaction via cell phone, they always took only the required amount of drugs with them. They believed that this strategy was safer, and it is possible they were right, because the great majority of the young men had steady customers and did not sell to random people on the street. Those who did sell to strangers in public places (usually only those who were just starting out or those who were trying to reestablish a network of customers) often stored drugs at a nearby location. For example, young men selling in the local park stored their drugs under a bush and only retrieved them when they made a sale. Ümit, for example, knew his limits: "I would never walk around with more than 20 grams [of cannabis]. Most of us just bunker [it] and get it when needed. If you get caught with more than that, you can't claim it's for your own consumption. And if the cops search the park or whatever, they can't prove it's yours."

The young men obviously preferred selling to established clients, a practice that had enormous security advantages for them. Becker has observed that regular clients inevitably become an integral part of the drug-trafficking scene and therefore guarantee a certain degree of safety: "In becoming defined as a member, one is also defined as a person who can safely be trusted to buy drugs without endangering anyone else" (1955, 215).

The young men did not use a fixed common location to conduct business. Drugs were exchanged at places agreed upon during the first meeting with a client—usually a street corner, a particular square, or a café, but never the dealer's apartment[20]—and these sites seldom changed. Decisions about where to conduct business were based on risk assessment, but the young men had various opinions about their respective places. Some felt that public spaces, such as bars and cafés, were the best locations for conducting transactions because no one would suspect drug dealing in those spots. Other felt that it was too risky to conduct transactions in cafés and bars because undercover police could easily blend in with other patrons.

One event drastically influenced the opinion of many of the young men about selling in public. Inanc and Reza had sold small amounts (2–3 grams) of cocaine to a previously unknown client a couple of times during a period of three weeks. After three weeks, the client asked for 200 grams. Feeling good about the connection, they agreed to the transaction and arranged to meet the client in a local café. Aissa recalled what happened and how Reza was busted:

> They were warned by three people that day. Mentor called Inanc and told him that he saw tons of undercovers on campus. This must not have happened. But Inanc went anyways to check out the situation, and he told Reza to wait at the Future [a different café]. And he met the guy at the Hemmingway [Café]. Reza was basically supposed to wait until Inanc would call him, but the idiot just came over with the stuff. So when the guy put the money on the table, like 7,600 euros, you could see people get up from twenty different tables at the place and run toward their table. No chance. The guy was an undercover, too.

Another strategy was to deliver drugs directly to customers. This technique was primarily used by dealers who sold large quantities of drugs to steady customers who did not want to be involved in shady transactions on the street. These customers were mainly professionals and sometimes students or sex workers, and their drugs (especially cocaine) were usually delivered in large quantities. The sex workers worked in brothels, out of their apartments, or in massage parlors/spas.[21] Besides the fact that these customers often purchased larger quantities, they often provided sexual services in return for a line of cocaine. Ümit's take on it was: "You give them a line for themselves, and you get a fuck. That's a good deal for everyone." Aissa agreed it was good business:

> The girls buy lots, and they sell to their customers. Some consume themselves, but they mostly just sell to their customers. And they take lots from us . . . like 50 grams or something. I just sold [some] for 44 [euros] a gram. . . . That's 12 euros for me per gram, [and] that's OK. They can ask for 50, 60, 70 euros, depending on how much and to whom they sell.

This was a good deal, because Aissa had bought the cocaine for 32 euros and resold it at 44 euros per gram. As he pointed out, it did not matter to the young men if the sex workers resold the drugs at a higher price.

The young men sometimes stored drugs at the community youth center as well as in basements, in public garages, or at the homes of relatives; some even rented bachelor apartments to store their drugs,[22] but they generally did not ask customers to come to the community youth center for transactions. They all stated that selling out of the center would make their job easier but agreed that the center should be reserved for hanging out and that dealing from the center would unnecessarily attract even more police attention. The community youth center was under constant surveillance, and the young men knew that it would be a dealbreaker to sell there. As Elvis explained, they felt that as long as customers did not come to the location, the police would merely observe but never enter the center:

> The cops never come in, but I am convinced that they know exactly what's going on in here. They are outside all day long and are always looking up. They must have a reason for doing that—otherwise, why would they always park a car right down there [pointing to the police car], as if that's the only place to park a car in this neighborhood? I think as long as we play by their rules, they leave us alone. If people here start going crazy and start dealing from here, the cops will come in.

While the young men did not ask outside customers to come to the center, and even vigorously sent away people who came there looking for their dealer, they did sell to regular visitors within their group at the center. However, these transactions generally only involved small amounts of cannabis products that were used for day-to-day consumption. Such exchanges were, as Erol, pointed out, a lot easier: "I like selling here, it's just easy. There are always enough people who'd like to smoke but don't have marijuana themselves. It's just the easiest way to sell stuff. It's only small money on the side, but money is money, you know?!"[23]

Cutting and Pricing Drugs

Prices did not vary dramatically over the course of my research. When they did, the changes were usually related to availability, quality (especially the purity of cocaine and heroin), and risk assessment. Policing sometimes seemed to be more strictly enforced, and some of the young men quit dealing during these times (which never lasted longer than a few weeks). Those who carried on with business during these periods had more opportunities for selling and sometimes raised their prices in response to the increased risk. Some prices, however, were set and never changed—for example, the price of a bag of marijuana never changed, although the quality of the marijuana in that bag might, as described in this exchange with Aissa, Ferdi, and Akin:

> AISSA: The bag is always 10 euros. But sometimes it's amazing pot. Then I just don't put 1.5 grams into the bag. The clients notice immediately that the shit is great, [and] they do come back.
>
> FERDI: Anything else would not make any sense. Everyone knows that it's 10 euros. They always bring 10, and there's no politics. Imagine it would be 11.70. . . . How the fuck would you deal with that? Give change? That'd be fucked up. This way, they know what they pay, and I know what I get.

Generally, the young men did not negotiate with customers, especially not in the marijuana and hashish business. As Akin said: "If they want to have it cheaper, they just have to go elsewhere. If you start negotiating, people will know, and everyone will want to negotiate. You need to be the boss." Prices for hashish were generally a bit lower than prices for marijuana. "Fake" hashish was often sold, especially to university students who, as Akin said, "had no clue what they're talking about." The young men often used the kitchen at the community youth center to "bake" fake hashish using henna (hair color) and other substances. The first time that I saw Akin, Inanc, and Erol in the kitchen, they said they were about to "cook." I was surprised and asked them what they were making; they gave me some vague answer. Later that night, I mentioned to Georgio that I was surprised that Akin had not asked me to cook *for* them. Georgio burst out laughing; he could not believe that I had really thought they were cooking food.

Over the years, the young men taught me all their tricks and tips on how to distinguish fake hashish from real hashish, and I was always surprised at how many customers did not know the difference. While they would sometimes come back and complain about the quality, changing dealers was uncommon. It was not easy for university students to find a dealer, so the threshold that needed to be met for a customer to look for a new dealer was quite high, even when he or she was unhappy with the previous dealer or his products. The young men at the community youth center very rarely consumed hashish themselves—they did not fully trust the drug, and they were concerned about health risks, as Erol said: "You just can't know for sure. There can always be glue in it or something strange."

In the cocaine market, prices depended not only on the purity of the drug but also on the knowledge a specific customer had. As Erol told me, some people "just have no clue." According to him, the customers who were generally less knowledgeable about the drug trade were "the suit fuckers who are just afraid to get caught." As they did with prices, the young men used varying criteria for cutting cocaine (diluting it with milk-sugar products like Edelweiss or lactose) depending on the knowledge of the particular client. Generally, they did not cut cocaine as much as they would heroin, as Nermin explained:

> You can't compare H with cocaine. It's a different game. Totally different customers. With H, you can cut like crazy . . . but powder? That's different. With powder, it really depends on the customer. Some really know their shit, and they refuse to pay if you cut too much. Generally speaking, I'd do one to one if I have really good stuff. But I also have customers who'd only take three to one. But the other way around . . . not like with H. Like three cocaine and one Edelweiss.

Heroin was usually cut more because the customers were more vulnerable and needy. The young men used very business-oriented strategies to attract and keep these customers. Georgio described his approach:

> In the beginning, you give them good stuff, like one to one, and the junkie knows, "Ah! He has good H." Then you wait until he starts buying from you exclusively and talks to other people and so on. Then you give him one to two—he does not notice, then one to three, and at some point, one to four. Some even sell one to five. . . . I mean, the junkies complain, but then you just give them a bit better, so that he's happy, and then you go down again. And if you want to get rid of them, you give them only shitty mixes or just pure color.

While the young men were willing to sell large amounts of cannabis products (usually in quantities exceeding 100 grams) on credit when they knew their customers very well, they would not arrange such deals for customers buying cocaine or heroin, because the risk of never seeing their money was too great.

CONNECTIONS TO THE FORMAL ECONOMY

The informal economy is often perceived as being completely separate from the formal economy, though I observed clear connections between the two. The young men all built up an active network of collaborations with people in the formal economy who supported their drug-dealing activities in one way or another. As mentioned earlier, the neighborhood had many cafés and bars that the young men occasionally visited. While not all owners appreciated these visits (as Yilmaz said, "Well, that's kind of understandable—who wants to have *Kanaken* in a café. I'd rather have other guests"), some had a very strong relationship with the young men and even assisted them in their drug-dealing business. These café and bar owners profited greatly from the young men, who always spent a lot of money when they went out and left huge tips. As I mentioned in chapter 2, many owners also gave the young men certain signals if cops were around.

> FADIL: The owner of this place here [pointing to it] gives us signs when the cops are around . . . and then we know: be careful!
> SANDRA: What kind of signs?
> FADIL: He'd open that window, the one over there. When that window is open, we know to pay attention.
> SANDRA: Are there other business owners who do similar things?
> FADIL: Yeah, for example, the woman over there, the one who owns that little newspaper kiosk. She always puts her ice cream flag out when the cops come around asking questions or sit in one of the cafés. We make sure to buy all our cigarettes at her kiosk.
> SANDRA: Did any of these business owners ever turn on you?
> FADIL: No, quite the opposite. For example, the other night, remember . . . when Mesut fell out of the window in that bar [pointing to it], or was pushed out . . . or whatever happened—no one knows . . . but the window broke—remember? Others would have called the cops at that point because the guys just left without paying and were really drunk. . . . It was bad, just bad! But he [the owner] was super cool. He basically went to Akin and said: "Tomorrow, one of you will come and pay, OK?!" And, of course, Akin and Mesut went there on the next day and took care of everything. The owner said that he doesn't care about the window, but that he just wants his money and that we also have to pay for the window.
> SANDRA: Why do you think he did not call the cops?
> FADIL: He'd be stupid. He knows we have honor and we'll come and pay. He'd lose us . . . and I don't think he wants us to be against him. But really . . . the guys just spend so much money when they go out, and I think a businessman can't say no to that.

Another important group of collaborators from the formal economy were medical doctors. Some of the young men from Kosovo were in Germany illegally, so they had to go to doctors who would not report their status to the authorities. While the other young men were in Germany legally, they also sometimes needed doctors who were willing to be paid "under the table" when treating wounds resulting from violence. In Germany, doctors are legally obligated to report victims of violence, so the young men avoided going to hospitals. Nevertheless, they sometimes ended up in the hospital if they were severely injured and onlookers called for an ambulance. If this occurred, they tended not to provide any information about what had happened, even if they had clearly been victimized. Yakut explained to me that he left the hospital one day after being admitted for a serious head injury that was evaluated as life-threatening because he wanted to make sure to "take care" of his opponent himself: "I ripped off all these tubes and machines as soon as I could. My mom pleaded that I should stay at the hospital, but I just could not. The guy would have been gone had I stayed."

Markus, who was severely injured by another young man in the group three years into my research (the only serious injury caused by someone from "within" during this period) was also brought to a hospital. A primary blood vessel in his thigh had been cut with a knife, and he was bleeding very heavily. The emergency workers later told me that their vehicle had arrived just in time to save his life. Although Markus was obviously a victim—his girlfriend had had a fling with Mahmut but then decided to return to Markus; Mahmut was upset and attacked Markus on the street when he saw the two together—and many witnesses had seen the incident happen, he did not provide any information to the police, who visited him several times while he was in the hospital.

A third group of very important collaborators were cab drivers, who often transported drugs to customers. Some of these drivers had been part of the previous generation of dealers, and even though they had stopped actively dealing drugs, they still wanted a "piece of the pie." The customer paid for the cost of transportation, and cab drivers would commonly receive about 15 percent of the net cost of a deal. The young men considered this to be one of the safest methods of conducting business, as cab drivers were usually not subject to street patrols or random police checks. Working with cab drivers was also a preferred method when buying drugs from wholesalers and transporting them to storage. This approach meant there was no direct contact between the young men and the wholesalers, which minimized police attention. Yakut confirmed the safety of this system: "I really have to think about this . . . but I don't think we ever had a cab driver getting caught. Ever. No . . . I can't think of anyone."

The social workers at the community youth center were obviously also important collaborators, but they were not the only ones who were aware of the young men's activities in the drug trade or that drugs were sometimes in the community center. It could be argued that the police facilitated the drug trade as well. They observed the place regularly, so they must have known about the activities going on inside, and they definitely knew about the clientele visiting the center. I am convinced that the police chose to ignore these activities for social control purposes.[24] Because the young men were confined to one hangout spot, they did not loiter in the neighborhood, which might have led to complaints by business owners or neighbors. At the same time, the police knew where to find the young men if necessary.

"DON'T GET CARRIED AWAY"

The young men used various strategies to avoid risk (e.g., preferring steady to irregular customers, conducting larger transactions, not carrying substances on them). Generally, they assessed the risks of drug dealing as quite low and considered the German police to be inefficient. As long as they "did not get carried away," they believed that they had nothing to fear.

Rationality and risk avoidance figured not only into how the young men conducted business but also into how they used violence—which was usually not the preferred way to handle conflict (see also Desroches 2007, 751) and was seen as likely to attract unnecessary attention from the police. The violence that I witnessed or was told about was almost never related to conflicts over money or turf, but almost always related to "honor" and "losing one's honor," which led to "shame." Most of the young men only resorted to violence if someone had committed a serious violation in the drug business; non-payment of small sums of money was usually not considered sufficient grounds for such retaliation. They differed, however, in their assessment of what constituted "small" sums. Aissa shared his perspective on this issue when talking about another young man in the group who had bought a large quantity of drugs from him for reselling purposes:

> If it's just a few hundred euros—whatever . . . that happens. I don't make a big fuss out of that. I'm annoyed if someone owes me that money, of course, but that's not much money. I would not go out and stab someone because of that. I'd pressure that person, and if nothing comes of that, so be it. Professional risk. That person is done here—no one would do business with that person again.

People who owed money had a very hard time getting back into the business, because "word got around." To the young men, putting someone out of business was punishment enough and was seen as restoring their honor.

It was generally accepted that they would not retaliate for drug business issues, and the young men considered themselves smart for not attracting attention.[25]

Over the period of my research, five of the fifty-five young men (Gezim, Erol, Ulun, Faton, and Jo) were incarcerated. Three others (Ferdi, Milot, and Emi) were incarcerated at the time when I started my research and were released during my first year. Gezim was incarcerated as a result of his illegal status, but he was released after just three months with the condition that he apply for legal status. The other four young men were incarcerated for drug-dealing offenses that had accumulated over the years. Because of the many offenses that they had accumulated, none of the four had any chance of probation, and Faton was deported to his parents' country of origin. None of the charges had been pressed by a teacher, neighbor, social worker, or customer who had observed the particular man's drug-dealing activities or felt victimized; all of the charges were pressed by police after long observation. When I asked Cafer if customers ever pressed charges, he replied:

> That's bullshit. I really want to see the customer who presses charges against you. Well, yes, if it is an undercover . . . but otherwise? What do they want to say: "Hi, I'd like to press charges against my dealer, the quality has become really bad?" Most customers are already chicken-shit when they are buying stuff— they won't go to the cops. Ever. . . . They're more afraid of us than of the cops.

Small offenses that were prosecuted but did not result in incarceration occurred more frequently; over the course of the five years, each young man had to deal with an average of 2.2 charges,[26] on grounds that varied and were generally unrelated to drug-dealing activities. Two very common charges were driving without a license and driving under the influence of drugs or alcohol. Charges for assault were relatively rare—only eight of the fifty-five young men faced this kind of charge over the course of the five years. Most offenses had no real consequences and the charges were either dropped or the young men had to pay a small fine or do a certain number of social work hours (e.g., cleaning a park or helping at a hospital).

In terms of risk, the American and German drug markets differ significantly. Levitt and Venkatesh (1998, 25) reported that the American dealers they studied had a 25 percent chance of dying within the study period. Reuter (2004) reported that 38 percent of all the dealers participating in his study thought that they would be incarcerated within the first year of drug dealing. Another 50 percent assumed that they would be either killed or seriously injured during their work as dealers. Of the 24,000 dealers in

Reuter's study, 200 were killed, 1,000 were seriously injured, and 3,000 were incarcerated. The market in Frankfurt was obviously not as risky as those in these American studies. The young men did not associate drug dealing with any risk of being killed (as Aissa said, "This is not America! There are no guns here"), and none of the young men were seriously injured for drug market–related offenses during the five years of my research (although four had been seriously injured before I began my research in 2001).

Overall, the young men assessed the risk in the drug market to be quite low, and thus the anticipated gains were perceived as outweighing the risk. Furthermore, they saw the financial benefits of drug dealing to be far better than what they could hope for in the formal economy and saw the informal economy as opening up chances for them, in terms of both profits and self-respect, and not as putting them at risk. While Gezim, for example, was certainly wary of facing charges for being illegally in Germany, he often pointed out that he was not afraid to get caught for drug-dealing offenses: "What should I be afraid of? What for? The police are stupid. Nothing ever happens. . . . I am not afraid of anything."

For the young men, the greatest risk lay in the possibility of "getting carried away" by agreeing to "crazy deals." As long as they abided by the rules that had proven to reduce risk over time (e.g., not carrying drugs, using cab drivers as collaborators, etc.) and did not get carried away by the prospect of making big money, the risk, as Aissa argued, was judged as minimal:

> If you ask me, I think the risk is so slim, nothing can really happen to you. I mean, just look around, there is tons of business going on. But the worst thing that can happen to you is if you get carried away. . . . You always have to evaluate the situation. But if you get carried away and you're suddenly into stupid deals, the cops will get you—but only then.

My observations agreed with Aissa's assessment. Each time that one of the young men faced serious charges during my research (e.g., when Jo, Reza, and Inanc sold drugs to the undercover policeman), they seemed to have gotten carried away and to have dropped their usual safety measures.

At the same time, the drug-dealing network acted as a support group, and their "profession" helped the young men to develop the social identity that they needed: they were "someone" on the streets. This was something that Akin recognized: "Sandra, if you tried something, they'd bust you the minute you tried something serious. This is my turf—I am the king of this [laughing]."

Overall, then, drug dealing allowed the young men to not only meet their financial needs more easily than they could have in the formal economy but also develop a positive sense of self by fully mastering their profession. Akin expressed this belief in the following conversation:

> Akin: All these students out there, they may have the brains for their office job, but they would never be able to survive on the streets. They'd get fucked the minute they'd tried to make any money. This is what we are good at. And all these old guys, they just went crazy with this. We know how to run things. I think we just perfected this shit.
> Me: Are you proud of yourself?
> Akin: Yeah. I'd say so! I'd say we really have a good thing going. We're just smarter than the old guys.

The transformations that their drug-dealing activities underwent throughout the years to make drug dealing "less risky" are reflective of the fact that the young men did not view their involvement in the drug market as simply a youthful way to "act up a little." In contrast, the young men made many of these changes consciously, knowing that they were not likely to take up jobs in the formal economy any time soon. Given their structural limitations in mainstream society, the young men definitely viewed the drug market as the best of their options. Dealing drugs, of course, was not in line with the moral belief system that surrounded them, and thus they had to invent strategies that allowed them to maintain their positive sense of self despite their engagement in this activity. I will describe these mechanisms in more detail in the following chapter.

CHAPTER 4

"I'm Not a Dirty Crack Dealer"

Purity and Impurity in the Drug Market

The guys at the train station are just fucked up, they're dirty hustlers. Selling pot and cocaine is a different game. I'm not a dirty crack dealer—I don't do chemical shit, I don't make my hands dirty with H. No one dies because of me. I keep my honor.

—Aissa

One late summer night about one and a half years into my research, Akin and I went out for drinks. Sitting on the Bockenheimer patio, we were soon joined by Jo, Erol, and Inanc, who had been wandering through the neighborhood and noticed us. Erol wasn't even quite sitting in his chair yet when he looked at Akin, nodded in Jo's direction, and asked, "Hey, you in on this or what?" Akin immediately replied: "No way, dude," and a long and heated debate followed about the pros and cons of doing a specific deal.

I had no clue what the young men were referring to—clearly, I was not in the know, even though I had spent the past several hours with Akin and had also seen Erol earlier that day; neither of them had mentioned anything noteworthy. At the same time, however, the young men did not seem to mind discussing this obviously important topic in front of me. If this had been a discussion about Germany, girls, or family, they would have asked my opinion and engaged me in the conversation, but in this particular scenario, I felt that they had forgotten that I was even at the table.

From the conversation, I understood that Jo felt he had an opportunity that he called "the deal of his life," and he was trying to persuade the others to collaborate with him. Though they agreed that this business opportunity was potentially very lucrative, they were reluctant to take part in it. I knew that Akin was highly selective of the people with whom he would work, but Erol had never struck me the same way. I knew Inanc was constantly in debt and desperately needed money, which is why I could not believe my ears when he announced: "I know you will probably get rich and drive around in this big fat BMW, but I just can't do it. I'm out."

This is when I jumped in to ask what they were actually discussing. It turned out that Jo had established a very promising heroin connection that would allow him to buy from a wholesaler for about 3 euros less per gram than the young men had ever heard of. At the same time, he had entered into an informal agreement with one of Frankfurt's brothel owners to have the exclusive rights to sell heroin to the sex workers in that particular location. While many of the young men sold large amounts of drugs to sex workers (who acted as middlewomen between the young men and the sex workers' clients), none of them had an official agreement in place with the brothel owners. From everything I knew and had learned over the first year of my research, this was indeed a unique and promising business opportunity. Nonetheless, Akin, Erol, and even the most financially needy of the group, Inanc, refused to participate. Their hesitation was not based on fear that the deal was fishy or could go bad—in fact, Akin commented several times: "This is fucking incredible. You lucky bastard"—nor was it based on not wanting to work with Jo. Rather, it came from a place of morality.

Many of the young men refused to sell drugs other than marijuana and cocaine. Heroin, to most of them, was a game changer—it was viewed as a real drug that was sold to dirty people. These opinions trumped any financial gains the young men might expect. At the end of the debate, which Jo eventually left in anger, Akin looked at me and summed it up: "Never forget, Sandra, even assholes like us have limits."

The behavior of actors in a market, formal or informal, is typically explained according to models of economic rationality. These models do not tend to address how beliefs[1] (or irrationality) (see Weber 1964) affect the behavior of these actors, and hence affect the market itself. This issue is probably omitted either because many theorists do not consider it to be important, or because it is too difficult to incorporate, or because the relevant data are too difficult to collect. Nevertheless, drug dealers—just like everyone else—act within a belief system: their choice of clients, business partners, localities, and drugs to sell can be highly influenced by irrational factors and beliefs.

Many examinations of drug dealers have applied economic theories and methods (Levitt and Venkatesh 1998; Mohamed and Fritsvold 2006;

Murphy, Waldorf, and Reinerman 1990; Reuter 1983; Reuter, MacCoun, and Murphy 1990). This kind of approach stems from the assumption that dealers are driven by rational economic calculations and act solely on the basis of utilitarian reasons. Analysts who apply an economic perspective tend to assume that dealers' actions are mainly influenced by the quest for money and/or respect (a quality that is associated with their ability to function in a competitive market) (Levitt and Venkatesh 1998; Reuter, MacCoun, and Murphy 1990; Williams 1989). For example, for the past twenty years, there has been an ongoing debate about whether the drug business is really a sensible business opportunity for street-level retail sellers. Some researchers have argued that the actual income of dealers is never as great as mainstream society generally thinks it is (Levitt and Venkatesh 1998), while others have argued that dealing drugs (e.g., powder cocaine) is financially worthwhile for disadvantaged and unprivileged people, even if they might have to spend time in prison (Freeman 1996, 32).

As addressed in the last chapter, the young men discussed in this book largely conformed to this rational or utilitarian model, but their particular cultural background differentiated them from other drug dealers in important ways. Akin, Aissa, and their group were trying to maximize their income and earn respect just like American crack dealers (Bourgois 2003), but their actions were based on more than just economics. Their motives and market-related behaviors suggested that their beliefs and particular situation as second-generation immigrants in Germany had a considerable (although perhaps diminishing) effect on their drug-dealing activities.

It is important to note that the young men did not see their delinquency or crime to be generally positive or morally correct. It would be incorrect to assume that they simply had very different values and norms than mainstream society and that these allowed them to participate in the drug market without feeling guilty. Like other criminals (Sykes and Matza 1979), they felt ashamed when they were caught, especially in front of older family members, and did not wholeheartedly reject the values and norms of mainstream society.

In contrast to Weber's (1947, 125) assumption that criminals find the law legitimate but not morally valid, the young men discussed in this book agreed that the law was morally valid. They were also aware that their actions in the drug market did not reflect the values of German society or those of their own cultural backgrounds. Essentially, they were attempting to negotiate a space for their criminal behavior between the forces of their Islamic and parental values and the values of the German mainstream. As such, they tried to neutralize and legitimize their actions as much as they could in order to safeguard themselves against permanent feelings of guilt and doubt. As Sykes and Matza (1979, 365) argue, neutralizing their criminal behavior was a prerequisite for said behavior; in this way, "criminals" are not purely driven by economics but must also negotiate and make sense of their actions, knowing that they may contradict cultural, parental, or legal expectations.

In this chapter, I will describe the young men's attempts to adhere to their cultural and religious obligations, while at the same time being successful as drug dealers. In particular, I will examine their concepts of purity and impurity, which significantly influenced the way they did business and helped them to self-identify as a "good dealer" as well as to distinguish themselves from those whom they viewed as real criminals. Furthermore, I will describe the young men's legitimizations for their participation in the drug market, especially with respect to their views on Germany and their interactions with their opponents, the police.

ON BEING A GOOD MUSLIM: PURITY AND IMPURITY

The drug trade provided the young men with a way to sustain themselves and their lifestyles in the face of their marginalization, but they had to find ways to be at peace with their own actions. To do this, they abided by principles that they believed would make them "good" drug dealers.[2] Many of the principles that helped them to neutralize their behavior were built upon ideas that they believed to be Islamic. Even though the young men had little factual knowledge about Islam or the Koran, they had very distinct ideas about what their religion meant to them. Only two of the young men—Rahim and Gezim—had any real knowledge about the text of the Koran, and, as Tarik explained, they passed on to the others the important rules of behavior:

> I think those two are the only ones here who have ever read the Koran. It's too complicated for most of us. But those two explain a lot to us . . . and also our parents and so on. When I have more time, later on in life, I'll read more from the Koran and pray and so on. But for now, this is fine. It's enough to know what I should and should not do as a Muslim.

None of the young men were fanatically religious. They rarely went to the mosque with their families, but many of their actions were strongly influenced by their moral and religious beliefs, especially their ideas about purity and impurity. The young men used this distinction, which they believed to be Islamic, to differentiate between pure and impure drugs and impure customers inside the market, as well as between pure and .nen outside the market. Abiding by this rule sometimes meant .ey made less money, as, for example, when they did not take on a ᴜmising deal because the drug to be trafficked was "impure."[3]

Many of their beliefs would never hold true in a traditional Islamic context. For example, their distinction between pure and impure only worked as an internal legitimization within their own group; I doubt that their parents would have agreed that it was OK to sell drugs as long as they did not sell to other Muslims or children. Faced with the need to balance their Muslim background and their drug-dealing activities, the young men often had to adjust their beliefs to justify their own behavior. Georgio recalled conflicts stemming from this issue:

> The other day, Gezim and Aissa were fighting big time, because Gezim said to Aissa that he is not a real Muslim because he is not doing Ramadan. And Aissa completely lost it and told Gezim to shut the fuck up because he is also just a pseudo-Muslim. Because Gezim says that while having a joint in his mouth, and he sells cocaine in the evenings.

Although the issue of being a "good Muslim" always loomed in the background and was highly debated, small personal disagreements like the one between Aissa and Gezim often turned into big debates about basic principles that involved many of the young men. Georgio continued:

> Most agreed with Gezim, because he said that one needs to continue to work when it's Ramadan and that he only sells at night and that the Koran only forbids food and drinks and sex but there's no mention of pot. . . . Aissa completely freaked out, he lost it big time . . . I tell you. Big time! He said that just because someone claims to be the better Muslim, . . . Allah would not think that he is a good Muslim, because he still smokes pot and sells cocaine and so on. You know, somehow Aissa is right, but you know, Aissa also does not have a clue about the Koran and stuff . . . and Gezim knows a lot about the Koran, and I think that's why people agreed with Gezim and not with Aissa.

Aissa's statement that Ramadan was a time to "fast and concentrate on Allah and nothing else" that left "no room to be stoned or to sell drugs" was not taken seriously by the other young men. Aissa's opinions about "either doing it the real way or not at all" were disregarded because he did not observe Ramadan at all (he was not a strong believer and often made fun of the "pseudo-belief," as he called it, of the other young men). During Ramadan, many of the other young men fasted during the day for a week or two and then decided that it was too tiring. Many continued to sell drugs and smoke pot during the day, while others decided only to sell or take drugs after sunset.

While I often sympathized with Aissa's opinions during my research, I came to understand how important religious identity was for the young men. Even though their beliefs had little to do with Islam, being Muslim and identifying with some agreed-upon core concepts (like the purity/ impurity dichotomy) allowed them to think of themselves as "good" people or "good" drug dealers and gave them a sense of belonging. Even the six group members who did not have an Islamic heritage (those with German and Croatian backgrounds) claimed to be more influenced by Islam than any other religion. Markus, who was one of the six non-Muslims and was technically Catholic, commented: "If you only hang out with Muslims, you start becoming one. . . . I know more of that religion than of my own. And most things make sense. It's not like to say the Lord's Prayer a thousand times and God forgives you and that bullshit. You can't tell me that the pope has everything together."

Interestingly, the other young men accepted their non-Muslim friends as quasi-Muslims. Within the group, being Muslim really meant being different from the mainstream—in other words, *not* being German, as Inanc explained:

> They are just like us: *Kanaken* and Muslims. I mean, they are not real Germans. . . .
> I mean, no one would think of them as Germans, and the Croatians are no differ-
> ent than us. . . . I mean, they say themselves that they are kind of like Muslims . . .
> and that's how they behave, so I'd say they're a bit like Muslims, too. Unofficially.

The young men often stated that their parents only associated with people of the same ethnic background, but among their generation, ethnicity did not seem to play an important role. Apparently, ethnic affiliation had evolved into religious affiliation, defined as being Muslim (along with being a Bockenheimer). This meant that the young men had a wider group of potential associates; for example, Albanian youths could easily join the group even though they were in the minority in terms of nationality. In the end, as Selim pointed out, ethnicity didn't matter: "I still remember when the Albanians came to Bockenheim—because they are the ones who came later. Like some of them who knew some of us. That was weird, but at the end of the day, the Albanians are also Muslims." As discussed in the last chapter, ethnicity no longer determined with whom the dealers would conduct business and what drugs they would sell. However, the young men still talked about different ethnic groups in terms of purity. Mahmut held a firm opinion about Moroccans: "I can't help myself—Moroccans are somewhat dirty. But, you know, Aissa and Nermin, for example, they grew up with us. . . . That's different."

Within these discussions, there was always a very fine line between joking and seriousness. Common themes included whether Kurds were "real Turks" or even whether they were "real Muslims." One of the group members, as Talat pointed out, was Kurdish: "Well, I can tell you something. . . . The place where he came from, those are no real Turks, you know. They are pseudo-Turks. They are wood gnomes . . . you know, like, really backward . . . like retarded. . . . It's like . . . there is nothing. They are also not real Muslims; I think they believe something else than real Muslims." This kind of statement was often made in heated debates and was generally forgotten relatively quickly; it had no influence on the choice of business partners or the formation of friendships. The fact that these arguments were forgotten quickly was certainly related to the young men's awareness of their common status as "Muslim foreigners" and as marginalized minorities in German society, as well as in other countries around the globe. That their Muslim identity mattered even across borders became quite obvious to them in the aftermath of 9/11— they often commented on the fact that increasingly, Muslims were being treated with suspicion in all Western countries.[4] This commonality was more important than differences between Alawites and Sunnis or between Turks and Moroccans.

The young men were completely aware of their status in German society and felt that the constant labeling of them as "Turks" and "foreigners" distinguished them as a group that was separate from mainstream German society. In a sense, they all had hybrid ethno-national-cultural roots (Mecheril 2000) and did not belong to any group fully. This observation is particularly interesting when one considers the purity concept that the young men shared. For them, Germany, Germans, and non-Muslims were impure; mainstream society, in contrast, classified the young men as a threat to German purity (an identification that fed into discussions both among the general public and among policymakers about how much "Islam" German society can endure). This attitude was something Ibor understood well:

> Well, honestly, whether I have a passport or not, what difference does it really make for the Germans? I will always be a Turk. All foreigners are Turks here . . . or *Kanaken*; we will never be Germans. Never. I have more in common with a Turk or a Moroccan than with Germans. They hate foreigners. . . . They don't want black hair to mix with the blond hair.

While the young men were aware that they were seen as a threat to German purity, they themselves let their actions and identity be heavily influenced by their own understanding of what is pure and impure and their agreement about what constitutes a "good Muslim." These ideas allowed them to distinguish themselves from "bad dealers."

CONSTRUCTING AN IDENTITY AS A GOOD DEALER

The young men explicitly championed their own lifestyle as "good," distinguishing between good and bad dealers and drawing clear boundaries between themselves and those deemed to be bad. The distinctions they drew were always relational and worked only when they compared themselves to others. By creating and abiding by their own set of principles, they were able to view their actions in a more positive light. Their distinctions between good and bad were important because—against all odds—they felt they had a future in Germany (see chapter 5). By maintaining principles that they evaluated as "good," the young men could save face and demonstrate that they still cared for their surroundings and the people around them, in contrast, as Talat said, to "other, real criminals."

The young men tried to portray themselves as better than others with regard to the area they chose for drug dealing. Although the police and most others would probably not consider the exact location where dealers sold drugs to be important, the young men attached great importance to this decision, as Selim explained: "Bockenheim has this really rough reputation and so on . . . and everyone . . . you know, when you mention that you're from Bockenheim, everyone thinks you're a really tough guy and so on. But if you say that you deal at the main train station, that's completely . . . how should I put it? . . . it's completely below the bar!" Like Selim, the other young men had negative opinions about the open drug scene at the main train station. As described in chapter 3, the drug market that the young men served and the drug market at the main train station differed in many other respects, including the drugs being sold and the customers being served. These differences meant that the business of dealing itself differed. At the main train station, many dealers hustled on the street by actively approaching potential clients, but the young men discussed in this book usually served steady customers. They absolutely condemned the practice of approaching clients actively not only because this tactic was thought to characterize the lowest step of the dealing ladder but also because, as Akin pointed out, "no one here really sees what we're doing. Kids and stuff. There is no hustling going on. We keep this place [Bockenheim] clean." "Keeping it clean," according to Erol, was as important as keeping it respectful: "All this . . . shh . . . psst . . . do you need something, do you want something . . . shh . . . that's like the lowest dealers. . . . It's like the ones who did not make it."

The best customers were those who were "honorable" and had a good reputation in society. The young men generally assessed these qualities based on traditional ideals. For example, they were very proud to have lawyers, police officers, and medical doctors among their clients. Students, the most common kind of customer, were considered to be more honorable than unemployed people or young men who were similar to themselves (Bucerius 2008).

The young men's belief in the pure/impure dichotomy was especially apparent with regard to heavy drug users. Heavy drug users were considered impure, and contact with junkies was to be avoided as much as possible. Fadil expressed this contempt: "They are just disgusting. You know, they're not even humans." They even condemned the somewhat-progressive drug policies of the city of Frankfurt and could not comprehend why anyone would finance safe injection sites or free needle exchange programs. Even though they made a living from drugs, they had very dated ideas about what drug policies should look like.

> TALAT: That's really fucked up to provide rooms for them and so on. In Turkey, this would not be possible . . . they would crack down on them. But the Germans, they do everything for the junkies. "Here's a room, why don't you make yourself comfortable, I'll serve the food in a minute." That's completely fucked up!
> SANDRA: But you're making your money off drugs as well!
> TALAT: But not with these disgusting creatures. That makes a huge difference!

The young men distinguished between themselves and "bad" dealers on the one hand, and between themselves and junkies on the other, placing themselves above both groups. Consistent with Michele Lamont's (2000) observations, despite the structural limitations and symbolic violence they face, the young men developed a sense of self-worth and dignity by interpreting differences between themselves and those above (Germans) and below (junkies and bad dealers) them. The moral criterion they used (purity) served to draw these distinctions between them and the individuals below them. In their eyes, Germans, bad dealers, and junkies lacked the morals that they believed in and valued the most. Thus, they could create a stronger bond among themselves as being the good ones, drawing boundaries to separate themselves from everyone else and illustrating differences across class and ethnic lines.

People were considered good only as long as they were pure and were doing pure things; if they came in contact with something impure, then they would also become impure. Mary Douglas wrote extensively about purity and impurity and argues that impurity is always relative (Douglas 1966, 53). As such, dealers can be pure in some contexts and impure in others; at the same time, they can be contaminated by impurity through association. In other words, contact with junkies—who, for the young men, were the epitome of impurity—would make a dealer impure. Consequently, the young men desperately avoided contact with such customers. As described in chapter 3, a small minority of the young men still sold heroin to heavy users, though never to crackheads, who were considered even worse, but the other young men openly demonstrated their disapproval of this decision by refusing to shake hands with those dealers or telling them to wash their hands first before greeting them.

Even the young men who sold heroin drew a clear boundary between themselves and those who sold in the open drug scene at the main train station. As Metin said, "You would not sell there if you didn't have to." The bad reputation of this scene worked both ways: many of the heroin customers who were served by the young men also did not want to be associated with the open drug scene and its shadiness, preferring to buy their heroin in a different neighborhood. Aissa explained:

> It's just that some of the customers—I mean, the ones who are not real junkies . . . would still take H. You know, once in a while. I think that they only sniff. And then [there are] the prostitutes who buy and sell to their clients. They don't want to make business with the guys from the train station . . . especially those who don't work there [as sex workers]. Often, people also say that quality is much better here. The customers, I mean. They get lots of crap at the train station.

In many ways, the separation between the open drug scene and the drug market served by the young men existed only in their minds. In effect, they were often indirect suppliers to the open drug scene, as some of their customers resold sold their drugs at the main train station—although this didn't seem to bother them, as Mahmut explained: "Personally, I don't give a shit about that. I mean, we also go to the prostitutes at the main train station. . . . I just don't want anything to do with it . . . I mean, selling there or having to deal with the junkies there . . . no thanks! But what customers do with the shit, I don't fucking care."

Separating themselves from that scene might have been important to help the young men see their work in a better light, but they sometimes visited the main train station in their free time for different reasons, one of which was to visit sex workers. Their views about visiting sex workers exemplified the flexibility of their ideas about purity and impurity. The dichotomy was more rigid with regard to work, in relation to which the young men were less willing to compromise and had strict ideas about pure and impure dealers. In this sense, work and how they conducted and rationalized this work were very important to identity formation, as it was through this act of boundary keeping that their own identity became solidified and accepted (Lamont 2000).[5]

Because heavy users were considered to be disgusting and impure, the young men tried to keep these users out of their neighborhood, to the point of actively banishing them. As mentioned previously, Akin took pride in what they had accomplished: "We really cleaned up in Bockenheim. All those disgusting creatures are gone. We don't want them to hang out here, and the cops are doing nothing. We took it in our own hands. Bockenheim is now junkie-free." The young men had an exceptionally strong attachment to the neighborhood (discussed in chapter 2), and so it was natural for them to exercise a form of social control in the neighborhood—especially with respect to children. Frank explained how they applied this control to kick out the junkies: "We made sure that they don't hang out here anymore. Back in the day, they did. We beat them all up and told them to get lost. Just imagine, the little kids, they should not see these monsters." Relating their actions to children was another way to portray themselves as "much better than real criminals." Rahim continued this discussion: "Of course, this is criminal. But doesn't your dad trick with taxes? Don't you download movies? That's all criminal, Sandra! But really, there are people out there raping women and bastards molesting children and shit like that. *That's* what I call criminal." In the young men's eyes, children had to be protected from all aspects of the drug market as much as possible. For example, selling to children, as Nermin emphasized, was considered a complete no-go: "I'd have a really bad conscience selling cocaine to children, but, of course, I would never do that." I even witnessed dealers turning away teenager customers because they were considered too young to be taking drugs. Being a "good" dealer meant not selling to customers who needed to be protected, especially children, even if that meant losing out on profit.[6] Akin emphasized this point: "If you don't sell to children, it's not a problem. I'd beat up the child who'd want to buy something. I'd say: Go home and play with your toys."

Similar to their ideas about not selling to children, the young men also thought that Muslim women should be protected from drugs. According to their logic, Muslim women were sacred and should be protected from defilement (Douglas 1966). The same was true for good male Muslims who had not previously been involved in impure things like drugs. According to Gezim, Germans ranked the lowest on the purity scale: "Well, I'd say it's entirely different. I know you're German and so on, but we believe that it's a greater sin to dirty Muslims. I mean, honestly, Germans don't really care about religion, they just do whatever they want to, and they never think of other people anyways."

Essentially, the young men took on the role of moral dealers who would not sell to children or Muslim women and who tried to keep younger brothers and cousins out of the drug-dealing business. This was not because they feared competition; they were, as Milot expressed it, acting as savvy adults who educated and protected the younger ones: "They have no clue, and they'd just do any kind of shit. We were worse, but look, they still have options. They could still do school and learn a trade or something. So it's up to us that they learn to listen."

When it came to product, the young men preferred to sell cannabis (marijuana and hashish) and cocaine in powder and crystal form (but not crack), drugs that were not generally purchased by the heavy users they were trying to avoid. In the young men's eyes, selling these drugs was morally justifiable because they were not as addictive as heroin or crack and were not associated with the same kind of impoverishment. The literature about drug dealing does not offer many explanations for why dealers avoid certain substances (see, e.g., Adler 1993; Bourgois 2003; Maher 1997; Williams 1989). Researchers usually assume that the choice of what to sell is made through an economic calculus involving estimated profit margins or is dependent on the type of market or personal connections that allow access to particular drugs and not others. Most of the young men I got to know talked about personal connections as an important factor in their decision to sell specific drugs, but they also talked about the moral implications of choosing to sell certain substances over others. Jawad drew the line at heroin:

I don't sell H. I would never do that. You'd basically have to live with the fact that some junkie kicked the bucket because of you. But cocaine, that's no big deal. I mean, no one can die from that. It's really not harmful in any way. . . . You know, all the lawyers are on cocaine. I don't have a bad conscience about that, but if you're doing H, you have to.

The young men were very much against selling chemical drugs such as ecstasy or LSD. They did not like the customers who bought chemical drugs or the music scenes with which they were often associated, and they were also convinced that chemical drugs were only sold by dealers with no conscience. According to the young men, you could never be sure what was in these drugs. Following this rationale, responsible dealers only sold drugs derived from plants, as Cafer explained: "It's all organic . . . you know . . . it's all nature, it's pure, there are no chemicals in there. Who knows what they put into the chemical stuff. No one can control that, believe me. And you have weird customers who listen to techno music and stuff."

Just as they had very strict rules about which drugs were acceptable to sell, the young men had very distinct ideas about drug consumption. Most of the young men consumed marijuana regularly. For some, that meant smoking one or two joints a day, while others seemed to smoke marijuana more or less constantly. Consumption seemed to subside when they were going through phases in which they wanted to better themselves—often initiated by a serious conversation with a parent or because they were in trouble with law enforcement. For most, these phases only lasted temporarily, and smoking pot soon became the norm again. However, they controlled their level of intoxication and rarely appeared to be "stoned" during the day; for the most part, this was also the case during the evening.

While legal, alcohol had a much more profound impact on the young men's lives. Many of them temporarily lost their driving licenses as a result of driving while intoxicated during the course of my research, and most violence-related charges that the young men faced were committed under the influence of alcohol. Usually careful to not draw any unnecessary attention to themselves, the young men quickly discarded their normal "safety measures" when consuming alcohol and often picked random fights with each other or with people at bars or clubs. They would also often get into cars so drunk that I literally doubted they would make it home ok—several car accidents and an incident in which Akin ran over a pedestrian whom he had not even noticed (causing life-threatening injuries) proved that my concerns were usually justified. I often took issue with the young men's drinking behavior, and learned to go home early when they started drinking. The young men usually drank once or twice a week, having a "when we drink, we drink" attitude, to use Erol's words. There seemed to be no limits when it came to alcohol consumption. Furthermore, they not only got themselves in trouble with the law but also engaged in very childish behavior when drinking. I will never forget one particular evening fairly early on in my research, when it came up that I once had a rabbit. In the middle of the night (I had been home a long time), my doorbell rang, and

I found Akin, Erol, and Kamer standing at my door—completely wasted—proudly announcing that they had stolen two rabbits for me from the zoo. I did not believe them at first, but I did go to their car with them, mainly to keep their noise away from my small apartment building. Indeed, they had two animals in the car, which turned out to be huge hares. While I laughed at first, it turned out to be extremely difficult to convince them that I could not take those two hares into my apartment, and I asked them to leave. They were quite upset about my "rejection" and became even louder, trying to argue with me about "German appreciation for gifts." I lived in a residential neighborhood, and one of my many neighbors became very interested in what was going on outside, even telling my father when he came to visit about the "dubious people" with whom his daughter was associating. Eventually, the young men left with the hares. When I asked what had happened to them, I heard very different stories, ranging from "We took them back to the zoo" to "We let them loose on the highway" to "We killed and ate them."

Very few of the young men used cocaine, and those who did generally tried to keep their usage hidden (e.g., using in the bathroom or some other place in secret), so I rarely observed anyone snorting cocaine. Nor had any of the social workers at the youth center ever seen the young men using cocaine at the facility. The young men condemned the habit (although not the practice of selling it), and those who did use it were looked down upon. Similar to their feelings toward junkies, they were very judgmental of anyone who could not control their drug consumption. Cocaine was clearly seen as a drug that could make one dysfunctional as a person and a dealer. Becoming "your own best client" was a fear that was very prevalent among the young men. Erol emphasized this point: "That's the worst; that should never, never happen to you . . .. Never become yourself the best client. You can just pack your stuff and leave if that happens. For better or worse, the cops will definitely get you, because you're not capable of thinking straight anymore."

The young men's attitudes about cocaine consumption changed over the years. When they were younger and the older generation was in charge, drug consumption was not looked down upon to the same extent. According to the young men, this was the case with regard to not only snorting cocaine but also snorting heroin (although injecting heroin was a different story), which was certainly not common when I conducted my research. Selim was aware of this history:

> Back in the day, everyone took a line. . . . That was just normal. But that does not exist anymore today. I don't know anyone who still does H. And the ones who do

cocaine, they basically make a secret out of it. Today, you're not seen as the king anymore if you have money for it—much rather, you're the loser if you spend your money on that!

As Selim noted, attitudes toward drug consumption (except for marijuana) had shifted completely, and drugs were often talked about using the same language of purity and impurity. People who used drugs were considered "dirty losers who can't control themselves," according to Akin, and "stupid for spending money on shit." The young men's negativity was influenced by their experience observing many members of the older generation becoming drug addicts. Rahim recalled his experience:

> I saw many of them doing really shitty. It's bad, real bad. . . . And you start think-ing: this can *never* happen to you. It's disgusting. . . . People are just very weird, and you cannot have respect for them anymore. Honestly! I am honest, doing H or cocaine, that's just very close to being a junkie. You know, you sit behind the curtain and you have paranoia because one of the idiots thinks the cops are coming into the apartment. . . . It's just not normal. Back in the day, we all did that. But today, it's just something for dirty losers.

Similarly to their very negative opinions about selling chemical drugs, the young men also viewed the consumption of chemical substances negatively. To them, consumption of chemical drugs was even worse than using cocaine or heroin because of their insecurities about what might be in the drug (as discussed in chapter 3, they themselves made fake hash, so they knew first-hand that drugs were being altered). Akin emphasized this point: "I would never sell that shit, but take it myself? I am not a complete idiot."

Haram Para

Besides having distinct ideas of what kind of substances were acceptable to sell to which customers, what selling places should be avoided, and what substances were OK for consumption, the young men had strong feel-ings about how the money earned through drug deals should be treated. Such money was considered *haram para*—dirty, impure, and non-religious money. It was treated very differently than money earned through legiti-mate means. *Haram para* could only be used to purchase things for them-selves and could not be spent on the family, the most sacred and pure of all things on Earth, a belief Omar held strongly: "*Haram para* is dirty money. You don't give something dirty to your family, you know?"

Research about drug dealers contains very little information about their attitudes toward the profits made from the drug business. Dealers are typically described as financing their lifestyles without giving much thought to the money's origin (Adler 1993; Bourgois 2003; Maher 1997; Tertilt 1996; Williams 1989). In contrast, the young men I got to know claimed that they would only spend *haram para* on non-durable goods. Ilber echoed Omar's comment: "You're not allowed to do honorable things with *haram paras*, you know—you're not allowed to buy something for the family, for example. It will definitely bring shame to your family. I only spend the money for myself and the guys, and, you know, the normal stuff: cars, women, partying, and so on." It could be argued that this opinion helps legitimize an excessive lifestyle, protecting dealers from criticism about their inability to save money or support their families. However, such an interpretation does not entirely capture the underlying dynamics of the young men's profit making and does not incorporate the strong influence of beliefs on their behavior. Among the young men, the few who reported weak relationships with their families and felt fewer religious obligations were the only ones who saved the profits from their drug business and spent them on durable goods.

There were times when the young men had to break their own rules, such as when their families asked them to pick something up from the store. In such cases, they did spend the money earned from drug deals on the family, even though they always claimed that this was a no-go. When I asked him about it, Aissa explained: "Well, I'd never take money from my parents. You just don't do that. That's shameful. So what can you do? You somehow have to pay." In other words, taking money from parents was considered even more shameful than spending the money earned through drug deals on the family. Again, the young men adjusted and amended their concepts of purity and impurity to fit the situation.

Germany as a Dirty Country

Conceptualizing Germany as a dirty country that does not warrant protection against adversity was used as a strategy by the young men to legitimize their actions in the drug market. Faton expressed this outlook clearly:

> Germany does not deserve any better! This country is almost as fucked up as the US. Germany is just . . . this is just such a dirty country. Just look around you. Girls fuck around as soon as they are out of elementary school, parents throw their kids out when they are 18, everybody is a cold-blooded robot or a Nazi. This

is fucked up. I don't sell to Muslims—so, whatever, you know! I mean, it's not my fault that Germans use drugs, is it?

Attitudes like this allowed the young men to confer guilt on Germans rather than on themselves. Because of their experiences in and perceptions of Germany, they felt that German culture had no boundaries and seemed to allow everything. At the same time, they could sometimes bend their own self-created rules about dirty money by pointing to the fact that they had made that money in a dirty country. In other words, as Yakut explained, they would at times claim that Islam allowed money to be made from drug deals in Germany because the transaction did not take place in a pure country: "Germany is a dirty country anyways. It would be a whole different story if you were to sell cocaine in an Islamic country. No one from us would ever do that, I swear on my mom. But it's not a sin in Germany, it's very different."

Strictly speaking, the Koran does serve as the basis for law in several countries while also providing religious guidelines. Obviously, one could argue that the Koran is not law in Germany and that thus the young men could not be held guilty under Islamic law. Following that assumption, the young men would always be free of guilt if they committed crimes in Germany. However, even if they were found not guilty under Islamic law, they would still have acted against the Koran's religious rules by engaging in illegal behavior, regardless of the purity of the place where that behavior occurred.

It is important to note that the young men had very infrequent contact with members of the German mainstream population—I was one of the few Germans they had ever gotten to know well—so their opinions about Germany and the German lifestyle were not necessarily based on firsthand experience. However, their presumptions were deeply rooted in their families and beliefs, and "being German" certainly had a very negative connotation among them. This was also shown by the fact that the young men always referred to me as an "exception" and as "not being German." In their minds, being German and being friends with them were mutually exclusive. At the same time, the three group members of German background identified as "being *Kanaken*"—a term that is mostly associated with minority youth—"just like everyone here."

Negative experiences of political, economic, and social exclusion probably played a role in shaping the views of the young men's parents. Schiffauer wrote, "In immigrant families, Germany is associated with broken homes . . ., sexual libertinage, alcohol and drugs, and Nazism and violence" (2004, 95). Because they were very close to their parents[7] and identified their own frustrations with mainstream German society, the young men were able to rationalize their actions in the drug market to themselves. Despite knowing that dealing was illegal (as Kaner said, "Of course, this is criminal. No one doubts that!"), they convinced themselves that it was a form of rightful retaliation or punishment: "Injury not wrong in the light of the circumstances" (Sykes and Matza 1957, 668). To them, not only had Germany caused them much hurt making it "deserving" of punishment, but Germany also was, in Mahir's words, a "very shitty and crappy country" that, in their eyes, was already impure. Research has shown that it is common for drug dealers and gang members to view "their involvement as an act of defiance against a society that has abandoned them," which is "often directly linked to profound feelings of injustice and social exclusion" (Wortley and Tanner 2008, 205).

The young men said many times that they would not be involved in the drug market if Germany treated them more fairly. At the same time, they argued that they'd stop their involvement if the law were more strictly enforced. They interpreted Germany's lax law enforcement (or the fact that not many of them got "caught") as a sign that Germany did not care much about drug dealing. This led them to the rationalization, as Selim argued, that "if the police don't really even have anything against it, why would I have to stop?"

Germans also did not meet the young men's religious purity requirements, particularly those rules against the consumption of pork and those rules prohibiting women from having sex before marriage.[8] Additionally, they felt that Germany lacked "culture" and "honor" and that the German people did not display important character traits such as sharing and hospitality. Ilber recalled how his mother was treated at her workplace:

> My mom always told us about her work—you know how the German boss bossed the foreigners around, just because they're foreigners, and she was super slick to the Germans. And the Germans never brought in cookies or something, but they always gorged on the ones the foreigners [brought in]. The Germans are just not warm or anything, they are just not hospitable at all. And all these other things, for example, that the girls are just fucking around and no one really cares. And the way they dress . . . just like prostitutes, I mean, honestly! My dad even said: "It's no surprise that they get raped." My parents would never allow my sister to walk around like that!

As Ilber noted, the sexual liberation of German girls was seen as a clear sign of Germany's impurity. This impurity reached beyond the act of sex itself: the young men could not comprehend how German parents could tolerate the sexual activities of their daughters or allow them to dress as they did. Allowing overnight class trips (a common practice in Germany) and sleepovers at a boy's home was also beyond their comprehension, leading them to the conclusion that Germans had "no honor" and put no emphasis on purity. Talat recounted that he had dated a German girl who wanted to spend the night with him and explained that he saw this as a clear sign that the girl's family had no honor whatsoever: "I once had something with this German cunt. She was like 16 or 17, and her parents would have let her stay over at my place. I basically told her: 'You're insane, what should my parents think? Don't you have any honor?' But she really did not care. She was a real slut . . . ridiculous."[9]

To the young men, honor and, relatedly, shame were two of the most important components of their identity. The loss of one's honor (which typically brings shame) was seen as a very bad fate. Without honor, one was perceived to be "dirt" or "shit"; in other words, losing one's honor and bringing shame upon oneself or one's family was closely related to becoming even more impure. Ayan described just how important honor was to him, exaggerating its significance to the point of being insulting:

> I'd say my honor is the most important thing. Well, fundamentally speaking, there is nothing in this entire world that you need to protect more than your honor. Because you're nothing without your honor. You'd be dirt, just dirt and nothing else. If someone tried to take my honor, then I'd do anything to get it back. Literally anything. That's just the way it is, at least if you are a man. But honestly speaking, the Germans don't even know what that is. You could fuck a German woman and rape her and so on, and the husband would literally not care at all. Just not at all! If anything, he'd say: "Oh, please, please, police, find the bad guy." Just because he does not have a dick in his pants and can't take care of his own wife.

As discussed previously, the perceived lack of honor (and thus purity) among Germans justified the young men's involvement in drugs; they were not dirtying a pure country, as Mahir said, because it was already damaged:

> I just think: in a country in which no one has any honor, I don't feel bad if I sell drugs. Don't you see that the Germans are buying it? It's really not my problem if the people can't control themselves. I mean, who am I? A psychiatrist? The Germans have always been like that, even before we got here. Dirty and stuff. I don't have to be considerate. Well, that's at least my opinion.

Many of the young men went a step further, claiming that they would not deal in their parents' country of origin. This assertion also highlights the importance of not "dirtying sacred things" (Douglas 1966, 17) while being free to take advantage of what is already impure. As Inanc noted,

> No one would deal in our own countries, no one! They would hang us immediately! But here? No one cares! The police are too stupid and Germany is just fucked up, they don't deserve any better. Girls are fucking around when they are 15, and the parents don't give a shit, no one has any honor . . . and you know, I don't sell to Muslims. I can tell you: in a couple of years, Germany [will be] no better than America.

It was very important to the young men not to sell to pure Muslims. Most of their customers were Germans, and the young men could absolve themselves of guilt by blaming these customers for being responsible for the drug-dealing activities in the first place.[10] As Gezim said: "It's [the customer's] own fault. I never said: 'Take heroin.' He did that himself, this disgusting junkie! It's his fault when he takes heroin." Or as Mesut said: "The people buy it. You know, they want to have it. I mean, imagine what would happen if we did not sell? All your student colleagues would get a crisis. That's what would happen!"

Often, the young men would legitimize their actions by saying that they were just "helping out a friend." When faced with a choice between obeying the law and helping someone close to them, they would always choose the latter; they had experienced so much marginalization in Germany that their loyalties were obviously with friends rather than with the state (see also van Gemert and Fleisher 2005; Wortley and Tanner 2008). Appealing to a higher loyalty (Sykes and Matza 1979)—as Mahmut did with Akin in the following statement—allowed them to deny responsibility: "I mean, they keep Akin under surveillance, and so it's not a problem for me to bring the shit to the customer. I mean, we would not usually do that, but if push comes to shove, you help out a friend. I mean, I make some money and Akin doesn't get into more trouble. I have no conflict with the cops."

Interestingly, even though all the young men felt that their involvement in drug dealing was justified given their marginalized position in society and was based on their opinion that Germany did not deserve any better, they still often blamed others or their environment for their actions, trying to release themselves of feelings of guilt. As Akin told me, "Sandra, if I had had friends like you, I would also have taken craft and piano lessons, and I would not have smoked." Similarly, Mahmut reported, "Everyone in Bockenheim is a criminal. You have no chance when growing up in Bockenheim. It's obvious that you'll be a criminal, too. Also, when you go to school here. My parents should have never sent me to the Clinton School, but they just had no clue." While the young men would usually glorify Bockenheim and their friends, when trying to legitimize their own actions, they referred to growing up in Bockenheim among impure friends as an explanation for their involvement in crime. Bockenheim and their friends, then, became "the bad place" with "bad people" that allowed them to lose their own purity.

Their need to justify and legitimize their actions demonstrated that they were well aware that drug dealing was against the law and opposed to German, as well as their own, cultural and religious expectations. However, they were looking for excuses and justifications and often claimed that despite being against the law, their illegal activities allowed them to take care of themselves and did not require them to call upon the state for social assistance. In fact, as Akin explained it, they often saw themselves as *supporting* the German welfare state: "Look, if I did not do anything, I'd make Germany poor. They'd have to pay me social assistance and welfare and unemployment money and all that shit. No one would ever employ me. You know, I'd rather make my money like this [drug dealing], and the welfare can go to a nice elderly grandfather."

INTERACTIONS WITH THE ENEMY

Perceptions about, and interactions with, the police greatly contributed to the young men's impression that Germany was not worthy of protection. In general, they felt superior to the police. Outsmarting law enforcement brought enormous joy to the young men, and being a step ahead of the police was certainly a "seduction of crime" (Katz 1988). At the same time and as discussed previously, participation in the drug market for a long period without any severe consequences was interpreted as proof that the German police were not to be taken seriously. The young men continuously made fun of the police and ridiculed their powerlessness. Mahir scoffed at what he was able to get away with: "Well, honestly, they'd have hanged me in Turkey a long time ago, or [thrown] me in jail. . . . This shit would not work there . . . but here? They have no clue! I mean, you know what they're all up to and how much shit is going on, and when does anything happen?"

The lack of serious consequences gave the young men a feeling of invincibility; over time, they felt that the local police were completely powerless. As Rahim said:

> The problem with the cops is that they have no fucking clue. They are just really not capable here in Germany; how can you possibly have any respect for them?

They are complete pigs, Nazi pigs, who basically check your IDs because you have black hair and then they find something . . . just out of pure luck! Just out of luck! But not because they really know something.

Not being tough on crime seemed like an invitation to the young men and, according to Erol, highlighted how the country was unable to take care of its reputation and honor: "If a country only does the minimum, it's its own fault if things are how they are. The Germans want us to be on the streets, they want that. No one can tell me that no one could do anything against the drugs, if they wanted to. Aren't Germans usually great at everything?"

Because the young men viewed the police in such a disparaging and sarcastic way, anyone who actually got caught was looked down upon. Most of the young men were never caught for a serious offense, so they viewed those who *were* caught as having been stupid. Getting caught meant losing face; it was always seen as a severe personal failure. In their opinion, being arrested was not the result of skilled law enforcement; instead, young men who got caught were seen as having done something so out of the ordinary that the police—independent of their ineptness—just had to catch them. Ulker took great delight in this fact: "I have to say that really nothing happens to you if you're smart. And that's not how it's supposed to be . . . you know, that the dealer is smarter than the cops. But here, it is the way it is!"

When arguing that the German police were stupid and unsuccessful, the young men often neglected to mention that they took a number of safety precautions to avoid getting caught. Still, in their opinion, a successful country would have a police force that could stay on top of the criminals; in other words, any safety precautions that the criminals took would not be successful.

Furthermore, they felt that the police and politicians actually supported their dealing, at least to some extent. Mahmut was one of several young men who told me that the only way they could interpret the lack of success among the police was that it was an attempt to maintain peace in the district, an agenda that included keeping the junkies happy:

Well, I think if not even the cops have an issue with it, it's not a problem. Because they just let us run wild. If they were really against all this, they'd do something. But they have no interest in the junkies being out in the streets and all going cold turkey and stuff because they have no supply. In Turkey, this would not be possible. They still do their jobs there. . . . They'd hang us all.

Despite having such negative opinions about the police, they did not brush off any interactions they had with the police as unimportant. To the contrary, they felt they were treated unfairly and were marginalized in many of their interactions, which Ayan attributed to ethnic profiling[11]:

> In Germany, it's not like they screw blacks . . . well, maybe, but there are just no blacks around . . . just at the main train station and some Americans [referring to American GIs who used to be stationed in Germany]. Mainly, it's about whether or not you have black hair. If you look like a Turk, you've lost. It's just like in the US, they'd fuck the blacks, and here, they screw the Turks at every fucking checkpoint.

If one young man had a negative experience with the police, it was instantly shared with the others. The police were described as "Nazis" or "fucked-up dicks," whereas the young men viewed themselves as victims of a racist, power-driven, and unfair police organization. Often, individual experiences were interpreted as mistreatment of the entire group or even as acts against immigrants or Muslims. The young men reacted by labeling the police force in general terms, not as individuals.

The police often tried to demonstrate their power over the young men openly and publicly. Given their limited success in "catching" the young men for illicit activities, police would often demand their IDs in places like public cafés, which the young men found embarrassing and emasculating. Mahmut felt that the police just liked to take out their frustration on them: "Just because they're too fucking stupid to work properly and their proofs are just not good enough or whatever, they have virility issues and need to bully us." The young men knew that the police had limited options when trying to ID them in public. Often, they would refuse to comply. According to the young men, the police were "chicken-shit" when they were outnumbered. Also, the young men were very aware that any attempt by the police to take them to the police station would be a highly bureaucratic and probably unsuccessful endeavor. Therefore, the young men tended to be very uncooperative and even impertinent in interactions with the police and rarely lost control of the situation, as Aissa described in this exchange:

> AISSA: I was sitting in this café with a friend and these two cops come around. I knew one of them, he's a wimp—I know him from the park. So they go: "Your IDs?" and I'm like: "Why?" So he says: "Just because. IDs!" So, I said: "Did we do anything? We're sitting here, having coffee." You know, it's embarrassing. I'm just sitting there having a coffee and they need to check on you in a public café? But they don't fucking care; it's pure bullying. . . . They just want to fuck with you. So the other cop is saying: "I know you! I want to

see your ID right away!" So I said: "If you thought you knew me, what would you need my ID for?"

SANDRA: Why do you always address them informally?[12]

AISSA: What do you mean, informally? He started it! They always address us informally! And he's insulting! So, he told me something about that law that says that you need to have an ID on you at all times. I said: "I live 20 meters from here, I am not going to carry an ID with me." So he goes: "That does not matter, we live in Germany, and this is your obligation. Do you have drugs on you?"

Aissa essentially dared the police officer to search him, which the officer did not do. Finally, the two police officers left. When I expressed my surprise that they had not been searched, Aissa explained that from his point of view, the police officers were afraid of the young men, especially "because it was only two of them." Interestingly, the young men sometimes sympathized with the police because of their lack of power. Generally, the young men considered interactions with the police to be based on discrimination, and they often commented on the rudeness of the police. One might contend that the young men behaved rudely themselves, but in my experience, the interactions were based on a give-and-take model. If the police were polite, the young men behaved the same way. This tendency highlights how the young men were not generally opposed to the police; on the contrary, they very much believed in police forces. However, they were frustrated by discriminatory treatment (like demands to show IDs in public cafés without cause) and were often disappointed and annoyed, in an odd way, by the inability of police to do their job effectively. Again we see Lamont's (2000) boundary work at play. The young men were drawing clear boundaries between themselves and the police (who were horrible at their job, according to the young men) and using these boundaries to strengthen their solidarity and essentially justify why they were dealing. Aissa described these interactions as a give and take:

It's not that I don't like the cops. But I don't agree with just randomly bullying people because you're frustrated. They are not good at their job—well, then, work on that. Don't take your frustrations and play power games in situations that don't require your attention. That's what losers do! This is pure harassment. And why would they always be rude? I think we treat them the way they treat us. Why do I have to show respect if they don't? If they do, I swear, everyone shows respect, too. Because we all have honor; we don't randomly treat people shitty, unless someone is, like, totally wasted or something like that. It's all give and take, you know?

The young men never spoke about discriminatory treatment by the police as a reason for engaging in drug dealing, but other researchers, including Sherman (1993), have made this argument. According to this theory, exposure to police behavior that is perceived as illegitimate can lead to criminal behavior in the future. Sherman argues that the weaker the relationship between those affected and mainstream society, and the more the sanction is viewed as illegitimate, the higher the likelihood that an individual will legitimize illegal behavior by him or herself and others in the future (448). While Sherman's work focuses on judicial sanctions, his theory is applicable to some of the young men's experiences; it is possible that their perceived marginalization undermined not only the legitimacy of judicial sanctions and the police, but the legitimacy of the entire society.

The young men did not talk about their concerns about Germany in terms of legitimacy, but in terms of purity and impurity. However, their argument is similar to that observed by Sherman: they felt that German society was impure and without honor and thus did not need to be protected. To them, this impurity was exemplified by what they considered to be the inefficiency of the police, the overly liberal parenting style of German parents, the sexual promiscuity of German girls, and the absence of hospitality in German society. These German "failings" allowed the young men to legitimize their actions in the drug-dealing world and, more importantly, to see themselves as good dealers, a crucial aspect of their identity formation.

CONCLUSION: BEING GOOD AND BEING SOMEONE IN GERMANY

Being a good dealer was crucial, because despite their illegal occupation, the young men saw a future for themselves within German society. By abiding to the rules that defined good dealers versus bad criminals, they demonstrated that they still cared. In contrast to the general perception of drug dealers, these young men still wanted to be seen as good members of society and not as ruthless criminals. While they sought to legitimize their actions by pointing to their exclusion from the formal economy and their marginalization, they still tried to find their identity within German society. Their feelings about Germany encouraged them to enter the drug market, but their self-perception as men of honor meant that they abided by their self-created rules for being good dealers who would not sell to children or sell bad drugs. Interestingly, the drug market helped them create a positive identity for themselves: it compensated for their exclusion on many levels and allowed them to gain respect in the streets. "At least here,"

Yakut said, "you are someone. Here, people have respect for you." Most importantly, this identity allowed the young men to feel superior to other marginalized populations, such as heavy drug users, dealers who had no choice but to take on any deal, and, to some extent, even the police officers who were—often unsuccessfully—chasing after them.

The young men did not only apply their concepts of purity and impurity to drug market–related decisions. They also distinguished between pure and impure women, a distinction that was particularly important to them when making decisions about dating, casual sex, and marriage. For the young men, marriage to a pure woman was seen as a way to find a place outside of the drug market and essentially represented their ultimate goal in life. In the next chapter, then, I will examine their hopes for the future and their decision-making process with respect to achieving their future dreams.

CHAPTER 5

Muslim Virgin Wanted

In Search of Reasons to Quit Dealing

You either have this life, or you get married. There is no other option. Otherwise you can just shoot yourself.

—Cafer

Ayan came to the youth center and showed a group of us five photographs of young women. Proudly, he told us that these were the women his mother had selected for him as potential marriage partners. No one but me thought that this was strange. The young men usually took charge of their own lives, defying most forms of authority, yet they were only too willing to relinquish their autonomy to their mothers when it came to finding a spouse.

As Ayan explained to me: "My mom carried me in her womb, she fed me as a baby, she raised me to be who I am. Who else but my mom would know better who's good for me?" This perspective was shared by the other young men in the room, who could not imagine marrying a woman of whom their parents did not approve or finding their spouse on their own; this was their mothers' responsibility. Eagerly, Ayan told us what he knew about the young women in the pictures and asked which one we all found most attractive. To me, it seemed as if he knew very little about his prospective wives, except that they all came from "good families" in his mother's village.

Conversations like these always made me feel awkward. It was in the context of women and marriage that my own ideas and those of the young men seemed to clash the most. Not only did we disagree about the role of women (and men) in relationships and about gender roles more generally, but I also could not understand how Ayan could pick out his future spouse from a bunch of photographs. I believed that one ought to marry the person one loves. He, on the other hand, was convinced that marriages based on love don't last, or, at the very least, that love should not be the deciding factor when choosing a spouse:

> AYAN: Love, love . . . that's all bullshit. Love dies. You might be in love today, but six months later or a year later, that's not the same thing anymore. It's going to be different. . . . It's not this hot thing anymore. So you're then stuck with this person that might not even have the same politics like you, or the same culture, or the same religion. You're stuck because you gave in to love, even though love always blows away. So choosing someone that is a good match because she has your religion and because your families get along and all these important things . . . because in the end . . . that is what matters in the end . . . that is what you should base your decision on. Because you are choosing someone for life and not someone you find interesting at a certain point in your life, you know?
>
> SANDRA: But what if you fall in love with someone, would you not try to make it work?
>
> AYAN [SLIGHTLY ANNOYED]: Sandra, I *know* what's going to happen with that. You know that, too! You *know* that this feeling changes. You can't tell me you don't know that. It makes no sense to let this influence everything. It's bullshit. *This* is the only way it works.

I had a hard time accepting the young men's belief that arranged marriages are the only successful marriage model, a tradition that differed significantly from that of my own culture. It also took me some time to appreciate how important an event marriage in early adulthood was for these young men. This practice differed from that of my own circle of friends, many of whom delayed marriage well into their thirties or decided not to get married at all, despite being in long-term relationships. On the contrary, the young men again and again identified marriage as their main future goal. For them, getting married was not just a religious or cultural obligation. As we will learn in this chapter, getting married was closely related to their idea of a life without drug dealing.

For most dealers, especially those with lower status in the drug trade, selling drugs is only meant to be a temporary occupation. For example, the Brooklyn-based dealers studied by Sullivan (1989) in the 1980s left the drug market as soon as they could find real jobs, and Williams's (1989) "cocaine kids" more or less aged out of dealing. Padilla (1996) recounts that the dealers in his study sought employment in the formal economy as their disenchantment with the empty promises of the street increased.

So what might the future look like for the young men in this book? This chapter explores the young men's thoughts about getting out of the drug market and what it would take for them to give up the benefits associated with their place in the informal economy. Will Akin, Rahim, and Inanc eventually decide that dealing is not a lifelong opportunity and try to find jobs in the formal economy? If so, what would be the motivating factors? A wedding? The birth of a child? Or simply "aging" out of crime?

When thinking about why someone might quit dealing, we have to consider what options he might have in the formal economy. Much has been written on potential incomes within each economy and whether and *when* crime pays (e.g., Reuter, MacCoun, and Murphy 1990; Freeman 1996; Levitt and Venkatesh 2000; Reuter 2004; Noveck 2007). While researchers have spent considerable energy disagreeing about whether average incomes in the drug market are higher or lower than those in the formal economy, the dealers I got to know made it clear that their participation in the drug market was driven by more than economic cost-benefit analyses. An individual's decision to get out of the drug business cannot necessarily be reduced to the event of securing a "real" job. In this chapter, I will show how numerous factors came into play each time one of the young men took up employment within the formal economy. More often than not, they soon returned to drug dealing.

Before exploring the issues that influenced their participation in the formal and informal economies, we need to consider what chances they had to obtain legal employment, and what motivated them to keep it.

EXPERIENCES IN THE FORMAL ECONOMY

As outlined in chapter 2, the young men's opportunities for getting well-paying jobs in the formal economy were severely restricted. Several German studies have reported that employers strongly prefer to employ native Germans, reducing the employment chances for immigrants from the outset. In addition, most of the young men in my study had not graduated from high school or completed vocational training. Consequently, the great majority were only qualified for unskilled labor.

During the five years of my fieldwork, many of the young men tried at various times to find positions in the formal economy. Not surprisingly, they were most successful at obtaining low-paid positions as unskilled workers, but none of them lasted very long in these jobs. Some were laid off; some quit. Rather than the goal of self-betterment, their primary motivation for seeking real jobs was almost always driven by short-term goals—appeasing their parents or making themselves look better for law enforcement following a run-in with the police or in time for an upcoming court appearance.

Jo, for example, tried desperately to improve his standing with law enforcement by searching for a job. He was being tried on various charges of violence (both against his girlfriend, with whom he had regular physical fights, and against strangers) and drug offenses and had no hope of avoiding jail time, but his lawyer advised him that showing serious efforts to turn his life around before the trial might allow him to cut a better deal with the judge. Jo had the social workers at the neighborhood youth center call almost every car dealership in the region, trying to find an employer who would not only give him a job but also provide him with some vocational training, since he figured that the court would look favorably on any attempts to further his education. Eventually, the social workers' efforts were successful; they found a car dealer who gave Jo a full-time job and the much-needed vocational training at the dealership that he needed in order to become a certified mechanic.

How Jo went about getting this job is worth commenting on, since it typified the application process for those young men who did seek jobs in the formal economy and revealed their obvious sense of entitlement, particularly in their interactions with the social workers. Throughout the entire application process, Jo placed none of the phone calls himself, nor did he try to write his own cover letter or résumé; instead, he expected the social workers to do all of these tasks for him. It could be argued that the young men lacked the "cultural capital" to manage these tasks themselves, but while this was essentially true, their feeling of entitlement was also very clear, as illustrated by Jo's comments: "You know, they get paid lots of money to hang out here and do nothing. I mean, look at them—they play pool and table tennis with the kids—that's not a job! The least they can do is to find us a job. That's their job! They get paid to do that. . . . That's what social workers do."

Jo's opinion was shared by the others; I often overheard the young men order social workers around, saying things like, "Hey—write a résumé for me." Their sense was that the social workers needed to justify the decent income they received for their "work," which was not the physically challenging blue-collar work with which the young men were familiar. To the young men, the job description for social workers consisted of "hanging out" and "playing pool," which in their minds did not qualify as work. Not only were the jobs the men had worked in the formal economy mainly blue collar, but so too were those of their family. For them, working meant "getting up early," doing physically challenging, intensive work, and earning relatively little money. Neither the social workers' job nor my work as a PhD student resembled any of their own experiences of work. Moreover, they believed themselves to be the reason that the social workers had their jobs in the first place and felt entitled to make claims about what they should be doing, despite the fact that they didn't pay their wages. Rahim put it this way: "If we weren't hanging out here, what would they do, eh? They only get paid because we hang out here. No other reason. So they should be fucking doing something for the money."

Although, as a PhD student, I did not earn as much as the social workers, the young men expressed essentially the same feeling of incomprehension about my work, as Akin pointed out: "I know you're smart, but really . . . what do you even get money for? You're not even doing anything." At one point I got into an argument with Rahim because I refused to write résumés and cover letters for the entire group. He seemed to be having a bad day—his father had just given him another long speech about how he should find legal employment and stop hanging out. Thus, when he encountered me at the community youth center, he was already in a very agitated state and started yelling at me for sitting around with some of the guys.

RAHIM: Sandra, if you're hanging out here, then do something useful! Go to the office and write applications for the guys. Don't just sit there and do nothing. That's not helping anyone! Start writing cover letters.

SANDRA: Well, for whom should I write a cover letter? Nobody is applying anywhere as far as I know.

RAHIM: You can just write cover letters. Just write cover letters for everyone! Just write lots of them. Then they're there and we can use them when we need them.

SANDRA: Come on, Rahim, I am not randomly writing cover letters. That's bullshit. If someone asks me for help, I am always writing the letter—you know that. But I am not randomly writing letters if no one is applying anywhere. I'd need to know what job someone is applying for to write a good letter, you know?

RAHIM: That's bullshit! You're just as lazy as the social workers. You can just write letters for everyone. We're not applying for big jobs!

AKIN: Yeah, Sandra, I think that's a good idea—just write letters for everyone and then put them in a folder or something. The social workers should be doing that, but they're lazy bastards. So just do it—you can't just hang out here every day and do nothing.

SANDRA: Well, as I said, if someone is applying, I am going to write a letter, no problem . . . but I am not going to write letters randomly.

At that point, Ayan came in and said that he believed Inanc and Lemir had just sold cocaine to an undercover police officer (which turned out to be true). Thus, the conversation shifted away from whether or not I was responsible for writing random cover letters. Nevertheless, this situation exemplifies how the group members clearly felt entitled to receive help (from the social workers or from me) with their respective application processes. By blaming the social workers for not always complying with their orders, they could avoid taking full responsibility for their inability to find a job. At the same time, their feeling of entitlement and the way they acted this feeling out were used to hide or shift focus away from the fact that, because of their structural and systemic exclusion (from school, specifically), they could not rely on their own agency to get themselves a job. So while they had this sense of entitlement and expressed it rudely, it was a facade that hid a sad and unfortunate reality: when I cut through the aggressive tone of their demands, I could hear both frustration and disappointment in their voices.

I came to realize as well that the young men's families did what they could to encourage them to look for work but were not always successful. For one thing, while families put pressure on the young men to look for work in the formal economy, this pressure was inconsistent. As Özgur described in the following conversation, even though his father put pressure on his brother, it was not strong enough to have any long-term effect in getting him to look for work:

ÖZGUR: My dad gives my brother headaches about doing something useful and stuff . . . but it's just not often enough. You know . . . I mean, he knows he's getting older and stuff, but he also knows that he can get away with it. They would not just let him down.

SANDRA: But do you think Rahim would actually get a job if your dad pressured him more?

ÖZGUR: Yeah . . . I mean, you know . . . we're all living at home. I don't want to say it's the family's responsibility, because it's not. But if they give you headaches . . . like every day, let's say . . . then you'd probably start taking it more seriously, you know? Because it's annoying, it gives you headaches, you know, if your dad is unhappy with you and stuff. But the way it is . . . .like, talking about it every, like, month or so, that's not doing anything, that's no pressure, you know?

The young men were aware that they did not meet their families' expectations about legitimate work, yet they did not feel pressured enough to secure jobs in the formal economy. Although I did not interview family members, I sensed that the young men's respective families kept the pressure low because they were frustrated with the formal economy themselves. For example, Akin noted, "When my dad came here, they promised him this and that, flowers and getting rich and shit . . . and none of that became true. He worked like a donkey for this fucking country." Also, some families indirectly benefited from their sons' income in the informal economy, which may have stopped them from insisting that the men find legitimate employment. Erol related how having a car came in handy: "Now that I have a car, I can drive my mom to go shopping. That helps her a lot."

Let us now return to Jo and his attempts to improve his résumé by working in the formal economy. For quite a while, Jo seemed to have found his true passion—he never missed a day of work, and he told everyone that working in the formal economy was the only true way to live and tried to persuade others, especially the younger men, to do the same. It seemed as if he had really found a new purpose in life. Interestingly, Jo's reflections on his former use of time echoed his diatribes against the social workers' lack of productivity:

JO: Yo, Sandra, that's great what I am doing, right? Tell them—tell them! I can't believe I was just hanging out all day long before. You're doing nothing; you just rot when you hang out here. It's awful. But I am doing something now. I'll get my degree—you will all see and marvel!

AKIN: Don't bullshit us, Jo. You're only doing this because of your story. If the lawyer hadn't told you, you would not be working right now. You're just bullshitting.

JO: You're a bullshitter. I'm doing this for myself, not for my fucking lawyer. He told me . . . but I am doing this for myself now. I never do anything because other people tell me to. You know that! What are you talking about? You'll see, I'll get my own shop one day and then you'll regret what you said!

For nearly three weeks, everything seemed to be working out, but then Jo's lawyer informed him that his case would not come before the court for another three months. At first, Jo took the news lightly, maintaining that he had changed and had found his true calling working as a mechanic in the formal economy. However, two days after the conversation with his lawyer, he came to the community youth center early in the afternoon, obviously not having completed a full day of work. When I asked him why he had left early that day, he complained about his boss, about whom he had always raved:

JO: This bastard is a racist. He always asks me to do things that others are not supposed to do. And he just fucks with my head—do this better, do that better. He only messes with me, never with the other motherfuckers. He is just a racist. I am not going to go to this fucking place anymore.

SANDRA: What happened? Didn't you always say that you liked this guy? Maybe he just had a bad day. . . .

JO: Well, he was OK in the beginning, but now he started to boss me around like a little puppy, and he complains about my work. "Paint this again," "The lacquer here is bad," blah, blah, blah.

SANDRA: Well, but you're in vocational training. Of course, he's going to try to teach you. He wants you to learn something, you know. I'd try another day.

JO: Well, then, why don't *you* go and work for this bastard? I don't care anymore.

Jo's story was very similar to that of his friends who tried their hand at working within the formal economy. Why did most of their attempts end quickly? The majority were very enthusiastic about their jobs at first, but the reality of having employment hit the young men very quickly and, combined with perceived discrimination from employers or co-workers, having to play a subordinate role in a mainstream company, the potential for having a female boss, and the need to get up early to make relatively little money, pushed them away from these positions and back into dealing. Inanc described his experiences working for a landscaping company for a couple of weeks as follows:

Well, for me, it was just totally fucked up. The boss was an East German and just totally racist. Not just to me—to everyone, to all the foreigners, you know? Except for the Polish! For whatever reason, he treated them just completely normal. And then you always had to get up early, just so that this guy could fuck around with you. We always had to do the shitty work, you know . . . like digging, and the Germans were allowed to plant and stuff. And for nothing; I could not even pay rent from it. So I just really didn't want to do this any longer. All the nonsense and, like, getting up at six for nothing—no, thank you!

Many researchers have reported that dealers usually have jobs in the formal economy while also being involved in drug deals, but this was certainly not the case for this particular network of young men (Fagan 1991; Adler 1993; Freeman 1996; Mohamed and Fritsvold 2006; Murji 2007). I could count on one hand how many of the young men kept their jobs for longer than a month.

Similar to the experiences that Bourgois (2003) described in his study of crack dealers in East Harlem, "going legit" was difficult for the young men in my study—not only because of their poor credentials and lack of cultural capital, but also because they didn't know how to play the role of subordinate workers in a mainstream company if and when they eventually did find a job. Having a female boss, for example, was inconceivable to them. In the streets and at home, they had learned that women should play a subordinate role to men. One day, Talat reminded me of this: "I don't understand why you would go to school for such a long time. What if your husband does not want you to work? Then all of this was for nothing. If I don't want my wife to work, she's not going to work."

They were clearly perplexed when they encountered female bosses. More importantly, they had not learned how to respect or behave around female bosses or how to cope with the fact that some male bosses they encountered would never be able to maintain a respected position in their own world of the street. To the young men, the formal economy seemed to reverse the rules of the streets: women could hold superior positions, bosses could be people who could not stand up for themselves physically, and obedience took precedence over the street value of "showing balls." For Inanc, the contradictions were too much to handle:

Well, when I tried last time [to work full time], my boss was this little weasel. You just know that he would just be beaten up if he wasn't sitting in his big chair [and was] German. I just can't do it. . . . I just can't take that seriously, you know? It's not that I can't take these people seriously in the beginning; it just [happens] when they start bossing you around and are trying to play big and stuff. I mean, you know that [your boss] would be a total loser on the streets. . . . [He's one] of those people who never had friends and who would send in his wife if there was an argument . . . or who would call the cops if someone hit on his wife because he doesn't have the balls to just beat that person up. Well, if someone like this always shows respect and stuff, then I do what he wants, even if he's a joke. But most of them are just trying to play big and pretend to be something they're not. And then I can't take them seriously.

Like Jo, who imagined having his own mechanic shop one day, most of the men dreamed of becoming their own boss at some point—of, for example, opening up a little shop or corner store. It would be a mistake, though, to conflate these dreams with a deep commitment to entrepreneurialism; rather, the young men simply did not want to deal with the hassles and difficulties of working in a company. As Erol described, they liked the idea of running things:

> If you have your own newspaper kiosk or something like that, at least you can decide yourself when to open and when to close and stuff. And you don't need to deal with these Nazis who work in every company—I swear. But all this responsibility, like having to make the money and stuff, that is scary too. So I don't even know whether it's better to have your own place—and you'll have to deal with all these headaches, like who's going to buy your newspaper or whether it's better to just work for an asshole. But I get too frustrated with these assholes, so I guess I would still prefer to have my own place.

Aissa also recognized the difficulties of company work but, like many of the young men, was realistic enough to understand that his credentials didn't make him a prime job candidate. Still, in his opinion, family life was a consolation for the losses associated with giving up the drug trade:

> When I think about the future, I think you're lucky if someone hires you. I mean, it's like you haven't done anything in so many months or years, right. So what do you expect? You can't expect nothing. You just need a job that pays for your family, then. I mean, you can't have . . . like, high expectations. You can't expect to be the boss, you know. It's a different life then—you just have to know that you will never be the person who makes the calls. That's over when you quit [dealing]. But you have a family then.

None of the young men expected to have a future career in the formal economy that involved a high income. Essentially, they were realistic enough to understand that they did not have the best credentials and that getting a job, and not necessarily securing a high income, would be the key to a stable life in the formal economy. Overall, though, these thoughts about permanent legitimate jobs were directed toward the future. During the five years of my study, the great majority of the young men never made any attempt to find a job in the formal economy; most of those who did had completed vocational training and should have had better prospects. Even so, they were generally unsuccessful in securing employment. Nermin was one example:

> NERMIN: Seriously, I sent out over 100 applications within the past fourteen months of being unemployed. Written by the social workers. No bullshit. Good applications. I mean, you saw them, I don't need to tell you. Good applications! And nothing. Niente. Nada. Nothing at all! And really . . . I have no clue what they want . . . seriously. . . . I never had to repeat a year. . . . I graduated from the middle stream, I graduated from vocational training, with good grades, actually. You saw my transcript; you saw it . . . no bullshit . . . no bullshit! I worked for two years straight after that. Straight! Nothing awkward in my CV, seriously . . . nothing! So . . . if I can't find anything, how are the others supposed to get anything? The only three times that I was invited for an interview was when I said I was Italian. Remember that bullshit?
>
> SANDRA: Yes, I do. That was . . .
>
> NERMIN: Crap! That was crap! I sent three CVs out saying I was Italian. Three! . . . and I was invited for two of the three jobs. . . . That's two invitations out of over a hundred applications! That's just crap, right? I mean . . . am I supposed to say that I am Italian so that they will finally consider my application? Just because Italians are not Muslims? That's just bullshit! That's this whole 9/11 shit. It only got worse after that.

Nermin's experience, of course, is just one example and does not prove that all German employers favor non-Muslim applicants. However, the young men perceived German society in general and German employers in particular to be very exclusionary and racist. Generally speaking, the experiences that Nermin blamed on the post–9/11 era have been supported by American studies that have reported that fear of terrorism among the general public has resulted in increased surveillance of immigrants by non-state actors such as neighbors, public transportation workers, co-workers, teachers, and classmates (Rodriguez 2008). These everyday practices of surveillance have intensified the social marginalization of immigrants, especially those perceived as Muslims, and excluded them from mainstream society, perhaps most notably in the labor market (Rodriguez 2008). Experiences like Nermin's—whether experienced directly or indirectly through a friend—further discouraged the young men from seeking employment in

the formal economy and served as a justification for not quitting dealing—
at least *not quite yet.*

THE EVERLASTING QUESTION: DOES CRIME PAY? OR IS IT A QUESTION OF LIFESTYLE?

When asked about the future, almost all the young men indicated that they imagined a future life *outside* the drug market and *within* mainstream society. However, these thoughts and plans were reserved for the future; for the time being, the drug market provided them with the opportunity to pursue a specific lifestyle.

The formal economy provided the young men with few opportunities in general, and even fewer opportunities for earning a comparable amount to what they could make in the informal economy. They were obviously much better connected in the informal economy, which meant that for the vast majority of the young men, the drug market was a much easier way to obtain the funds necessary to maintain their lifestyle. This lifestyle was generally quite expensive, and a job in the formal economy would probably not generate enough money to support it. One day, we were hanging around, talking about everything and nothing, and Jo came along, pointing to the pockets of his jeans.

> JO: Look how full they are! I'll buy the BMW today.
> AKIN: Shut up, man, what BMW?
> JO: Oh, I found it last week. It's in great shape and [has] only 40,000 kilometers [on it]. I love that baby!
> SANDRA: And you're going to pay cash?

At that point, Jo reached into his pocket and proudly and slowly counted out 24,000 euros (approximately US$30,000). This encounter occurred only four months into my research, and I was shocked at the amount of money these young men apparently made in the informal economy. I had never seen that much money before. A couple of months later, I learned that not all the young men made such huge quantities of money and that their incomes fluctuated greatly. However, at that moment, I must have looked very startled, and Jo immediately commented on my expression:

> JO: What is it? Have you never seen money before? How much money do you have in your pockets?

SANDRA: I don't know. Definitely not 24,000 euros—I know that much!

JO: Well, you're not buying a car, right? But how much, then? It's Friday, you must have *some*. The weekend is around the corner. Are you not going out on the weekend?

SANDRA: Yes, I will. I just went to the bank, so I actually do have money on me. [Reaching into my pockets and taking out 100 euros] I don't think I will need all of that.

AKIN: What do you mean? That's not going to be enough for a weekend! Are you crazy?

SANDRA: Eh? I am not going to spend 100 euros on a single weekend. That's a lot of money. I am still a student. How much money do you spend on a normal weekend?

AKIN: A normal weekend? Like, Friday night, Saturday night, Sunday night? At least 500 euros, if not 1,000 euros. I mean, you'll go [to a] party, [there'll be] the cover, alcohol, food, you'll open a bottle of champagne or two, or whiskey—they are like 100 euros at a bar, [you'll need a] hotel for the night . . . [laughing] or brothel. Maybe you rent a car . . . [or] the girl. Life is expensive, Sandra.

This conversation left me puzzled. Here they were talking about a cost ranging from US$128 to US$1,200 for an evening's worth of entertainment. At that point, I still thought of the drug dealers I was studying as lower-class immigrants who dealt a little bit on the side simply to get by. I was aware that they all wore designer clothes and always had the newest (and most expensive) cell phones, and that some of them drove expensive cars, but I had assumed that the young men saw these as important status symbols and spent all their money on a few expensive items (which were also sometimes secondhand, like the car Jo was purchasing). Taylor (2000) has noted that status symbols and consumer consumption are especially important for the identity formation of those groups in society that are chronically underemployed. Similarly, Hayward has observed: "What is unique about the last few decades of the twentieth century is the way that the creation and expression of identity via the display and celebration of consumer goods have triumphed over and above other more traditional modes of self-expression" (2004, 144). I had been heavily influenced by the academic literature and assumed that the young men I was studying saved every cent to spend later on status symbols. Although my assumptions about how the young men spent their money turned out to be true, my concerns about whether they were living beyond their means were ungrounded. I realized during the conversation with Akin and Jo that the young men did not focus on saving as much as I had thought.

At that stage of my research, I also hadn't yet observed how the young men spent their time outside the community youth center. Naively, I had assumed that most of their stories about excessive nights at bars with many bottles of expensive whiskey were exaggerations—portrayals of themselves as being tougher and more powerful than they actually were. After this conversation, though, I realized that I had been too quick with my interpretations and overly influenced by studies reporting that incomes in the informal economy are generally lower, or not much higher, than those in the formal economy (Reuter and MacCoun 1992; Reuter, MacCoun, and Murphy 1990; Wilson and Abrahamse 1992).

Although the young men had a pretty good idea of how much money a weekend would cost them, they did not really engage in any rational cost-benefit analyses and didn't know how much they actually made in a given month. In other words, they did not deal drugs because they expected to make a specific amount. Sometimes (like that particular day for Jo), a dealer would have a lot of money in his pocket. On other days, the financial situation was completely different, as Aissa described:

> Usually . . . I mean, you have the money in your pocket and you spend it; you don't have a clue how much you're actually making. . . . This whole thing from like the beginning of the month until the end of a month . . . that doesn't make any sense when you're dealing. It's not like you get a payslip or something like that. You don't pay attention whether it's the tenth or the twenty-eighth, you know? That doesn't *mean* anything. You sometimes have a couple of thousand in your pockets, and sometimes you have nothing. That's just how it goes.

Aissa's explanation demonstrates that the young men did not particularly care—or know—exactly how much money they were making. This finding supports previous studies that have reported that the actual income of drug dealers remains a mystery (Jankowski 1991; Denton and O'Malley 1999). The gang that Levitt and Venkantesh (2000) studied kept detailed statements of their revenues and expenditures, which allowed the authors to comment on the income of individual dealers. When I asked the group members if they kept track of their revenue and expenses, they laughed the question off and stated that such a thing was improbable. Aissa expressed how absurd this idea seemed to them:

> OK, Sandra, that's just bullshit. Someone would have to be very dumb. . . . It's like shooting yourself in the foot. That will only count as evidence against you.

Once I heard of someone who kept track of people who owed him money, so he saved a list of the names and the respective amounts on his phone. The cops found that . . . so *that's* already really dumb! I mean. you have to be *really* dumb to do that. Think about what people would think if the cops paid them a visit because they were your list. . . . Well . . . I think the way it works is that you have a rough picture of what you're making and who owes you money, but I don't think anyone would ever write that down or save it on the phone or something crazy like that. . . . I don't believe that anyone would write that into a book. . . . That's a cock-and-bull story, Sandra. Unless it's a total retard, of course . . . but someone like that is not going to survive for a long very time.

How much, then, did the young men make in a month, and was drug dealing lucrative in comparison to the formal economy? Given that the young men could not really comment on their exact income and that their incomes constantly fluctuated, it was impossible for me to estimate how much they actually made in an average month. Nevertheless, I would agree with their claim that they earned more from their involvement in the drug market than they were likely to earn at the average job they could get in the formal economy (based on their level of education, these jobs generally paid around 1,000 euros (US$1,200) a month, equivalent to a single night out on the town). When asked how much he made in a month, Aissa replied:

That's too hard to tell. It really depends on supply and demand, what you're dealing with, and in what quantities. Nobody bothers doing these calculations . . . you know, as long as you have enough money in your pockets. And if you don't have any money in your pockets, all you know is that you need to get some deals done ASAP to get some money in. It's just the fastest way to get cash. You just always have more money this way . . . always. If you get really, really lucky and get a really, really good job at the airport, you'll make 1,200 max—but you would never make more than that. Never! And making more with drugs is no problem. . . . I mean . . . you can basically make the same amount in one day and then just chill for the rest of the month. You're making good money here, good money.

In other words, the drug market made it possible for the young men to make "good money"—*how much* that actually was seemed of secondary importance. Essentially, money was important insofar as it enabled a certain lifestyle: parties, women, cars, eating out, designer clothes, the newest cell phones, alcohol, and drugs. The young men never said that they could not quit dealing because they did not want to give up a certain income; instead, they expressed much more concern about not being able to engage in the *lifestyle* to which they had become accustomed, which included strong connections with their friends. At the same time, they—at times—gained deep satisfaction from "outsmarting the police" and "being on top of their game." To stop dealing would also mean losing this satisfaction, which made drug dealing even more seductive (Katz 1988).

While a simple *economic* cost-benefit analysis wasn't a deciding factor for the men when considering their future in the drug trade, a more nuanced analysis did come into play. Quitting drug dealing would allow them to meet the expectations that they and their families held about getting married and being a good Muslim, but their anticipated losses from leaving the drug trade were heavy. Although the loss of being one's own boss factored into the men's narratives about work in the formal economy, a more significant loss associated with quitting the drug trade was the fact that not having disposable money would mean that they could not hang out with their friends.

Because the young men generally shared their bills, a person without money could be covered for a while. For example, when five of the young men went out to the movies, one person would often supply the car and the gas, another would pay for refreshments for everyone, and a third would pay for all of the movie tickets. Nights out at bars in the neighborhood, which generally produced bills in excess of 200 euros, were covered by one or two individuals. However, "free riders"—that is, those who *always* went along at the cost of others—were quickly identified and talked about, which dissuaded them from coming along in the future. Aissa explained how this system worked:

> You can only do this so many times. At some point, you just need to realize that this is too much. People will get mad. I will get mad if I always pay for the same motherfucker. I mean, I have nothing against paying—you know that, we all pay for each other, we don't split bills and do this whole German thing, like, "You owe me two and a half euros." . . . I mean, that is just ridiculous. But if someone is just always coming along, always coming along and never pays for shit, then that's not cool. Then I'd say something. You can't have a free ride forever, you know what I mean?

The discussions I witnessed and in which I participated repeatedly showed that the young men's peer group was one of the most important aspects of their lives: they did not occasionally hang out together—they spent every single day together. Essentially, their close relationships with their friends provided them with the sense of community, place, and belonging for which they so desperately strived as marginalized second-generation immigrants. In fact, they often commented on friendships between individuals in other social milieus and claimed that *those* people (or me, for that matter) did not have any *real* friends. Akin explained the difference:

> What you have, like, meet people and drink red wine and talk bullshit for an evening—that's not what I call friends. That's like . . . *acquaintances*. My friends are my brothers. I see them every day, every night. None of us would ever move away like Germans do. Like, pack your stuff and move to Berlin. How could you do that? You just have no clue what friendship is. No one who has real friends would just leave them.

Most friend-related activities involved hanging out in the streets or at the community youth center. If the group engaged in special activities, like going to the movies or to a bar or club, they almost always did so on a last-minute basis. This made it very hard for individuals who could not constantly hang out and be on standby to participate. A decision to go to the movies, for example, was often made within two minutes. Similarly, plans that the young men had contemplated in the afternoon were often completely outdated by the evening. More than once, the group talked at length about going to a specific bar or club on the weekend, but by the time the weekend arrived, plans had completely changed and most of the young men did not even remember that the original plan was to do something different. Given these dynamics, it was very difficult for individuals who did not spend every minute with the group to stay in the loop.[1] Those who thought about quitting drug dealing or—more importantly—considered leading a different lifestyle that included less hanging out knew that they would most likely have a very hard time getting together with their friends in the future. Thus, quitting dealing was very much associated with *being on one's own*, that is, being isolated from the other Bockenheimers and eventually losing one's place in the tight community.[2] Aissa described this dilemma:

> One thing that makes this so damn hard is that you don't know if you'll ever see the guys. I mean, if you decide that you don't want to just hang out in the streets and just stop wasting all your time, but you do still want to be in touch . . . right. . . . I mean . . . that's really hard! So all you can do is hope that they will call you if they do something. Haha. As if that's going to happen.

Did the young men then view themselves as lifelong drug dealers? Although the peer group was very important to them, and quitting dealing was synonymous with becoming less involved with friends, the vast majority of the group planned to eventually find a job in the formal economy and consequently quit dealing. By the time I left the field, all but four individuals were still involved in dealing, so it was impossible to predict whether the other young men would actually quit dealing as they claimed they would. Still, the ethnographic material I gathered offers detailed insights into what the young men imagined for their own futures.

Of the fifty-five young men in the study, only Akin and Ferdi repeatedly stated that they would never leave the drug market. All the others talked about quitting dealing *eventually*. For these individuals, this expectation was not necessarily about wanting to quit; rather, it was their ultimate life goal of starting a family and having children that made them think about a life after drug dealing. For these young men, having a family and children was inextricably connected with pulling out of the informal economy. This did not mean, however, that the young men planned to work toward a life within the formal economy; in contrast, they clearly distinguished between their present and future lives and constantly claimed that they were not thinking about the future yet. Present and future were fundamentally separate, and the young men did not make any preparations for the future whatsoever, at least in the traditional or mainstream sense. As discussed previously, the few attempts some made to find employment in the legal economy were driven by the urge to look better on paper for an upcoming court case or in response to family pressure. None of these individuals saw these attempts as a turning point in their lives.

This clear distinction between present and future may seem strange to outsiders, but considering the young men's jobs in the informal economy, it is not that surprising. The young men simply did not know whether they could realize their goal of having a family and kids and living outside of the informal market. Many obstacles could get in the way, such as incarceration, deportation, and even death,[3] but the most important issue was whether they would ever find a wife and get married. Though most of them relied on their family to arrange a wedding for them, they did realize that they were not top candidates for such arrangements. Still, like Jawad, the young men were aware that some families in their parents' home countries sent their daughters to Germany because they had a good chance of marrying well there:

You just have to look at it this way: my parents can tell them whatever they want about me, because they don't actually live here and they don't know shit about what's going on in Frankfurt. My mom can tell them that I have been working with my dad forever and that's going to be that. And for those families, it is good to send the daughter off to Germany, you know. It's the country where milk and honey flows. . . . It's really good to have your daughter married there.

As a result, despite their involvement in the informal economy and the fact that most of them did not have much going for them in terms of education or careers in the formal economy, the young men's residency in Germany equipped them with enough social capital to be viable wedding candidates for some parents outside of Germany. As Talat summed it up: "I don't even need to think about that [marriage]. My mom will just find me a good wife when the time has come. There are plenty of good wives in her village, plenty. She will find me one—trust me."

However, even though the majority remained hopeful that their families would eventually arrange a wedding for them should they not find a partner themselves, Talat's total confidence was not the norm. Most of the young men didn't trust the arranged marriage process enough to quit dealing before getting married. Yakut described his situation as follows:

I will think about this when the time comes. Right now, I just want to live my life here and now. If the time comes for marriage and stuff, I can think about a job and so on. That would be way too early now. How should I know when this is going to start, when you find a wife and so on? You know, just imagine, I would find a job and earn crappy money and have nothing to do with the guys and so on, but I will not meet a woman for the next three years. Just imagine! What would I do for the next three years? Watch TV by myself because I won't have friends anymore and can't go out because I won't have money anymore? No thanks!

When I asked these young men what they would need to quit dealing, conversations like this one took place:

CAFER: You really need to have very strong arguments to quit . . . well, *very, very* strong arguments! Well, a wedding, you know . . . that would be a strong argument. 'Cause you want to be able to teach your kids something, you know?
SANDRA: Are there other arguments you can think of? Anything else besides getting married?

CAFER: Hmm . . . no, not really. I don't think that anyone could quit this without getting married.

INANC: Yeah, yeah . . . a wedding is . . . you know, it's kind of like a new start . . . it's kind of like a new life you get. It's a completely different life then.

SANDRA: But couldn't you have started that after prison?

INANC: What? What for? For myself? Not having money and sitting at home by myself? Leaving all my friends for nothing? No way!

CAFER: No one does that. You either have this life, or you get married. There is no other option. Otherwise you can just shoot yourself.

For the young men, the turning point seemed to be a wedding and the subsequent start of a family. A wedding was in fact the *only* reason they could think of that would entice them to quit dealing, so they viewed getting married as their *only* realistic chance to turn their back on the informal economy and its accompanying lifestyle.

From a theoretical perspective, this outlook is similar to life course perspectives (Laub and Sampson 2003), according to which certain events—such as getting married—can have a significant influence on criminal careers. By getting married, the young men hoped they could leave their previous life behind and start a new and "better" life. The future life they imagined was also in line with the religious beliefs that they all claimed to have but had put on the back burner, apparently to the dismay of their parents. They felt that Allah would forgive everything a young person did. Of course, they extended the period of "being young" much longer than even the most liberal scholars of Islam would accept: to the young men, "being young" (and thus having a "free pass" from Allah) could be extended until they actively chose to change their lifestyle, even if they were 35 at that point. However, to become a good Muslim, a good husband, and a good father, as they all hoped, would require them to change their life radically, which was a very difficult task, given the type of life they were living. Kash described how lonely it would be for him if he quit:

KASH: I just can't imagine it without a wedding, wife, kids. And then . . . what should I do? All the guys, your friends, the money . . . it's all there . . . so if you don't have anything that really draws you in, something that is really worth quitting all of that for . . . I mean, if you don't have something that is basically worth quitting your life for, *your life*, Sandra, then I would not do it. There is no reason why anyone would do that. You just must have a real reason. Nobody does that without a reason! Nobody! Never! What for?

SANDRA: What would happen?

KASH: It's not like in your life, Sandra, it's not like anyone [would come to our] place and play a board game with [us] and drink red wine [with us]—that's your life, not ours. [When you're out of the trade,] you're lonely. Real lonely! You can either walk to the corner and listen to the stories of the guys, or you can sit at home by yourself. Both are shitty, because you don't have anything to do with the guys anymore. If you have a wife and kids at home, at least someone is at home, you know.

Having a wife and children would justify leaving their friends, their tight community, their income, their status symbols, and everything else behind to find a steady job in the formal economy, even if that meant having to deal with the downsides of legal jobs such as having a subordinate position and making far less money.

If we take their arguments at face value, then, it seems likely that the young men will never simply "age out of crime," as suggested by Gottfredson and Hirschi (1990); rather, they will probably wait for certain events to occur that will make quitting the drug scene, and the lifestyle that goes along with it, worthwhile.

PURE AND IMPURE WOMEN

The young men's anticipated path out of the informal economy through marriage was not straightforward. Each of the young men had very concrete ideas about his future wife and the characteristics she should possess. First and foremost, a wife for whom it would be worth quitting dealing would have to be "pure."

As pointed out in the previous chapter, the pure/impure duality played a role in many aspects of the young men's lives, not just in terms of how they understood women: for example, the money they earned from drug dealing was regarded as impure, which hindered them from saving it for their pure future or from passing it on to pure family members. They also justified their involvement in the drug market by arguing that Germany was an impure and dirty country that did not deserve any better. Interestingly—and this is where interpreting ethnographic data gets tricky and less straightforward—this opinion also demonstrated their ambivalence. Although they viewed Germany as an impure and dirty country, they clearly envisioned a pure life after drug dealing *in* Germany.

When assessing their future, the impure/pure duality was important in two different ways. On the one hand, they distinguished between impure and pure women; only the latter qualified as marriage partners and thus could free them of their impure life. On the other hand, they could not imagine being involved in the essentially impure drug market while having a family life. A family was seen as a symbol of purity that ought not be brought into contact with impure things such as the drug market. Therefore, the young men envisioned making a radical break and abandoning all of their contacts and connections—even their closest friends—once they started a family. Ultimately, this would mean abandoning the community they had created for themselves—a community that had given them a sense of place and belonging in an otherwise-exclusionary and discriminatory society.

However, it is possible that some of the young men will never be able to accomplish the transition from a drug-dealing lifestyle to a mainstream existence through marriage because of their strong feelings about the purity and impurity of women. The vast majority of the young men emphasized that their future wives should come from the same country of origin as their parents, or that, at the very least, they should be Muslim. To the young men, pure women were Muslim women who had had a "good" upbringing and "good" parents.

> SANDRA: You always say that a girl must come from a "good" home. What do you actually mean by that?
> TALAT: That means . . . that means that the parents are good parents. A good family, you know?
> SANDRA: No . . . I am not sure what exactly you mean.
> TALAT: You're not stupid, Sandra. Of course you know what I mean. Like, good parents . . . like, who make sure that she does not hang out, that she has a good upbringing, like, she helps her mom and she is at home . . . and that she is a virgin. Like a family with honor, you know . . . a family that takes care of its girls and that teaches them how to be a good wife and so on. You know what I mean . . . that's a good family.

The young men invariably stressed the importance of virginity when talking about "good" girls. They labeled both liberal Muslim women who preferred a different lifestyle and all non-Muslim women as impure. In this way, the dichotomy between pure and impure was bound to religious and cultural backgrounds and was dependent on a woman's level of sexual activity (or non-activity).

The reader might wonder where German girls fit into this equation, given that the young men were naturally surrounded by them. A German girl with no sexual experience could never attain the same status of purity as a Muslim virgin girl, but the young men could attach the attribute of "good" to her to emphasize that she was an exception and that her background did not accord with her sexual experience. It was on these grounds that the young men would often state: "She's German, but she is a good girl." Using the label of "good" allowed them to loosen their stringent notions of purity and impurity and to make these notions slightly more compatible with their secular and mainly non-Muslim surroundings. However, moving from the theoretical acceptance of a German as a girl-friend to the acceptance of a German as an eligible marriage partner was still a big step. This leap would require further modifications to the purity/impurity dichotomy, an adjustment that might be necessary if the young men desired a larger pool of potential marriage partners. The young men's ideas about purity and impurity made it very difficult for them to find a partner for marriage; most of the girls they met in Frankfurt did not meet their explicit expectations of purity and hence did not qualify for marriage.

> ENVER: A German could never be like a Muslim. That's just impossible! But there are some good Germans too. Well, very, very few, but there are *some* . . . with a good upbringing and stuff . . . and a good family and stuff. That's a big exception though, I tell you!
> SANDRA: Would you marry a good German girl?
> ENVER: Never!

It's important to note that although the young men expected Muslim girls to remain celibate until their wedding day, the young men themselves led a very different lifestyle. Even though they hoped to marry a pure virgin and subsequently quit the drug trade at some point, this didn't mean that they had no sexual contact with women. The great majority had various relationships with women that mainly served to fulfill their sexual desires; none of these relationships were taken very seriously. Generally, the women in these relationships did not have the same cultural or religious background as the young men. On the contrary, it is significant that the young men preferred to have casual sex with women who did *not* share their cultural or religious background because they did not want to dirty their own women.

Since women of non-Muslim background were considered impure, the young men interpreted this to mean that they could have sex or "mess around" with these women without any conflict with their belief system or religion. They also felt no guilt about having casual sex with impure women because they fully believed that it was the responsibility of the woman to avoid sexual contact, as Mahmut explained:

> I'd never want to fuck a *good* girl, you know? Well . . . what does that mean? . . .
> *If* she is a good girl, she would never let anything happen in the first place, she
> would never let anyone lay hands on her—do you understand what I mean?
> She'd have her honor and her religion. and, you know, nothing could happen
> to her. But German girls—that's a *completely* different story. The Germans . . .
> they're all sluts, none of them are still virgins. They just fuck everything
> that comes near them. . . . You really don't need to feel bad when screwing a
> German girl.

Although the young men expected their future wives to be celibate, they had very different expectations of the women with whom they just wanted to be sexually active, explicitly favoring women with sexual experience. As Rahim said: "You don't want to fuck a virgin. That's no fun anyways."[4] The young men created a double standard by being sexually active while stressing that such activity was forbidden for female Muslims. In addition, they created a double standard in their evaluation of women by dividing them into the categories of pure and impure.

Perhaps unsurprisingly, given their opinions on these matters, they also routinely visited sex workers. Visiting brothels was often a group event and was never treated as a taboo in front of other group members (or in front of me). As a female ethnographer, I was not permitted access to brothels, but I was able to meet some of the "apartment sex workers" they frequently visited; these were sex workers who did not work in brothels but operated out of their own apartments. Many of the group members had had their very first sexual experience with a sex worker. They rationalized these visits by arguing that the pool of marriageable women was extremely small in their Western setting, so they simply did not have the same opportunities as their parents had had to live a pure life at a much younger age. Metin argued that his parents would understand his position if given the chance:

> I'd be *sooo* embarrassed in front of my parents. I can't even imagine. But you
> know, they are also from a village. I mean, they got married at 15 or so. . . . You
> know, there, you already had your wife at 16 or something like that. And here,
> that's a totally different picture . . . there are just no good women for marriage.

And, you know, you just can't expect that you don't have sex until you're like 35 and have one to marry. . . . And . . . I mean, if my parents were just thinking about this . . . like, logically thinking about this kind of situation and stuff . . . then I am sure they would agree with me.

Since all of the young men claimed that they would eventually quit dealing and its accompanying lifestyle as soon as they could find an eligible woman to marry, what did they do, then, to find a suitable partner? Most of them were actually not actively looking for a girlfriend, explaining that they did not have an immediate need to quit the lifestyle. The women they met when hanging out with friends clearly did not qualify as marriage partners for a variety of reasons, with one of the most frequent being that they felt that only impure women went out at night while pure women stayed at home. Although I quickly learned that talking about women (especially in sexually explicit ways) was a favorite activity among the young men, I never got the impression that women were part of their social circle—making it hard for the young men to meet potential spouses. Even outside the youth center, the young men engaged in purely homosocial relationships.[5] Thus, the most logical—and for most, the *only*—imaginable way to meet their future wife was through family networks.

Earlier in this chapter, I mentioned that four of the young men quit dealing drugs while I was conducting my research. Three of them had marriages arranged by family members, and one met his future wife by coincidence. Though these four essentially quit dealing and stopped hanging out with their friends once they were married, their marriage did not mean that they changed their sexual behavior and were monogamous from that point on. Even those who fell in love with pure girls and had relationships during the time I was conducting my research still visited sex workers and/or had sexual relationships on the side at the same time. This behavior would normally be interpreted as being unfaithful to their partner. However, I soon realized that this promiscuity could also be interpreted both as an attempt on the part of the young men to prevent their steady partners from becoming dirty and as a way of maintaining some type of contact with their pre-marriage community.

One night, the group and I were hanging out in a café and some of the guys decided that they wanted to go to a brothel. Enver was among the group that desperately wanted to go. He was out that night to celebrate his last evening with his friends, as his marriage to a woman from Albania had recently been arranged. He anticipated that his regular evenings out with his friends would soon be over.[6]

SANDRA: I thought you're happily married now. Why don't you just have sex with your wife?

ENVER: What are you talking about, Sandra? I can't fuck my wife. . . . Are you out of your fucking mind? What should I tell her? "Hey, baby, I want to have it this way"? No, no. . . . I'd feel really, really bad.

Mustaffer was also among those interested in ending the night with a quick visit to the brothel. He had recently started a serious relationship with a Turkish girl whom he would later marry. In contrast to Enver, however, this relationship was not arranged. He was the only one of the four who had met his future wife by coincidence and had fallen in love with her. Even though he was strongly committed to her, his opinion did not differ from Enver's: "Well, Sandra, think about what you're saying . . . . Enver can't go to his wife and say, 'Hey, baby, this is what I want.' If you're with a ho, you can do *anything*. She gets some money . . . done deal, you know. You can't fuck your wife like a rabbit. No one does that." His explanation exemplifies the ambivalence embedded in the young men's concepts of purity and impurity. On the one hand, the young men claimed that they needed to quit the drug market when they started a family because the impure aspects of their lives should not affect their family; on the other hand, they did not shy away from continuing to visit prostitutes or having casual sex on the side once they were married.

As mentioned previously, these actions can be interpreted as the young men's way of protecting their future wives or steady girlfriends from an impure lifestyle. In this sense, the young men were constantly aware that they did not always live up to their own standards of purity, yet they did try to keep their partners clean. Aissa, one of my key informants, tried to explain this behavior to me one night:

> Well, I can't really express what I mean. It's just a different kind of sex with your wife. That's just . . . you know . . . to make children, not for . . . not for, like, the purpose of having sex. You know what I mean? . . . I have no idea what's going on in, like, Turkey or Morocco. I think it is different there. But here . . . you know, you've already *had* lots of sex before [you get married], and then you just want to continue to have this particular kind of sex. This . . . you know . . . just having sex like you want it. And you just would not do that with a virgin who has no experience, you know what I mean? You would want to protect her from that. It's also the only thing you still do with your friends, you know. Like, you don't hang out anymore and stuff once you're married, but you just sometimes go to the brothel together.

As a side note, the idea that sex in marriage is purely for reproductive purposes has nothing to do with the Islamic notion of sexuality. The young men reinterpreted Islamic understandings of sex for their own purposes. By having sex outside of their relationships and/or marriages, they claimed to be trying to not bother or molest their wives, fiancées, or girlfriends with their impure sexual fantasies and thoughts, and thus to be attempting to keep their loved ones pure. They believed that this was their duty as Muslims, even though their ideas about purity and impurity were far removed from Islamic values and norms.

Douglas (1966, 7) has described pollution and impurity as *relative* and said that "sacred things and places are to be protected from defilement." In this sense, for the young men, girls were not inherently impure, but they could become impure if they were not protected. The young men fulfilled their sexual desires with women whom they already considered to be impure and reserved sex in marriage for reproductive purposes only. Only by doing so could they guarantee that their wives would not lose their pure status through impure sexual activity. This framework also exemplified the very different standards that they had for themselves and for their partners, as Rahim pointed out:

> First of all, she will be shocked when you're jumping up and down on her like a horn-dog . . . but I also don't want to be guilty of her becoming a dirty slut. If she's a good girl, like, from a good home, you do have some form of responsibility toward her and toward the dad of the girl. I mean, you do need to make sure that her upbringing wasn't just useless. I mean, you need to give a shit. You basically need to make sure that she's not going to do dirty stuff.[7]

CONCLUSION: "YEAH, IN THEORY YOU WANT OUT . . . BUT IN PRACTICE . . . "

The concept of quitting drug dealing after marriage only made sense if the young men actually married pure women. Because they believed that pure and impure things should not be mixed or brought into contact with each other, maintaining this distinction was their only way out of the drug trade. They wouldn't quit dealing to marry just *any* woman. If they considered the woman to be impure by their own standards, their rationale of not bringing those two worlds together would not make sense.

This left them with a very small pool of eligible women who could seduce them into making the transition from the drug-dealing world to mainstream society. Thus, quitting the drug-dealing lifestyle as a result of marriage was only a hypothetical possibility for most of them. It could be argued that some set the bar so high that it could never be reached and so had a justification for remaining active in the drug economy. After all, the young men loved their lifestyle and all it entailed. Having said that, the rationale of finding an eligible woman and quitting dealing was effective for four of the young men I studied, as well as for some of their older brothers and cousins.

Based on the experiences of their older peers, the young men saw only three possible life trajectories: a successful marriage to the kind of woman they sought, getting incarcerated or deported to their parents' country of origin, or staying active in the drug market until possibly being pushed out by younger dealers. The young men were most afraid of the last option and constantly stated that they did not want to be a loser who was still hanging around at the age of 40. Even so, quitting dealing by choice seemed not to be an option, even for the oldest members of the group:

> MESUT: You would have to be very strong. I mean, you'd lose every-
> thing. You'd lose your life. No one is that strong—at least no one
> that I know. You're either forced out, or you're lucky and you get
> a wife.
> SANDRA: When you say, "You're lucky," that sounds to me as if you do
> want out. So is there really no other option you can see?
> MESUT: Well . . . yeah, in theory, you want out. Because you want to
> be a good person and have a family and be a good Muslim and all
> that shit. And you're afraid that you're still here when you're 50
> and that you're the loser that everyone makes fun of, you know,
> like Rezal. But in practice, look at the life we're living . . . . No one
> leaves that for nothing. There must be a reason. A strong reason.
> You don't just quit your life—that would be the shittiest exis-
> tence you can imagine.

In the end, the wedding/quitting dealing formula (while irrational to outsiders) appears to have been perceived as the only way out among the young men I studied. For these young men, marrying the good and pure Muslim virgin was clearly associated not only with having to quit the drug trade, but also with essentially breaking entirely with their past, their friends, and their lifestyle. This event was also associated with becoming a practicing Muslim and living up to their families', and even their own, expectations. Essentially, and perhaps unconsciously, by marrying a pure woman, they hoped to become a little bit less impure themselves.

CHAPTER 6

Where to Go from Here?

What could make a difference? Sandra, I have no idea what you're talking about!

—Akin

People always ask me whether I liked the young men I studied. The underlying assumption of this question is that drug dealers are intrinsically bad people. While I definitely disagreed with some of the young men's opinions and could not sympathize with some of the choices that they made, the reader must concede that this is true for many, if not all, of the people we meet in life. So my honest answer is that I enjoyed spending time with many of the young men I discuss in this book just as much as I like spending time with academic colleagues (and in many cases, I would even prefer hanging out with the guys). Thinking about drug dealers as bad people per se is an oversimplification of a complex problem. The real questions are: Why are second-generation immigrants in many European countries overrepresented in criminal statistics? What can we learn about this overrepresentation by looking at the lives of the young men in this book? And in what ways does the German context play a role in ensuring this overrepresentation?

THE YOUNG MEN: THE LINKS AMONG SOCIAL EXCLUSION, IMMIGRATION, AND DRUG DEALING

The majority of Germans might not even be aware of the disadvantages that immigrants face in German society. As I have described, many German institutions cater to the German majority, safeguarding a good education, high-paying jobs, and citizenship for their own purposes. For example, the early streaming in the school system (and the associated lack of universal German-language classes for non-native speakers) can make it hard for immigrant children to measure up to the native-born students. Likewise, the official political rhetoric about immigrants might not strike the average German as odd, despite the fact that it instills a feeling of otherness and exclusion in immigrants. Even the wide use of the term "Ausländer," which—from the German perspective—is a technical term that just underlines the fact that the person does not have German citizenship, signals to immigrants that they do not officially belong to the country in which they were born and raised.

Amidst this landscape of exclusion, the young men have carved out a niche for themselves in Bockenheim, their neighborhood. Identifying as Bockenheimers has allowed them to create an identity within Germany without having to identify with the German state or the German mainstream. Being known in Bockenheim and having an extensive local network helped the young men feel that they had a part in actively shaping Bockenheim, which in turn contributed to their feeling of belonging. This sense of agency is important, because it allowed the young men to imagine a future in Germany despite the fact that they faced structural limitations in many areas of their lives.

The young men internalized the exclusion they faced from German institutions and in everyday life as being normal, and they started participating in the drug economy as a *reaction* to these structural barriers. Drug dealing seemed a natural choice for them: many of their older friends and relatives were involved in the drug market as well and provided access to the drug economy while at the same time serving as role models to the young men. The drug market provided them not only with financial resources but also with a way to gain self-respect. After all, they could take on leadership roles in the drug market, whereas they were relegated to subordinate roles in the formal economy. While the young men rationalized their participation in the drug trade as a reaction to their living situation in Germany, they also understood that their actions and activities strengthened and reinforced the stereotypes that caused them to be excluded. As such, they were aware that they were actively contributing to the continued perception of immigrant youth, and particularly youth with guest-worker and Muslim backgrounds, as criminals and consequently to the ongoing social exclusion of such youth.

Given that the young men turned to the drug market because they lacked better employment opportunities and not because they identified as drug dealers per se, they negotiated their drug-dealing activities in light of their perceived cultural and religious obligations. While scholars of Islam might disagree with the young men's interpretation of Islam, the young men took their self-ascribed religious obligations and interpretations quite seriously, which helped them to distinguish themselves from people they called "real" criminals. In this way, they were able to develop a positive sense of self by not dealing to people they identified as pure, like children or Muslim women, and by not dealing substances they labeled as impure, like LSD.

That the young men did not identify as drug dealers becomes particularly clear when examining their future plans and the fact that most of them wanted to leave drug dealing behind in order to turn their lives around, start families of their own, and become devout Muslims. They viewed the institution of the family as sacred, which is why they could not imagine combining their impure life as drug dealers with raising children (it is also for this reason that they did not have any children out of wedlock, an outcome that is often seen in American studies of similar populations; see Bourgois 2003; Anderson 2000).

The fact that the young men did not fully identify as dealers also becomes clear when we examine the way that they did business. While incarceration might reasonably be seen as a normal aspect of a dealer's life, the young men took many safety measures to avoid trouble with law enforcement. Certainly, this increased concern for safety was also possible because they did not have to provide for any dependents and were mostly still living in their parents' homes. The young men certainly desired the financial rewards of their business, but staying safe and "not getting carried away" were always given higher priority. They did not engage in many risky deals and often turned deals down even when they were financially promising. Again, their self-ascribed religious rules and the fact that they imagined a future life outside of drug dealing are probable explanations for these safety precautions. Essentially, they had too much to lose.

As immigrants in Germany, then, the young men faced structural barriers that limited and defined their opportunities in German society. It was within this context that they started participating in the drug economy while still trying to adhere to their perceived cultural and religious rules and to engage in deals that were considered relatively safe. It was because they were aware of the structural barriers facing them that they rationalized their actions to themselves and others and did not fully adopt the identity of a dealer.

What can be done about this situation? How can Germany keep young men in similar situations from engaging in the drug economy? And if the young men neutralize their actions by pointing to structural barriers, what can be done to ensure that immigrants evaluate the German system as more fair? While doing my fieldwork, I grew increasingly frustrated with many of Germany's policies and institutions, especially the school system, the formal economy, and the legal system involved in citizenship rights, which seemed to be putting the young men I got to know at a disadvantage. I also became increasingly irritated by officials' labeling of second-generation immigrants as the "lost generation" and debates over best practices for deporting them to their parents' country of origin when they became involved in crime (without ever considering the second generation as native-born citizens, as is the common practice in the North American context). While I do not want to draw attention away from the young men's participation in the drug market, I do want to emphasize that they became involved in this market even though they were born, raised, and educated in Germany. In fact, most of them had never spent any significant time in their parents' country of origin, and when I met them, many had not been back to visit that country in many years. The roots of their criminal involvement cannot be found in Turkey or Morocco. Rather, such roots need to be sought in Germany, particularly in the peculiar situation that second-generation Muslim immigrants of guest-worker backgrounds encounter. As the young men stated over and over again, not being wanted in the country they called their home was a common feeling for them, which, I argue, has significantly shaped their lives.

Islamophobia in Western Europe

This situation is not unique to Germany. In fact, the situation of immigrants in other Western European countries is similarly problematic, and while the context varies depending on the country, it seems that Muslim immigrants in particular experience numerous disadvantages in *all* Western European countries (Klausen 2008). Interestingly, Muslims in Europe are an ethnically diverse group, which speaks to the fact that it is not just predominately Turkish youth, as in Germany, who face barriers. In other European countries, Muslim youth of other ethnic origins find their opportunities similarly blocked.

While no systemic comparative research has been conducted on crime rates of Muslim immigrants in different Western European countries, single-country analyses are available. For example, research has shown that Moroccan youth in the Netherlands (Engbersen, van der Leun, and de Boom 2007; Junger-Tas 2001; Van Gemert and Fleisher 2005), Maghrebian youth in France (Tyler 2007), and Bangladeshi youth in Great Britain

(Klausen 2008) are particularly involved in the criminal justice system. Like the young men in Germany in this study, these immigrant youth seem to fare worse socio-economically, which likely contributes to their overrepresentation in crime rates.

How do the situations for Muslim immigrants in other European countries compare to that of Muslim immigrants in Germany? European Muslims are disproportionately poor in comparison to the native-born populations of the country in which they live, and many remain residentially segregated (for example, in France, 50 percent of Moroccans and Algerians and 40 percent of Turks and Tunisians live in social housing [Choudhury 2007, 81]). Socio-economic immobility, then, is of concern not only for Turks in Frankfurt or Berlin, but also for Maghrebians in Paris and Amsterdam and Bangladeshi in London.

A publication by the Institute for Strategic Dialogue (Klausen 2008), an independent think tank, argues that Muslims face socio-economic hurdles—such as poor access to education, lack of mobility to look for work outside of low-employment areas, and intergenerational disadvantage—in *all* Western European countries that create barriers to integration. These barriers are particularly detrimental to the second generation of immigrants, because they "prolong the income gap between Muslims and non-Muslims" (Klausen 2008, 9). Germany, Austria, Denmark, and the Netherlands have particularly low employment rates for both immigrant men and immigrant women (OECD 2007), and especially for Muslim immigrants (Open Society Institute 2009). In countries with high unemployment rates, like Germany or Britain, the unemployment rates for Muslim youth (especially those of the second generation, like the young men in this book) are generally twice as high as the unemployment rates for native youth, and are sometimes even higher (OECD 2006a, 73).

Like Germany, many other Western European countries also make immigrants' attainment of citizenship difficult. This again is particularly problematic for members of the second generation, like the young men in this book, because some Western European countries have also established new rules requiring employers to hire foreign nationals only in the event that no competent national or EU-national job applicant can be found. Citizenship, then, becomes important not just for social reasons (e.g., identification with the country) but also for economic reasons.

Contributing to these barriers are unfavorable views of Muslims and Islamophobia held by the public. Such views are prevalent throughout all Western European countries but are particularly pronounced in Germany and Spain. The Pew Global Attitudes Project in 2006 (http://www.pew-global.org/category/datasets/2006/) showed that 20 percent of the public in Britain admitted to a generally unfavorable view of Muslims, compared to 35 percent in France, 54 percent in Germany, and 62 percent in Spain (cited in Klausen 2008, 10).

While in each Western European country different factors play a role in the marginalization of Muslim youth, Islamophobia seems to be a contributing factor in all of them. Because it is generally hard to change attitudes and opinions through awareness campaigns, however, policy suggestions will have to be context and country specific. It is for this reason that I mainly focus on Germany here, but I do think that many of the following suggestions can be applied to Muslim youth in other Western European countries as well.

What Can Be Done?

As I thought about how to change the situation of the young men I had gotten to know, I felt increasingly helpless. Shouldn't I be able to come up with policy solutions? After all, I had gotten to know these individuals and understood their plight much better than many others did. Over time, however, I came to understand that there were no "easy fixes." Many of the policies and institutions that were particularly problematic for immigrants would need a major overhaul, and I was frankly not optimistic that such proposals would ever get the approval of the majority of the population. Even if one were to significantly change the school system to provide equal or at least better chances for immigrant children in contrast to what they currently face, would that really change the thinking of the majority? I also had little advice for the young men themselves. Could I really encourage them to do the morally right thing, stay in school, and get their degree after witnessing firsthand the reality that they might not be invited to job interviews because they were Muslim (or simply because they were not German)? I still feel torn on that question.

As I became more and more disillusioned about the right policy solutions, I often found myself asking the young men what they thought could be done to improve the situation for second-generation immigrants in Germany. One night, when hanging out with Akin at a bar in Bockenheim, he gave me a very typical response to that question: "Sandra, I have no idea what you are talking about!" He did not believe that any single policy could improve the marginalization and distrust that immigrants faced in mainstream German society; in fact, he could not even imagine "a different Germany." Policies that could really make a difference in their lives were, for the most part, beyond the imaginations of Akin and the other young men—Germany seemed like a static place to them. Akin's point is valid: isolated policies such as the integration of German-language classes into school curricula without getting rid of the tracking system, or educating the public about the country's guest-worker history without extending citizenship to second-generation immigrants, cannot adequately address the deep roots of the marginalization that immigrants face. In an ideal world, helping marginalized people would be possible if the structural, political, and economic roots *as well as* the ideological and cultural roots of marginalization and exclusion were addressed. I believe that only when solutions take into account the fuller framework of marginalization will policies actually make a difference.[1]

I will begin this chapter by discussing some of the most important areas that need attention in the German context. These policy recommendations are by no means comprehensive but can be considered important steps toward fostering "social cohesion and integration" among Muslim immigrants, a goal that was identified by the members of the German Islam Conference, an annual discussion forum bringing together Muslim representatives and German politicians founded in 2006 (see chapter 1). This conference's main objective is to promote cooperation and social cohesion between the German mainstream and the Muslim immigrant population. I will then focus on more general policy recommendations to address marginalization, not just in Germany but also in other Western countries.

FOSTERING SOCIAL COHESION AND INTEGRATION IN GERMANY

Unlike the United States, Germany is founded on values that center on "society" and lead to its perception as an elaborate welfare state. Individuals are not considered to be solely responsible for their failures, and the German state and society are supposed to step in if an individual is struggling. It is quite likely that this belief was ingrained into the young men in this book; consequently, when Inanc claimed that "there is nothing else we can do in Germany but be drug dealers," it signaled to me that perhaps he was more integrated into Germany than the German mainstream would ever admit. He was clearly adopting the German belief that he had been let down *by society* and not by himself. But in reality, when it comes to the Turkish-Muslim immigrant community, individuals and groups are blamed for their own misfortunes, which are supposedly caused by their lack of willingness to integrate. General public opinion may not be as extreme as Thilo Sarrazin's "leave or integrate" position, but second-generation Turkish immigrants who drop out of school and become involved in violence and drug dealing do not get much sympathy.

To maintain social order, the state needs to respond to criminal behavior, including drug dealing and violence. As noted in chapter 2, in Germany (and other European countries more generally), crime levels among second-generation immigrants drastically exceed the crime levels of the native-born population. In more traditional immigration-heavy countries, such as the United States and Canada, crime rates among second-generation immigrants are lower or equal to those of the native-born population. What are the reasons for these differences?

One common explanation is that traditionally immigration-heavy countries select immigrants based on more stringent criteria (e.g., education and work experience), which makes these immigrants a better fit and more prepared for Western society. When countries use education as an important basis of selection (which is especially true in the Canadian case), education is more likely to be a value of families chosen to enter the country, so parents are likely to pressure children to stay in school and off the streets. In contrast, many immigrants came to Germany and other Western European countries as guest-workers without any formal education, raising questions about whether they could (or would) support social mobility through education for their children. As discussed in chapter 2, Aissa's mother was afraid when his teacher offered to send him to the Gymnasium, because she had very little education herself and had never gone to school in Germany.

However, the arguments that "selection" is responsible for the lower crime rates in traditionally immigration-heavy countries and that the lack of selection explains the higher crime levels among immigrant populations in Germany (and other European countries) are disproven by the crime levels among first-generation immigrants. Crime levels among first-generation immigrants in Germany, as in traditionally immigration-heavy countries, are much lower than those among the native population. In fact, many studies have shown that on average, the first-generation immigrant population has stronger moral values, better health, and lower crime levels than the native-born population (Lopez-Gonzalez, Aravena, and Hummer 2005; Marmot, Adelstein, and Bulusu 1984; Ousey and Kubrin 2009; Palloni and Morenoff 2001; Portes and MacLeod 1996; Williams 2005).

The low crime levels among first-generation immigrants in Germany demonstrate that these immigrants are not "culturally criminal," nor are they criminal because of a lack of education. The difference lies in how immigrants are received in their new country. As discussed earlier, not only Germany but all Western European countries show some overrepresentation of Muslims (of different ethnic origin) in crime statistics. The weak socio-economic integration of these groups and the general Islamophobia that currently pervades Western Europe contribute greatly to their poor reception in these countries. More traditionally immigration-heavy countries have implemented many measures to help immigrants settle and integrate, and their political rhetoric also sends an important message to society that immigration is mostly wanted and desirable (see, for example, the common description of the United States as a "melting pot" and Canada as a "mosaic"). Few such measures are in place in Germany and other Western European countries, so immigrants there tend to face severe structural difficulties. Inanc's daily interactions with his German neighbor exemplify the way in which many of the experiences the young men encounter make them feel as if immigrants are neither wanted nor desired: "Almost every day, she makes comments like, 'Why do you lock your bike here, we're not in Turkey,' or she makes comments to my mom about food, she's like, 'The entire hallway stinks because of your food. You're in Germany, when will you learn to cook German food?'"

Germany's lack of integration policies—such as those found in Canada (see Reitz et al. 2008) and the United States—and its different ideology about immigration also sends the unequivocal message to society at large that integration depends on immigrants' willingness to overcome these obstacles, essentially putting all the emphasis on individual agency and ignoring the structural forces that limit integration. As Aissa pointed out, problems like the ones that Inanc had with his neighbor are almost impossible to overcome: "Germans have particular ways of doing things, and everything that is somewhat different is bad. They are not open for new things or different things. For Germans, it's not possible that food can smell different. Different means bad. You can't change that thinking. . . . it's the way Germans think." While Aissa's statement clearly borrows from stereotypes about Germans, he probably has a point that Germans are generally quite peculiar about how things ought to be done, having strict opinions and regulations on issues ranging from "quiet times" to the most appropriate time to do laundry. It is not uncommon to get into trouble with neighbors for running a vacuum cleaner between 1 and 3 p.m. (supposedly "quiet time"), for playing piano after 6 p.m. (supposedly "nighttime"), or for hanging up laundry in the shared backyard on Sundays (supposedly the "sacred day"). Locking a bike in a shared stairwell would likely get Germans into trouble as well, so Inanc's neighbor might not intrinsically be racist, but it obviously sparks deeper debates when it is the Turkish immigrant who does not abide by the rules. While the German locking a bike in the stairwell might be thought of as "deviant," the Turk might be thought of as not just deviant but also not willing to integrate. A similar line of thinking is likely common in other Western European countries.

There is no doubt that the demographics of the immigrant population in Western European countries *are* different than those of the populations in the United States and Canada (supporting the selection argument); however, Muslim immigrants in all Western European countries, including Germany, face more difficulties than their North American counterparts when trying to integrate and are not as well received by the mainstream (Klausen 2008). Policy recommendations only make sense if they address these structural difficulties and are simultaneously geared toward changing public perceptions about immigrants. Public perception, of course, cannot address the "demographics" of the immigrant population, but I argue that in the German case in particular, it is Germany's *historical responsibility* to integrate its immigrant population. Germany actively recruited guest workers without planning to integrate them. The German government has always claimed that no one planned for a long-term solution (speech by Angela Merkel, Nov. 2, 2011), but nor did it implement a successful rotation system or enforce the return of guest workers to their home countries in any other way. The integration of immigrants, including those who became "criminals" while growing up in Germany, has become a question of moral and social responsibility.

A small step into the right direction would be to change the vocabulary used to refer to immigrants. German politicians and newspapers continue to refer to second-generation immigrants as "foreigners," despite the fact that they were born in Germany and are fluent in German. According to Koopmans, the continued and derogatory use of this term "may have real and important consequences, both for the attitudes of the majority population, and for the self-identification of immigrants" (1999, 636). Throughout my fieldwork, the young men frequently commented on the fact that they were referred to as foreigners, explaining that the common use of the term instilled feelings of being a perpetual "outsider" and "not German." As Kaner emphasized: "We may get the fucking passport at some point, but we will always be foreigners—my kids will be foreigners, my grandchildren will be foreigners, my great-grandchildren will be foreigners. I don't think the Germans would ever look at a Turk and say, 'Yes, you're one of us.'" Ironically, Germans expect assimilation, yet politicians, the media, and the general public continue to refer to all immigrants as foreigners, constantly highlighting the impression that they don't really belong to Germany.

I also believe that including the experiences and plight of guest workers in history and social science classes in high school might make a difference in the long run. Recent history such as the country's postwar policies and its guest-worker program are usually not addressed in these courses, meaning that students are not exposed to Germany's postwar immigration policies unless they take a personal interest in the topic. This lack of awareness means that the general public is not very well informed about the country's guest-worker history, so important background information is missing from public discussions and integration debates, like those sparked by Thilo Sarrazin's book (discussed in chapter 1). I believe that including the history of guest workers in the curriculum would send the important message that this history is part of the country's history, and that the guest workers and their children belong to and are part of Germany.

I also think it would be helpful to offer Turkish-language classes in German high schools. Özgur often talked about how illogical it was that German schools did not offer classes in the language spoken by the largest immigrant population in the country, whereas Latin was still widely taught in the Gymnasium stream. For him, as for many of the other young men, it seemed strange that Germans would learn a dead language like Latin instead of a language that was widely spoken in their own country. They insisted that learning Turkish would put Germans in a different light in their eyes; as Özgur said, "I think that would be really cool, it would show me that they have some interest in me." Similarly, the young men always cheered me on when I learned Turkish words and were eager to teach me the language, despite the fact that they almost exclusively communicated in German with each other. With respect to the high school curriculum, I believe that the works of German authors like Goethe, Brecht, and Durrenmatt could be supplemented with works by immigrant authors to reflect the demographic makeup of German society and encourage a feeling of inclusion among immigrants, which might in turn discourage future generations from seeking out a feeling of belonging in deviant street groups. At the same time, this approach might foster understanding among Germans and hopefully—in the future—create a feeling of a "shared history." When I hosted a going-away party at my house before moving to the United States, a few of the young men commented that they had never been to a "German home," reminding me that despite attending German schools, the young men had always been segregated from German students. Akin added: "I've never been invited to a German kid's birthday party." This segregation only strengthens stereotyping on both sides.

As the young men endlessly pointed out, the German school system itself needs reform. I worry that Germans will probably never fully reject the streaming system for fear that they might lose certain privileges (Weber 1972); that is, they fear that middle-class German children might end up in the same classroom as lower-class Turkish children. But actually, the roots of the problem go even deeper than the streaming system. Unfortunately, Germany's teachers and early childhood educators are very poorly paid, and the younger the children are, the worse is the pay. Additionally, teacher education often involves random pedagogy seminars, which means that teachers are not necessarily prepared to teach in diverse classrooms. This is not to say that aspiring teachers cannot take courses on diversity as part of their university studies, but at most universities, this is not a requirement for graduation. Aissa recounted what happened during Ramadan one year when Muslim students were fasting: "My Grade 9 teacher was yelling at this girl in my class because she was hungry and could not concentrate. She said something like, 'It's illegal in this country to not give children food.' It was Ramadan, and so she constantly made these ridiculous comments." Appropriate education for new teachers is crucial in order to foster cultural competence and thereby promote change. Unfortunately, unlike in countries such as Finland (Prenzel 2004), in Germany, teaching is not a very desirable profession, so the criteria for entrance to university teaching programs are almost non-existent.

Making seminars about diversity a prerequisite for aspiring teachers may only be a small step, but it could make an important difference in the lives of Muslim students in German classrooms. The young men recounted hundreds of stories about schoolteachers who clearly were not equipped to deal with a multicultural classroom. Germany is officially a Christian country, and it expects immigrants to assimilate to German values and beliefs, so policies in Germany are not tailored to cultural differences. Turkish parents who do not allow their children to participate in school trips or physical education (which is often co-ed), or Turkish girls who wear headscarves to school or in public, are seen as being against both integration into mainstream society and integration into the German school system. Commenting on this, Rafet once noted: "My parents did not allow my sister to go on this five-day trip to a youth hostel. She was in Grade 6 in the Gymnasium. So the teacher said that they should send her to school in Turkey if they're unhappy with the way they do things. The next year, she was streamed down anyways." Furthermore, he went on to comment, "I never had a teacher who knew anything about Islam. I even had teachers making fun of Ramadan. This really needs to change before I send my own kids to school. . . . It is bad . . . ridiculous . . . mind-blowing."

On a macro level, the German Islam Conference is a good forum for all participants to discuss such topics and for the Muslim representatives to raise concerns, but on a micro level, teachers have to be better prepared to handle such debates and discussions. The young men in this book interpreted many of their experiences with teachers as "racist" and "exclusionary," which they certainly were, but blaming the teachers will not do anyone any good and certainly will not bring about change. It is the system in general—the pay structure, the lack of training and awareness on matters of diversity, and so on—that needs reform.

Being Muslim in an overtly Christian country and an overtly Christian school system clearly sends the message that Muslims are outsiders in German society. Mahir pointed out that exclusive religious studies in his public school contribute to this impression: "At my school, we had to take religion every year. But they only offered Protestant or Catholic [classes]. That's absurd to me. We had like 90 percent foreigners at my school—all Muslims." Mahir, along with many of the other young men, advocated adding a class on Islam to the curriculum as an option for fulfilling the religious studies requirement. Personally, I think it would make more sense to move away from religious instruction in public schools and replace those denominational classes with a class on "world religions." Given that most public schools require students to take religion classes from Grade 1 until they graduate from high school, this time frame would provide ample opportunity to expose students to other faiths and would foster meaningful dialogue among the different religious groups.

While the young men did not comment on their lack of kindergarten attendance as an issue, I believe that the fact that kindergarten is not mandatory in Germany imposes additional structural difficulties for immigrants. The argument against mandatory kindergarten (often championed by conservative Germans) is that this requirement would interfere with the right of mothers to raise their children at home, but a wealth of literature has demonstrated that mandatory full-day kindergarten is key to educational success (Ackerman, Barnett, and Robin 2005; Baskett et al. 2005; Da Costa and Bell 2000; DeCesare 2004; Cryan et al. 1992), regardless of socio-economic status (McCain, Mustard, and Shanker 2007). At present, immigrant children who do not attend kindergarten (or who attend a kindergarten with immigrant children of the same ethnic background) are not socialized in the German language or among Germans until they enter elementary school, which means that they often lack the social capital and German-language skills necessary for their integration into the school system, particularly when facing the streaming that takes place after Grade 4. Additionally, class differences become more apparent when children receive their (early) education mainly in the home.

Students in my undergraduate and graduate courses are always surprised that Germany only recently began to grant citizenship to second-generation immigrants. I don't believe that the young men I got to know would be better integrated if they were suddenly granted citizenship, but I do believe that this would be the morally correct action on the part of the government. Most of the young men said that receiving formal German citizenship would have symbolic value, and as an ethnographer, I am inclined to take these statements seriously. I was once asked at an academic conference whether I thought the young men would stop dealing if they were granted citizenship (retroactively). I had to answer "no," because too many other factors have influenced their present situation. However, it might help foster a feeling of belonging among these young men, which in many ways is a prerequisite for social integration, and social integration is an important indicator of crime prevention. Moreover, it would certainly not hurt if the young men's future children grew up with parents who felt a stronger sense of belonging to Germany.

Granting citizenship (retroactively, since the most recent law does not include second-generation immigrants born in Germany before 2000) to second-generation immigrants, even if they have criminal records, would address the reality that most positions of symbolic importance (e.g., those in the police, army, and judiciary) require valid citizenship (Koopmans 1999). This generates a cyclical systemic power imbalance that deepens the chasm between nationals and foreigners. Without citizenship, second-generation immigrants are also barred from voting in democratic elections, so German politicians regularly "leave the representation of immigrants and their interests at a minimal level" (Koopmans 1999, 635). Without citizenship and the right to vote, second-generation immigrants will remain politically unrepresented and unable to alter their own social, political, and economic well-being through the democratic process. Lastly, the denial of citizenship on the basis of having a criminal record underlines the strong political message that Germany has sent to immigrants for years: that even the children of the former guest workers who have been born and raised in Germany do not truly belong to Germany and that Germany has no responsibility for the courses their lives have taken. Instead of understanding how the structural limitations faced by second-generation immigrants, especially those from guest-worker backgrounds, influence criminal behavior, Germany has chosen to place the entire emphasis of the citizenship conversation on individual agency. However, as part of the German Islam Conference and more public integration debates, some politicians are now admitting that mistakes have been made in the past and that integration programs were simply not in place when they needed to be. Granting citizenship retroactively would, in my opinion, be a way to underline this realization with some much-needed action.

ADDRESSING THE DECISION-MAKING PROCESS OF MARGINALIZED POPULATIONS MORE BROADLY

While the previous recommendations are exclusively geared toward Germany, the following section will speak more broadly about addressing marginalization and street culture in Western societies. In all Western countries, many second-generation immigrants face marginalization and exclusion. Second- and third-generation immigrants are aware of social exclusion and marginalization, especially in the educational system, to a much higher degree than the first generation was. In the United States, for example, while the majority of second-generation immigrant youth are making educational and occupational progress, a significant minority are being left behind (Farley and Alba 2002; Kasinitz et al. 2008; Portes and Fernandez-Kelly 2008; Portes and Rumbaut 2001; Rumbaut 2008; Zhou et al. 2008). Policies need to focus on this minority.

In my opinion, cultural and ideological changes are a prerequisite for other sustainable and successful measures aimed at encouraging change at the street level. The participation of marginalized people in street culture is problematic from a law enforcement perspective and can also have serious long-term effects on society, leaving generations of marginalized young immigrants without hope. As Bourgois (2003, 326) has stated, for drug dealers, "fortune, fame, and destruction are all just around the corner." The most obvious way to encourage change is to address the discrepancies between the economic and status rewards of the legal, formal economy and those of the informal economy. As long as marginalized people like the young men I got to know are able to earn more money and respect in the drug-dealing world than in the formal economy, and as long as they are denied access to good jobs in the formal economy, the lure of the streets will always be stronger. When Aissa tried to turn and then stay "legit," he soon had to realize that despite having a high school degree and having learned a profession, his salary would not allow him to pay the rent for a small apartment he shared with his brother, eat, and have a car. Even after he sold his car, he could still barely make ends meet and stayed involved in drugs in order to "top up" his legal salary. As he said, "Sandra, I am not asking for much in life. I want my place, a girl, and a job that's decent. I don't understand why that's so impossible."

An important issue related to shrinking the drug market is decriminalization. A strong argument can be made for decriminalizing drugs (see

Bourgois 2003), but although this is a worthy long-term goal (albeit one that is merely wishful thinking in most countries), allowing underprivileged people to enter and remain in the legal labor market must always come before any attempts at decriminalization. Only when marginalized people begin to see (through the success of ex-dealers gone legitimate) that "steady money" can be made in the formal economy will they reevaluate the costs and benefits of trafficking. Failure in the legal economy not only discourages those attempting to transition into legitimate employment but also serves to reinforce their belief that the informal economy is their only viable option for making money and gaining respect. Repeated failure inevitably sends a broader social message to dealers and underprivileged individuals that they have no place in the legal economy. As 18-year-old Veli told me before he quit school: "There is no point. I can finish, but I would end up in the same spot. We all end up here. There is no point. Look at the guys: no one is successful—with or without a degree."

The absence of room for marginalized people in the formal system is certainly related to the emergence of youth gangs and drug-dealing street groups. Based on my research, I find highly questionable the classification of the young men I got to know as a "criminal enterprise" or a "criminal organization" as set out by the criminal code in most Western countries. While illegal activity and violence certainly need to be addressed by law enforcement, it is unlikely that the many current initiatives—particularly in the United States and Canada—aimed at cracking down on youth gangs and street groups are appropriate. In many ways, these groups act as a source of social identity that marginalized youth cannot easily find elsewhere. Understanding this fact and the marginalized position that many youth are in (for various reasons and in various contexts) would yield more adequate policy responses. However, tackling the root of the problem is a macro-level enterprise: marginalized youth need to be able to find positive representations of themselves in mainstream society. If mainstream society can only offer marginalized populations ill-funded schools, daily discrimination, and underpaid jobs in the legal economy, it should not be surprising that immigrant youth will try to find a more positive sense of their identity outside of mainstream society. As Fehim put it: "On the streets, you don't only get money, it's also that you can be someone."

Trying to be "someone" on the streets, however, often puts young and marginalized youth in direct contact with the police (who are seen, in many ways, as representatives of mainstream society). By "outsmarting" the police, being a step ahead of the "law" and thus "the state," the young men (and participants in street culture in general) gain dignity and self-worth, power and respect. But relationships with law enforcement are not purely negative: during my fieldwork, I encountered several police officers who had gained the trust of youth in marginalized communities over the years through initiatives focused on building trust between the communities and the police. Erol described one officer he knew from Bockenheim: "We've known him forever. He's one of the good ones." However, many of the law enforcement strategies implemented in the aftermath of 9/11 have undermined this trust.

At this point in time, I would argue that many of these strategies need to be reconsidered, especially those implemented in the United States that target immigrant populations. For example, under the recently passed Memorandums of Agreement (U.S. Immigration and Custom Enforcement 287g), trained state and local law enforcement authorities in the United States are now permitted to "question and detain undocumented immigrants suspected of committing a state crime" (Ismaili 2010, 78). This increases the likelihood that officers will stop immigrants to check their immigration status, even though they are not officially authorized to execute random street checks. This expanded authority sends a very negative signal to immigrant communities and undermines any trust that might have been established between immigrant communities and the police before 9/11. In short, the police can only make a community safe and counteract victimization and crime when they work *with* its residents rather than against them.

In the United States and Germany, many new law enforcement measures have targeted Arab Muslim communities, significantly undermining their cooperation with the police. Ironically, this means, as noted by Tyler, Schulhofer, and Huq (2010), that Arab Muslims are less likely to inform law enforcement about potential terrorism-related activities within their communities, the very intelligence the state is hoping to gather. Heightened suspicion of immigrants, especially Muslims, has had very serious consequences: not just undermining immigrants' trust in and cooperation with the police but also increasing distrust of immigrants and Muslims by non-state actors such as teachers and neighbors. The number of false reports about immigrants, particularly Muslim immigrants, being involved in crime and terrorist-related activities has significantly increased since 9/11 (Hendricks et al. 2007).

Essentially, both sides win if there is cooperation between the Muslim community and the police. This cooperation can only be achieved by building (and rebuilding) trust between these two groups. While I argue that some of these countries' recent policies have been counterproductive in this regard and should be reversed, there is much more that can be done. For example, police officers are often unaware of cultural norms that make an important difference in their interactions with people they are policing. I was once present when two police officers came to Nermin and Aissa's house to inquire about a stabbing that had taken place within their network of friends. After the police officers had left, both Aissa and Nermin were furious about the "racist cops." From my perspective, the interaction that I had witnessed was actually quite cordial, so I inquired about what exactly it was that had so upset Nermin and Aissa. It turned out that the police officers had not taken off their shoes before entering their apartment—an important cultural act that demonstrates respect. I had not noticed that the officers had neglected to do so, but it left Nermin and Aissa enraged. As Nermin stated:

> This just shows their disrespect. If they work with Muslims, they know this. I tell you, they do know this, and they do it on purpose. When they are rude to you . . . like, call you names or ID you in public or . . . you know . . . are treating you like shit . . . that's one thing, because it is against you. But this is disrespect against *everything*, against your house, against your family, against all Muslims, you know. Because they would do the same thing at the next house too. It has nothing to do with me . . . you know. . . . They know fucking well to take their fucking shoes off. I am sure people have told them this 1,000 times.

While I am unable to prove whether the police officers really knew that they should take their shoes off, it is precisely these little gestures that make a huge difference in the interaction between Muslim communities and the police. Essentially, then, cooperation needs to come from both sides: police officers need to become "culturally competent," show respect for the norms of the community they are policing, and be able to adopt those norms into their interactions. By doing so, they would likely increase the willingness of the community to cooperate with them much more than would punitive measures or increased surveillance. Ultimately, this would go a long way toward making German society, as well as other societies, safer.

A FINAL WORD

Despite all they have to face and the negative impressions mainstream society may have of immigrant youth, the young men in my study had formed a very close relationship to their neighborhood and were motivated to find better lives for themselves and their future families. This sense of belonging should send a very powerful message to stakeholders on both the local and federal levels. Instead of seeing this relationship with their "turf" as a threat of increased violence between different neighborhood gangs, this bond could and should be used for positive change. Engaging young men, like those I got to know in Bockenheim, in neighborhood-level decisions and issues will not only give them agency, but also instill the feeling that they are perceived as a group that can drive positive change. Most importantly, it will foster social awareness that these young men care about decisions involving their neighborhood and the larger society. Last, it will instill a feeling of belonging and recognition—and at the end of the day, that's what marginalized people lack the most. As Özgur once said, "I would like to have an influence, but no one would listen to a Turk."

Without broader structural changes such as those I have tried to outline in this conclusion—be they in Germany, other Western European countries, Canada, or the United States—we can expect little improvement in the lives of immigrant youth. Only when the state initiates long-term strategies and policies can these micro-level initiatives bring about positive change. Right now, the efforts being made to improve the lives of immigrant youth and marginalized populations amount to little more than beating a dead horse.

APPENDIX

"Somehow You're a Friend, Even Though You're a Woman"

Some Thoughts on Negotiating Access and Trust

You're just not a real German. Really, you're like a foreigner—I mean, you're not like us, like *Kanaken* . . . because you're like a doctor or something, but you're more a foreigner than a German. And you're like a sister. I don't have a sister, but I think this is what it would be like.

—Özgur

There is no "how-to" guide to help researchers gain access to their target population. Much has been written about ethnographic work in general, but the process of building trust and rapport is highly individualized and personal. Similarly individualized are the different roles that researchers assume when conducting fieldwork. Ethnographers have written extensively about these various roles and the implications they have for their fieldwork experiences and findings (Adler and Adler 1987; Asselin 2003; Brannick and Coghlan 2007; Coffey 1999; Gans 1968; Gold 1958; Whyte 1943).

While I formed very close friendships with some of the young men during the five years of my research and established good relationships with others, I would never claim that I was ever a "real" insider. Although my gender was the most obvious feature that set me apart from the all-male group, I was also distinguished by my German-Christian heritage, level of education, and class background. Frankly, while I shared five years with these young men, I could have walked away any day and continued to live my very comfortable upper-middle-class life, whereas they did not have such an option. Because of the many differences between us, I argue that I remained an outsider trusted with "inside knowledge." Yet, as Duneier (1999) reminds us, aspects of a researcher's identity may become more or less salient over the course of the research process, depending on the context. In his influential ethnography *Sidewalk*, Duneier recounts that he was at times seen as "a naive white man who could himself be exploited for 'loans' of small change and dollar bills" and at other times as "a Jew who was going to make a lot of money off the stories of people working the streets" (1999, 12). I had a similar range of experiences throughout the process of establishing a rapport: I found that my identity was fluid over time and that I was perceived differently depending on whom I was with and in what context we found ourselves. Ultimately, however, all of the young men treated me like a "buddy-researcher" (Snow, Benford, and Anderson 1986). This meant that I could behave as their friend while also retaining a certain degree of professional distance (see also the concept of "stranger and friend" in Powdermaker 1966).

Over the course of my research, many of the young men came to consider me as both a friend and an outsider. The research process was a constant give and take—a mutual exchange of ideas. Together we created a world that did not exist prior to this research (nor after) but allowed the research process to happen.

INITIAL CONTACT

Since it is common knowledge that youth centers in most large German cities are frequented by young men who are involved in illicit activities, I decided that the easiest way to gain access to my original target population—low- and mid-level dealers—would be through one such institution: I assumed that I would be able to hang out at the center and fairly easily engage whoever was there in conversation. One key benefit of this approach was that I would not have to try to engage young men for the first time in the streets but could use what I thought would be a safe and open space to make initial contact.

It took a lot of effort to persuade the three male social workers to let me use the facilities for my research (for a more detailed account, see Bucerius 2013). Officially, I was given the role of a "social work intern."[1] According to the social workers, this title would make it much easier to justify my presence to the young men. Mainly, my job as "intern" was simply to "be there" to write résumés for the men, help younger visitors with their home-work, engage in conversation, and play table tennis or darts. The tasks of the social workers did not differ much from mine. The facility had no struc-tured programs, but the social workers were supposed to be available to offer advice, often over a game of table tennis, darts, or pool. They also wrote résumés and job applications when needed and made many phone calls and wrote letters on behalf of the young men. In a sense, the youth center served "as the living room that these guys don't have" (in the words of the director of the center), a place where they could feel safe and com-fortable, and could meet their friends. Essentially, the youth center used a "low-threshold" approach, aimed at providing an at-risk population with social assistance without expecting them to comply with many rules or to participate in structured programs.

The social workers told me that the success of my research would hinge on what the "leaders" among the young men thought of me. They pointed out Akin and Inanc as the main leaders and stressed that I needed to under-stand the social workers' position and their inability to keep the young men in check. They also stressed that even if they wanted to, they could not really protect me: "You have to understand," the director said, "it's three of us and seventy, eighty guys who carry knives—there is no way we can really protect you."

Many of my early interactions[2] with the young men were influenced by how the "gatekeepers" told me to behave and what they told me about how the young men might react. In retrospect, I think that many of the initial perceptions the young men and I had about each other were influenced by the social workers' opinions, which they shared with me and the young men. For example, they openly discussed my initial inability to gain Akin's trust with other young men, trying to figure out how I could improve our relationship:

> DIRECTOR: Sandra would have it so much easier if she smoked. She could just sit down with Akin and share a cigarette. Smoking forms bonds.
> TALAT: Yeah, I agree. You could have a much more relaxed conversation.

These conversations emphasized the importance of my Akin's acceptance, both to me and to the rest of the guys. Furthermore, the message that I should impress the "alpha males" stuck with me long into my research, often obscuring the fact that I had gained the trust of some young men well before I had gained that of Akin or Inanc and influencing my behavior toward everyone else. For example, the social workers maintained that Inanc was one of the most powerful young men in the group, and the director told me on one of my very first visits, "If Inanc's thumb goes down, you'll be out of here in no time." As a result, I was very nervous to approach him over the first few days. What the social workers did not know, however, was that Inanc was already losing status among the young men. He had become a heavy cocaine user, a habit that was condemned by the majority of the group. Because cocaine consumption (or dealing, for that matter) was never discussed in front of the social workers, they continued to operate under the assumption that things were how they had always been. In other words, the social workers were not always current or "in the know" on intragroup developments and had relatively little knowledge about what was going on outside the community youth center, even though these developments often influenced the young men. In effect, because the social workers presented themselves as *insiders*, I initially trusted their analyses of the hierarchies among the young men more than I trusted my own as an *outsider*—a role I eventually came to realize had its own potential. The social workers' claims to insider status in fact often impeded their ability to obtain accurate knowledge of the young men. For example, they often refrained from asking questions about group dynamics or the drug trade since a "true insider" would likely already know the answers. In my presence, they often presented their assumptions about hierarchies and drug dealing as facts, thereby implicitly reinforcing their insider status. Yet I was probably in a better position to witness group dynamics and politics because I was not already enmeshed with the young men (Fay 1996). I could pose detailed questions that only an outsider could ask about group life and the drug trade, and the inside knowledge with which I was increasingly entrusted allowed me to gain a more complete picture of the young men over time. The young men readily told me about Inanc and his cocaine habit, for instance, when explaining the group rules by which they were expected to abide and which Inanc had evidently overstepped.

CONSTRUCTING MY ROLE AS A FEMALE RESEARCHER

The first few weeks of my research were very difficult for me, but it was an awkward time for the young men as well. I had simply shown up in their territory without any referrals from people they knew, so they had no idea of who I was or what to make of me. In the past, they had seen a few new male social workers come to the center, so they knew how to react to and test the trustworthiness of a male "intruder," but having a woman in their midst was a completely new situation. After he grew to trust me, Rahim told me:

> Let's face it, Sandra, you're just showing up but nobody knows you—not a single fucking person around here! And, of course, you're saying that you're a student and want to write a book about us and all that bullshit. I mean, that's all nice, but honestly, who is supposed to believe that shit? And how are we supposed to know whether you're cool or not? Let's face it, this could have been the biggest nonsense! . . . You are a woman. . . . We can't check you out the same way we'd do it with a guy. Nobody around here is going to beat up females or threaten them big time or something like that. That's why everyone was just staring at you for the first couple of days and everyone was waiting for you to leave again by yourself.

As some of the young men started to talk to me over the first few weeks, the focus of our interactions became less about me being a stranger and an outsider and more about me being a woman. They started to test me against their idealistic image of women in every possible way: almost every conversation we had was related to women, gender roles, and why I did not fulfill their criteria of a "real" woman. I was aware that many of these conversations were attempts to test my reaction and "impress" me (Kauffman 1994, 180), but I couldn't help feeling awkward when they made remarks about my physical appearance, my clothing, or my "female" personality. As much as I wished that comments like, "Sandra, did you gain weight? Your legs look a little fat today" would have no influence on me whatsoever, I caught myself thinking about the comments more than once.

During the first stages of my research, I even carefully selected my outfits (as in Maher 1997) and tried to avoid any allusion to sexuality by wearing extremely baggy sweatshirts, worn-out jeans, and no makeup at all. This strategy ended up backfiring, as I was constantly subjected to negative comments about my appearance and womanhood. I could endure this reaction because of my research goals, but I sometimes wished that I could appear as my usual self. The first time I wore a (long) skirt, several months into my research, the young men did not stop commenting about it all day—highlighting how my usual clothing was very "non-female." I started wondering whether I had made too strong of a statement with my chosen "youth center clothes," which had apparently facilitated the very conversations I was hoping to avoid (except that instead of discussing how sexy I was, all they talked about was how "un-sexy" I was).[3] Ironically, my perception of the young men's reactions toward women had led me to wear typical "male" clothing and thus to enforce gender roles myself. As many feminist researchers have pointed out, gender is *always* salient (e.g., Arendell 1997; Presser 2005); however, in those early days, I mistakenly believed I could somehow "ease the tension" by trying to efface the signs of my femininity.

The gender dynamics were also complicated and compounded by my age: when I started my fieldwork, I was 23, the same age as the group average. This meant that the men perceived me as a potential sexual partner, which undoubtedly influenced the process of establishing relationships with them. Some attempted to flirt during the first few months of the research; however, because I had not garnered their full respect yet, these attempts were always in one-on-one situations rather than in front of other young men. At the same time, the homogenous setting of the youth center allowed for many discussions of the "perfect woman." Since I clearly did not fit that picture (because of my different social and religious background, my ideas about gender relations, and my lack of resemblance to the pictures of women in the many pornographic magazines that circulated around the youth center), there was never a moment at which any of the young men overtly flirted with me.[4] Later in my research, I had become an integral part of the group, so viewing me as a sexual partner was not really an option anymore (as Özgur said many times, I functioned as a sister to many of them—sexuality was out of the question). However, despite the sexual overtones that are obviously always present in gender-mixed interactions, being a woman also enabled me to act as a sort of relationship counselor without having to act as a "wise adult."[5]

As torturous as it was to work through the gender dynamics during the initial stages of my fieldwork, this process was crucial to gain access to, and earn the trust of, the young men. Over time, I was increasingly trusted with "inside knowledge," and discussions about my "incorrect perception" of women and my "female duties" became less frequent. My femininity became accepted as part of my identity and was sometimes even seen as a positive attribute. As Jo wrote from prison, "The guys never write. Men don't write letters until they are locked up. With you, I at least know that I will get something back."

In many ways, I was saddled with the role of a sexual educator who was supposed to present the "female perspective." In contrast to Horowitz (1986), who was initially identified as "the lady" by the men she was studying (meaning that sexual matters were not discussed in front of her), sex and women (as long as they were "only" sexual partners and not steady girlfriends) were constantly discussed in front of me, and this did not change over the years. Discussions about sexuality helped me earn trust, as all the young men were interested in learning more about female sexuality. This gave me a chance to impress the young men: I had information to offer that they could not easily access from anyone else.

RAHIM: Sandra, come here, we're having an argument.
SANDRA: What's it about?
IBOR: We're talking about how often a woman has her period, and this moron thinks it's four times a year! I've been telling him it's just twice.
RAHIM: Whatever, you idiot! Sandra, tell him I'm right!

Given the young men's clear ideas about how women ought to behave, gender dynamics played an important role in my research. Such dynamics are always shaped by personal experiences and cultural background, so our views often clashed. Especially in the beginning, the young men took it as a personal offense that I constantly refused to fulfill my "female duties" or acquiesce to their demands to "go make coffee," "go clean the toilet," or "clean this fucking place." My "disobedience" was often followed by discussions in which the young men made comments that were stereotypically expected of them as they tried to get me to fulfill these "female duties." I don't believe that the opinions they expressed in these discussions always represented their true opinions; rather, I think these conversations served as a medium for debating the larger question of gender roles.[6] This topic was a constant undercurrent of the research project (given the gender divide between me and the young men), but it was also a result of cultural stereotypes. The young men generally felt that I, as a German woman, was not fulfilling the female duties that they expected me to fulfill based on their own cultural backgrounds (or their understanding of those backgrounds). Many of these discussions were staged and exaggerated; they only became heated debates when we pushed each other's buttons, as exemplified by my early field notes:

Talat and Inanc asked me whether I can pick up the trash on the pool table—I say "no." The typical "Why not?" "Because that's not my job" conversation develops and more guys join in. Akin joins and says "Why do you even discuss that with her, she's not a real woman. Having boobs does not make her a woman." I am annoyed by his remarks and ask why he thinks a real woman would clean the pool table. We get deeper and deeper into the discussion—what started off as a joke becomes a loaded discussion about their moms and how they respect everything that they do. They don't let me off the hook anymore. . . . I asked myself why I even tried being confrontational. Later on, Nermin and Mustaffer tell me to not take everything so seriously.

Most of these discussions occurred near the beginning of my fieldwork, highlighting how they likely did not always represent the real opinions of the young men (or my own, for that matter) but often exaggerated their views. These conversations allowed both sides to fulfill our "roles"—the young men expressed themselves in a stereotypically expected way, and I did the same. In a way, these discussions brought us closer and provided great possibilities for building trust by enabling both sides to express our emotions. Because we both held very stereotypical views about the other's opinions, many of the discussions served to test each other's "real" standpoint but also provided a basis for getting to know each other. We did push each other's buttons, but we also tried to understand each other's opinion. These young men had never before had the opportunity to ask a German woman about relationships (and vice versa), so we both used the situation to learn about each other's worlds: the young men who were living in Germany and me as a researcher embedded in their subculture. In many ways, then, being a woman actually helped me to negotiate access and trust.

I think the fact that I was Christian rather than Muslim also helped me. The young men's Islamic background was important to their identity, and they had very clear ideas of what actions they believed to be in compliance with their religion. Even though most of what they believed to be "Islamic" would never hold true in a traditional Islamic context, they took those self-created rules very seriously. They tried hard to keep women separate from their group and felt that women had to be protected from becoming "impure" by exposure to other men, drugs, or violence. This belief was particularly strong when it came to Muslim women, so being allowed access to their "impure" world likely depended on the fact that I—as a Christian— was seen as an outsider.

CONSTRUCTING DIFFERENT RESEARCHER IDENTITIES

The young men saw me as someone with "choices" in life, whereas their own experiences had clearly limited their options. My German background meant that I had more possibilities than the young men, who blamed Germans for much of the social, political, and economic exclusion that they had experienced. Thus, I initially represented what the young men called "bad people." However, fairly quickly, they decided that because I was genuinely interested in them, I was not like other Germans, who, according to the young men, were racist:

Gezim: A typical German?? A wimp . . . somebody who works like a robot, no feelings involved, no honor at all, no clue about family values . . . or simply a Nazi.[7] Let's face it: most Germans are Nazis. I don't mean Nazis like the Americans. . . . They are not so much against blacks, but just against foreigners in general.

The fact that I was also a PhD student meant that class played a bigger role in our encounters than it might have had I been a social worker (especially in the German context, in which educational attainment is hugely dependent on class). As a graduate student, I differed completely from the young men, whose main (and often only) source of income was through drug dealing; none of them had a steady job within the formal economy. Most didn't understand what a PhD was—they thought I was working to become a medical doctor—so I explained that I was interested in writing a book about their lives.[8] As other ethnographers have found—and much to my relief—the young men turned out to be quite excited about this idea. As Scheper-Hughes would say, I became the "minor historian" for people who otherwise would have no history (1992, 29).

The group's level of acceptance of me increased during the research process, but I was never accepted as a full member, becoming "one of them": after all, I obviously couldn't change from a female, German, upper-middle-class student into a male, migrant, lower-class drug dealer. Ethnographers are encouraged to immerse themselves into the native scene (Lowie 1937, 232), but Polsky warns that they had better not pretend to be "one of them" (1967, 124). No matter how involved in the young men's activities I became, I was never one of them. I could only become a friend to them: close enough to accompany them in their activities, but always a stranger from an entirely different *Lebenswelt* (Powdermaker 1966, 12).

While it took a very long time for the young men to fully understand my identity as a researcher and what I meant to each individual member, it was evident fairly quickly who I was not. As Ümit said: "I don't know . . . you're just not German. I mean . . . you're not a German. You're more of . . . I can't explain that . . . you're just an exception. You're actually more like a foreigner, but not German at all." I did not have to take on any predetermined gendered or ethnic role. Because I was different from what they had expected (i.e., a "German robot woman") and I was the first German woman with whom they had had close contact, they were interested in getting to know me. Their intense interest in my sexual life, for example, was rooted in their ignorance about female sexuality and the fact that they had never met a woman who would answer their intimate questions. I assumed the role of a "sexual educator" who presented the "female perspective." They were also eager to discuss cultural differences and their difficulties with German society. While many debates about gender expectations were certainly exaggerated, the young men were honestly interested in understanding my point of view. Because of this, as well as the fact that they finally came to view me as a friend, I was not constantly "hit on," as one might expect. A German girl had never been part of their group, so we mutually created a new and unique relationship, which was crucial for preventing sexual overtones from overpowering our relationships. They could treat me as a woman but not as a sexual object. As Özgür said:

> And certainly, most of the guys still want to lay you . . . but, you know, only in theory, only in theory. . . . But you know, that's just not a topic anymore, that is . . . how do you call it? . . . a "no-no." . . . It's a taboo. Just like a sister. If you think about it . . . you could have a sister who is a sexy chick, but you would never, ever have sex with her, never. 'Cause it would be disgusting!

CONCLUDING REMARKS

As stated initially, accounts of gaining trust as a researcher and the roles we have to assume to do so are always highly individualized, and my account is by no means any different. However, I believe a few concluding comments can be made that are relevant to ethnographic research more generally.

First, my research experiences challenge the long-cherished assumption in anthropological research that "the key to understanding . . . appears to be to build relationships of trust with people to gain privileged insider status," for without that insider status, one "learns less" (Tope, Chamberlain, and Crowley 2005, 489). Fay's provocative question, "Do you have to be one to know one?" (1996, 9) raises the question of whether membership in a group is in fact necessary or sufficient to gain in-depth knowledge (see also Mullings 1999). My fieldwork demonstrates that it is possible to develop an intricate understanding of research participants while remaining an outsider (see also Hill-Collins 1990). Importantly, my outsider status encouraged the young men to trust me with inside information that they would not otherwise have shared with "real insiders" (Fonow and Cook 1991), such as when Akin divulged to me the story of his parents' divorce.

Second, although gatekeepers are often regarded as providing points of entry into a field setting, my work reminds us that they can also hinder the process of gaining the trust of the group. The gatekeepers at the youth center were insiders who behaved as though they possessed "monopolistic or privileged access to knowledge" (Merton 1970, 15), which initially had a significant impact on my perceptions of the young men and vice versa. In many ways, the gatekeepers in this study misunderstood the young men's hierarchy and had minimal knowledge of the young men's activities outside the center, indicating that gatekeepers do not necessarily always have the inside knowledge that they think or claim to have. I discovered that it is smarter to test gatekeepers' assumptions rather than relying on them unquestioningly, as I did at the outset, which hindered my initial collection of useful data. A researcher is often right to assume that gatekeepers may be too enmeshed within the group to retain the distance necessary for analysis (Powdermaker 1966). They may also have ambivalent feelings or personal agendas that obscure their ability to recognize the reality of a situation, as in the case of Inanc, whom they continued to believe was one of the most powerful members of the group when in fact he had slipped in the ranks. Moreover, their repeated privileging of Inanc seemed to serve as their own privileging tactic—a way of reaffirming and justifying their insider status. In this sense, my work shows how being—or assuming that one is—an insider can actually be a liability, since it permits many assumptions to go unquestioned. Being an outsider trusted with inside knowledge, however, can be a great research asset (see also Powdermaker's [1966] motif of stranger and friend).

Third, very often, and especially in criminology, researchers believe that conducting effective research that crosses gender, ethnic, and class lines is nearly impossible. As a result, we often hire community-based research assistants to work with members of groups involved in illegal activities that we are interested in studying, or we at least attempt to match as many of our own identity markers as possible with those of our research participants. Gender is a particularly salient characteristic when considering the differences between a researcher and her research participants. When I give talks at criminological conferences, for instance, most people's first question to me is often, "How could you do this research as a woman?" It is generally assumed that studying drug dealers or gang members is a dangerous activity that should be left to male fieldworkers. What goes unnoted, however, is that even male researchers studying male-dominated groups that engage in illegal or illicit activities often feel that they have to prove their masculinity by engaging in stereotypically masculine behavior. For example, Ferrell (1998) joined his participants in spray-painting graffiti and was eventually arrested. Bourgois (2003, 127–28, for example) engaged in alcohol consumption with his participants to facilitate more open conversations, and Venkatesh (2008) even climbed the ranks of the gang he was investigating to supposedly become a gang leader. Moreover, male researchers are often either suspected of being spies from rival gangs (Venkatesh 2008) or undercover police officers (Bourgois 2003; Jacobs 1998). For the most part, I was not subjected to the same assumptions.[9] Female researchers may not have to engage in such activities precisely because they are not expected to perform "manhood acts" (Schwalbe 2005). For example, my research participants never urged me to consume drugs or alcohol with them and even indicated that I would lose credibility were I to partake because of their bias that women ought not to consume drugs.

In effect, being a female researcher who studies male-dominated groups occupied with illicit or illegal acts is not necessarily a liability to overcome; however, it does produce different points of access.[10] It is not surprising that being a woman at once facilitated access (by permitting me to serve as a relationship counselor, for example) and also impeded it in other circumstances (I could not follow the young men into brothels and observe their interactions with sex workers, who were among their biggest cocaine clients). Overall, however, being a woman allowed me to participate in conversations about women and sex and to serve as a sexual educator whenever required, all of which helped me secure the young men's confidence and respect. As a German woman, an identity upon which many in the group projected very particular and denigrating stereotypes, I could obtain certain information that a man or a non-German would likely not have been able to access. Importantly, the men I studied did not equate me with "the typical German robot woman" who, as Talat said, "only cares about her career, career, career and nothing else" and "never laughs, hates her children, and can't cook at all." In fact, they had trouble identifying me with all the negative and xenophobic connotations that they associated with what it meant to be "German," particularly since my interest in the group signaled to the young men that I was not xenophobic.

Unlike the assimilationist efforts the young men had experienced at school, my interactions with them never signaled a desire to promote their assimilation into German culture (Heitmeyer, Müller, and Schröder 1997, 21). They recognized over time that I was honestly interested in them, and they continuously asked me about "the book" (a phenomenon similarly encountered by Tertilt 1996, 81). In many ways, this study demonstrates that ethnographic research in criminological fields of inquiry across gender, ethnic, and class lines in fact opens up opportunities for gaining access and trust, and ultimately a deeper and more nuanced understanding of the research group. Researchers often make a mistake by assuming that the identity markers that render us outsiders will compromise our efficacy— that they are liabilities we must overcome. In fact, I discovered quite the opposite—these markers were key to garnering "insider" information and to facilitating effective research.

NOTES

INTRODUCTION

1. All of the young men have been given pseudonyms.
2. This likely stems from the fact that Turks comprise the largest immigrant group of Muslim background in Germany. In truth, Muslims in Germany represent a wide variety of ethnicities, as reflected in the demographics of the young men the youth center. Turkish heritage was the most common ethnicity among the young men that I studied (represented by twenty-seven men), followed by Kosovo-Albanian heritage (eight men), Moroccan heritage (six men), and then Croatian, Bosnian, Serbian, German, and multinational heritage. In the German context, "Muslims" denote a group with a specific religious affiliation. However, being "Muslim" or being "Christian" does not say anything about actually being "religious" or practicing one's faith. To differentiate between Muslims from different regions of the world, I refer to the different Muslims' "ethnic backgrounds." Within this context, "ethnicity" refers to one's affiliation with a specific country of origin. This is how the young men viewed the relationship between their Muslim and ethnic identities.
3. I do not intend to make an argument here against "social mixing"—however, one needs to carefully think about the consequences of "relative deprivation" before supporting socially mixed neighborhoods. The benefits that Wilson (1987) has in mind for "the poor," that is, the building of social capital and hence upward mobility through connections with and exposure to middle-income people, may not be realized. Research has shown that whether and to what extent people actually mix across income lines is rather questionable (Thompson, Bucerius, and Luguya 2013).
4. As was the recent case with Philip Roesler, a member of the Free Democratic Party.
5. It is certainly interesting to explore the question of why Germany's history has not prompted Germans to be more politically correct, not just regarding "Jewish topics" but also with respect to other minority groups. It is crucial to understand that the aftershock of World War II and the collective feeling of guilt shared by Germans have been so overwhelming, and the atrocities of the Holocaust so unique, that it is impossible to draw any comparisons with any other situation or any other minority group in the country. In other words, any suggestion that Germans should have learned from their experiences and should be more accepting of today's minority populations (a suggestion that the young men offered quite often) would be shut down immediately by arguing that *any* comparison

with World War II or the fate of the Jewish population in Germany would be absolutely outrageous and ignorant.

6. While Levitt and Venkatesh (2000) argue that drug dealers still live with their mothers because they do not have the financial resources to move out, I would stress that the majority of the young men in this book certainly had the financial means to make such a move possible. However, cultural reasons prevented them from leaving their families earlier than necessary (i.e., before getting married). Furthermore, it is almost impossible to get an apartment in Frankfurt without providing evidence of a work contract (something that the young men obviously did not have), often leaving landlords worried about the ability of these men to pay rent. Moreover, while most of the young men certainly made more money than they ever would have made in the formal economy, for various reasons, they also spent what they made almost immediately (see chapter 6).

7. I knew these unit commanders through previous research, so a rapport had already been established.

8. The social workers repeatedly tried to restrict marijuana consumption to the smaller room, but this could only be enforced for short periods. Over time, smoking marijuana throughout the entire facility would become the norm for a few weeks until the social workers re-identified the problem and convinced enough young men that it would be better to restrict pot consumption to one area.

9. This impression was shared by both the social workers and the regulars.

10. Given these observations, which clearly raise legal and ethical concerns, it is important to note that German universities had not established ethical review boards at the time of my research. To date, the German university system still maintains no ethical review of research as in the American context. As such, this study did not have any official institutional oversight. However, I was part of a national scholarship foundation that supervised the study at all stages. In addition to my supervisor and other faculty members at the University of Frankfurt, the scholarship foundation helped me sort through ethical as well as moral and legal concerns.

11. I had also originally intended to use NVivo for my data analysis, but I soon realized that the benefits of doing so were marginal. I soon developed a systematic strategy for analyzing my data each week, coding and trying to identify new emerging themes, and so on. As such, I was very familiar with my field notes and interviews throughout my research, and analysis without using a computer program (which occasionally misses important points) seemed the more viable option.

CHAPTER 1

1. This statement, made on November 21, 2005, reflects author Max Fritsch's famous quote: "We wanted a workforce, but people came." Retrieved 1 September 2011, http://www.carnegiecouncil.org/resources/transcripts/5280.html.

2. In an effort to create a long-term dialogue between state and Muslim representatives, the German Islam Conference was founded in 2006 with the explicit objective of promoting cooperation and social cohesion between German mainstream society and the Muslim immigrant population. Theoretically, these conferences should provide a forum in which the general integration debate can be shifted away from the perceived *unwillingness* of Muslim immigrants to integrate, yet what is actually happening is that the discussions are strengthening the perception that the beliefs and values of Muslim immigrants are incompatible with

those of the German mainstream. The main discussion points for this year's meeting, for example, were "religious education in Koran schools and state schools, the headscarf issue, the training of imams, the role of women and girls, halal butchery, and prevention of radicalisation and extremism" (retrieved 2 June 2013, http://www.deutsche-islam-konferenz.de). In other words, instead of focusing on issues of inclusion, acceptance, and understanding, the conferences tend to touch upon "problem topics" associated with Turks that only serve to strengthen stereotypes of Turkish immigrants and their supposed ability or unwillingness to adopt German core principles and beliefs.

3. The popularity of Italians has increased considerably since the 1980s. Currently, Italians are viewed as members of the European Union who are welcome in Germany. When I grew up near Frankfurt in the 1980s, Italians were mainly referred to as "Spaghetti-Fresser" (spaghetti feeders).

4. For example, Canada currently has an agricultural migrant-worker program with a very similar format.

5. Former guest workers also boosted the economy in the following years. For example, twenty years later, in 1992, 66.9 percent of all Turkish households in Germany owned a car, compared with only 52.7 percent of all German households; 20.4 percent of all Turkish car owners chose a Mercedes, compared with only 7.4 percent of all German car owners; and 61.5 percent of all Turkish households had a hi-fi unit, compared with only 47.9 percent of all German households (Sen and Goldberg 1994, 29).

6. Polls in the early 1990s indicated that as many as 57 percent of former guest workers found the immigration process too complicated and too expensive (Thränhardt 1994, 227, 236) and therefore had refrained from even applying, even though they met official requirements. Brubaker (1992) argues that the naturalization rates were low because of a lack of political support and the official exclusionary discourse. In 1995, Bavaria, the most conservative state in Germany, had a naturalization rate of 0.63 percent; Berlin, one of the least conservative states, had a rate of 1.7 percent.

7. In an effort to be consistent with the international literature, I will use the terms "foreigners" and "immigrants" interchangeably in this chapter. However, one should note that the term "immigrants" is not commonly used in the German context.

8. While German citizenship law has made it nearly impossible for the young men in this book to ever receive citizenship, it has not been as restrictive for all foreigners. Citizenship law was, and continues to be, very inclusive to people considered to be "ethnically" German, even if they do not live in Germany, speak German, practice German culture, or have German citizenship. This was mainly the case for *Aussiedler*, or individuals of German descent living in the Eastern bloc. Their chances of receiving German citizenship were very high, even if most were not directly related to a German citizen:

> The large majority of recent Aussiedler are descendants of German-speaking settlers who migrated hundreds of years ago and long before the creation of a German nation-state (in the case of the Siebenbuerger Sachsen as much as 800 years ago) to areas that have never been part of Germany" (Koopmans 1999, 631). Citizenship was even granted to ethnic Germans who had never lived in Germany: in 2000, approximately 200,000 *Aussiedler* who had obtained German citizenship were living in Poland. (Green 2001, 37)

Unlike guest workers, ethnic Germans did not have to be permanent or temporary residents of Germany, did not need to demonstrate sufficient means of subsistence, and did not need to relinquish their former nationality (Hailbronner, Renner, and Kreuzer 1998, 573). Most importantly, in the process of granting such individuals citizenship, there was also "no room for discretion by the responsible authority, not even regarding the assessment of a security threat" (which was the case for anyone else applying for citizenship, a situation that often made people dependent on the subjective opinion of one person at a municipal office) (Koopmans 1999, 631).

9. Germany was ruled by a conservative–liberal coalition made up of the CDU/CSU and the Free Democratic Party (FDP) from 1982 to 1998; these parties certainly did not push strongly to reform citizenship law. A nationwide poll in 1997 indicated that nine out of ten immigrants would vote for candidates from the Social Democratic Party (SPD) or the Green Party if allowed to participate in elections. This may be one reason why citizenship law was only reformed after the SPD and the Green Party had the majority in the Bundestag (parliament).

10. Many previous polls had indicated that former guest workers wanted to obtain citizenship and remain in Germany, but the various political parties could not find common ground in terms of what rights should be granted to these individuals.

11. While this is a significant change, it only affects children born after 2000 and cannot be applied retroactively. Hence, the children of former guest workers are not affected by this law. Additionally, citizenship is only granted on "probationary terms" (called the Optionsmodell). At the age of 23, young people must decide whether they want to maintain their German citizenship or their other citizenship. If they fail to declare their choice, they automatically lose their German citizenship (Beauftragte der Bundesregierung für Migration, Flüchtlinge und Integration 2005, 12).

12. Furthermore, applicants had to demonstrate that they could fully sustain themselves and their family members without having to rely on social assistance or unemployment payments. They also had to possess an unlimited residence permit. Young adults aged 16 to 23 had to show that they had attended a German school for at least six years, four of which had to be after elementary school.

13. Composing about 80 percent of the Muslim population, Sunnis are the largest immigrant group within Germany, while Alevis compose about 17 percent and Shiites only 3 percent of this population. One-third of Muslims living in Germany self-identify as "strongly religious," and about one-half characterize themselves as "rather religious," with men more likely than women to consider themselves religious.

14. Research has shown that "the odds of being married to an imported partner [are] higher for the middle than for the first generation" (Lieven 1999, 734; see also Familienbericht 2000, xvi). Wanting to marry someone with the same religious background is frequently identified as one of the main reasons for this phenomenon. In 2010, a total of 54,865 people moved to Germany to reunite with family, 13.7 percent more than in 2009 (Bundesamt für Migration und Flüchtlinge 2011, 90). Presumably, many of these moves were made for marital reasons, although statistics do not differentiate within the category of family migration, so it is not clear how many immigrants migrate to marry, compared to, for example, those who bring a parent to Germany. Of these new arrivals, 15.2 percent came from Turkey, 6.6 percent from Russia, and 5.2 percent from Kosovo (91). Of all Turks

immigrating to Germany, 27.1 percent were the wives of non-Germans, 16.2 percent were married to Germans (who may or may not have been of Turkish origin), 25.2 percent were the husbands of Germans (again, who may or may not have been of Turkish origin), and 10 percent were the husbands of non-Germans (93).

15. It has been shown that it is not the immigrant background itself that puts students at a disadvantage in the German system, but a weak socio-economic background, which is the case for the majority of immigrants in Germany, given their social position in society (Baur and Häußermann 2009).

16. It is sometimes possible to switch school tracks later if certain requirements (e.g., grades, outstanding behavior) are met.

17. When looking at this number, one has to keep in mind that many of the immigrants who came to Germany through family migration had very low levels of educational attainment and no knowledge of the German language (Castles and Miller 1998, 195).

18. In 2013, the German government introduced a new bill called "Betreuungsgeld" (caregiving allowances), which essentially provides monthly financial compensation to parents who choose to keep their children at home as opposed to sending them to kindergarten. I would argue that this policy will further disadvantage low-income families, and especially low-income immigrant families. If a family is already poor, this money might be seen as an additional incentive to keep children at home, which would further delay the children's exposure to the German language (and subsequently put them at a disadvantage as early as Grade 1).

19. Generally speaking, the immigration literature refers to the "first generation" as those individuals who immigrated to another country. "Second-generation" immigrants are the first generation born in the new country. Some researchers refer to "1.5-generation" immigrants as those individuals who were born abroad but immigrated during their childhood and spent most of their childhood in the new country.

20. For example, Goldberg's (2006) study of high school students in Bochum found that 21.7 percent of all students of Turkish background reported having committed a violent offense over the past year, compared with only 11.1 percent of all German students and 15.2 percent of all students of Polish background. Wetzels, Enzmann, Mecklenburg, and Pfeiffer (2001) surveyed high school students in nine German cities and found that students of Turkish background were most likely to report being involved in violence over the past year (34.2 percent, compared with 18.6 percent of their German counterparts and 29.4 percent of those of Yugoslavian background). Obviously, these studies all focused on geographically restricted areas and only on specific types of crime.

21. Goldberg (2006) claims that non-German students in general, and Turkish students in particular, have much higher media consumption rates but are also more involved in sports than their German counterparts. She found both factors to be correlated with increased rates of violence (885). Oberwittler (2003) argues that the higher violent crime rates can be explained by the disadvantaged social environment of foreign students, particularly the neighborhoods in which they grew up. Babka von Gostomski (2003) argues that the experience of discrimination and racism plays a huge role in criminality committed by "foreigners" in Germany—a finding with which the young men in this book would certainly agree. Oberwittler (2003), Schmitt-Rodermund and Silbereisen (2004), Reich (2005), and Müller (2000) find that foreign students have much closer friendship networks and cliques than do German students, and that these groups often encourage students

to participate in violent acts. Wetzels et al. (2001) and Wilmers et al. (2002) claim that Turkish students in particular are much more likely to witness and experience violence in their families and therefore are more likely to view violence as legitimate. Windzio and Baier (2008) report that juveniles of Turkish background are affected by more risk factors (e.g., they are more likely to have violent friends) that predict violent behavior.

22. http://www.druginfopool.de/gesetz/hessen.html. Retrieved on March 5, 2012.
23. http://frankfurt.de/sixcms/detail.php?id=3834&_ffmpar[_id_inhalt]=7524.

CHAPTER 2

1. As a nickname, they called me "Bullock," as in Sandra Bullock.
2. This is true across borders—that is, we can see this phenomenon in all Western countries that collect crime data related to immigrants (Bucerius 2011).
3. It is important to note, however, that while the crime rates of second-generation immigrants rise in comparison to the first generation, in most Western countries, they do not necessarily exceed those of the native-born population. In Germany, however, the crime rates of the second generation clearly exceed those of the native-born population (this also holds true for ethnic groups in other European countries such as the Netherlands and France). Moreover, while immigrants who engage in crime tend also to experience *some* form of social, political, or economic disadvantage, not all disadvantaged immigrants are drawn to crime like the young men in this study were. Other factors that contribute to the choice of a criminal path are clearly at play.
4. In the United States, for example, "immigrants, especially those from Latin America, have lower rates of adult and infant mortality and give birth to fewer underweight babies than natives despite higher poverty rates and greater barriers to health care. But their health status—and that of their children—worsens the longer they live in the United States and with increasing acculturation. The children and grandchildren of many immigrants—as well as many immigrants themselves the longer they live in the United States—become subject to economic and social forces, such as higher rates of family disintegration and drug and alcohol addiction, that increase the likelihood of criminal behavior among other natives" (Rumbaut and Ewing 2007, 2).
5. Being able to form a positive sense of self—that is, a positive social identity—within a given context (in this case, German society) enables feelings of belonging to develop. Without the feeling that one belongs, integration is much harder.
6. In other words, parents can overrule the teacher's recommendations in some states, but schools are unlikely to accept students who have not been recommended. In other states, the recommendations of teachers are binding and parents cannot try to send their child to a stream if that child has not received a recommendation.
7. At the time, Aissa was making a serious attempt to quit drug dealing and had gotten a job at the Frankfurt airport. His parents had moved to Spain, so he and his brother Nermin needed to pay rent and meet other financial requirements on a monthly basis. Thus, the outside pressure to become more responsible increased significantly. Interestingly, even though he was successful at securing the job at the airport and continued to work there for an extended period of time (to my knowledge, he is still employed there), he never fully quit dealing. Although he made a regular net income of around 1,100 euros/month, his expenses were significantly higher, so he continued to be involved in drug deals. (Only a handful of

the young men who held a job in the formal economy remained involved in dealing, unlike the dealers studied in other research, who were frequently simultaneously involved in both.)

8. Some German Bundesländer (states) require at least one parent to be fluent in German for the child to enter the Gymnasium stream. If that requirement cannot be met, children are automatically excluded from this stream, regardless of their elementary school grades. Most German states do not have this rule in place, but teachers appear to be hesitant to recommend for the Gymnasium stream students who are lower class or from an immigrant background. Studies have shown that students from poorly educated families (defined as families in which the father lacks a degree from the Hauptschule) must perform 50 percent better than students from well-educated families (defined as families in which the father has an Abitur) to receive the same recommendation for a secondary school stream (i.e., Gymnasium, Realschule, or Hauptschule) (Lehmann and Peek 1997). Recent OECD studies have confirmed that the social background of students in Germany is the strongest single factor associated with school performance (OECD 2004, 14; see also Isserstedt et al. 2010, 72, 101).

9. In Germany, being lower class and having an immigrant background are usually correlated.

10. This difference becomes even greater when students' grades do not objectively warrant placement in the Gymnasium stream. Only 11 percent of all lower-class parents whose children's grades average B or B– consider sending their child to the Gymnasium, whereas more than 75 percent of all upper-class parents of children with the same grades plan to do so (Ditton 1992, 130). While these studies cannot demonstrate whether upper-class parents are more likely than lower-class parents to be encouraged by teachers to send their children to the Gymnasium, the ethnographic material clearly shows that the young men's parents tended not to oppose the advice of the teacher if he or she suggested entry into a lower stream. Upper-class parents, in contrast, have access to more social, personal, and cultural capital and are more likely to fight a teacher's recommendation if it opposes their own plans for their child's educational trajectory. It is possible that lower-class parents hesitate to send their children to an upper-school stream if they (like Aissa's mother) did not receive a similar education or—as is often the case—received no education at all. In this sense, lower-class parents may not desire upward mobility; they seem to be more comfortable having their children attend schools that their friends' children are attending.

11. A lack of kindergarten attendance is often cited as the reason why children with immigrant backgrounds lack the social skills and maturity necessary to perform successfully at school and would thus "benefit" from being kept behind for an additional year—the remedy usually recommended by the school. As mentioned earlier, kindergarten attendance is not mandatory in Germany, nor do all cities or counties provide enough kindergarten spaces for all children. Thus, arguing that a lack of kindergarten attendance justifies the delay of a child's educational career seems quite ironic, unless one really believes that children from an immigrant background are collectively less mature than German children.

12. Some, but not all, of these special schools allow students to graduate with the same kind of degree that they could obtain at the Hauptschule (the lowest of the three regular school forms).

13. Note that only 19 percent of all people living in Germany have an immigrant background (Gomolla and Radtke 2009).

14. The studies cited here all confirm this impression; it is not clear, however, whether immigrant status itself results in additional disadvantages for students from an immigrant background in Germany. What is clear is that being lower class puts students, regardless of whether or not they are of immigrant background, at a significant disadvantage. In this respect, it is important to keep in mind that the majority of immigrants in Germany, or at least those with a guest-worker history, are considered lower class.

15. The 2000 law states that children who are born in Germany to foreign nationals and have at least one parent that (1) has legally resided in Germany for eight consecutive years and (2) has been in the possession of an unlimited residence permit from Germany, an EU member state, or Switzerland at the time of the child's birth can automatically obtain German citizenship by birth. However, they must declare by the age of 23 whether they will retain German citizenship or the citizenship of their parents' country/countries of origin. If they fail to declare one or the other, they automatically lose their German citizenship.

16. While the reformed law does make it easier for immigrants to naturalize, one of the requirements for naturalization is a clean criminal record.

17. As mentioned in chapter 1, PISA is a study conducted by the OECD (2006a) comparing the school performance of 15-year-olds in sixty-five countries/economies. The test has been conducted every three years since 2000, and results have consistently shown that no other country/economy in the world has such a great gap between the school performance of students with a migrant background and the school performance of students without a migrant background as is found in Germany. Students with a migrant background in Germany tend to be two to three school years behind native Germans.

18. In this quote, we can see again that the young men were aware (at least in retrospect) of the symbolic violence and social closures they had experienced.

19. Perhaps not surprisingly, most of the businesspeople who had these sorts of informal arrangements with the young men were not German.

CHAPTER 3

1. Of the three who were not involved in dealing during my study period, only one had never sold drugs, and the other two had quit before I began my fieldwork in 2001.

2. For a long time, I assumed that Akin was not very good at pool and was afraid of losing to a younger member. I was shocked when Akin took second place out of almost eighty participants at the youth center's holiday season pool tournament.

3. At the same time, he was embarrassed about things he had done. One night at a bar, when I mentioned the masturbation, he looked at me and said, "Sandra, do you think I would have done that if I had known that we would ever sit here, having a drink? Don't ever mention that again, please! I could die when thinking about it."

4. Originally, the street gangs formed as a response to the right-wing violence that emerged in the 1990s in Germany, especially after reunification.

5. My impression was that the young men with whom I spent time, and the people with whom they interacted, still talked a lot about the "rough guys from back then," often appearing fearful of and fascinated by them, but that others had no such associations with Bockenheim.

6. Every neighborhood in Frankfurt has a local drug scene that is often served by young male immigrants. The drug market in Bockenheim was believed to be bigger than any of the other neighborhood markets, probably because of the presence of the university in its district.

7. While young men starting out would often receive assistance from others who were already in the business—including access to some clients—they still all had to build up their own network of clients if they wanted to deal on a bigger scale.

8. The young men would always claim that they were "brothers" who would "be there for each other, no matter what." However, in many ways, their "brotherhood" was dependent on the physical presence of individuals—as soon as someone got incarcerated or hospitalized, for example, the former "brothers" would rarely ever visit.

9. Losing one's license was "the norm," and hence it was understood that everyone could, at some point, be in a position to need a ride. Thus, the young men were generally very generous with giving others rides. Even when a car owner did not know someone well, he would generally still give him the ride.

10. The young men of Albanian heritage seemed to make greater profits than the majority of the other young men. However, this was mainly a function of their legal status—they could not, like the rest, visit bars and clubs as freely. They tended to spend more time at their apartments (usually shared by three or four young men) and had limited opportunities to spend money. Additionally, these young men were the only ones who planned to return to their country of origin. Their plan was to save money, get rich, and go home: they saw the informal economy in Germany simply as a way to make money, whereas it filled a very important social function for the other young men.

11. Obviously, ethnicity is a highly complex concept that mattered for the young men at certain times and in specific ways (as when choosing one's future wife), but not at other times or in other ways (as when choosing a business partner). Essentially, being close to each other and having grown up together trumped ethnicity—thus, the young men could easily decide to team up with business partners of different ethnic backgrounds. Ethnicity mattered, though, when the young men were unfamiliar with the people involved in a transaction; arguably, they did not know wholesalers as well as they knew their own friends and business partners. In the same vein, marriage was a concept that had little to do with their present life, being reserved for the future. Because marriage was very removed from the young men's current life, it made sense for them to again put emphasis on ethnicity, underlining that once "unknowns" entered the picture, they started to trust others who shared their ethnicity more than those from other ethnic groups.

12. Over the course of my research, the youth center organized three such outings. Interestingly, two of them were held during my first two weeks at the youth center. In retrospect, I could not help but wonder whether the social workers had organized these outings on purpose to create the impression that they were doing lots of social programming for the young men.

13. The weight of our clothes pulled both of us down, and it was almost impossible to get back into the canoe. Gezim was swearing the entire time, but he was also very concerned about my safety. He immediately swam over and grabbed the collar of my sweater. Even though I told him that I was a good swimmer, he wouldn't let go and tried to pull me over to the canoe, as if he were rescuing me. It was so hard for me to move that I had to fight him off—verbally and physically—so that we could both get back to the canoe. I learned something about gender relations on that

day: as a woman, I was supposed to be saved (regardless of what they thought of me at the time).

14. It was Reuter (1983) who deconstructed the "organized drug market." The title of his work *Disorganized Crime* is actually inaccurate: drug markets like the one in which these young men participated might at first appear chaotic and seem not to fit the classic Mafia model, but they all have a basic organization and are not "disorganized" in that sense. Some basic organization is required for two or more people to work on transactions together. Reuter probably wanted to refute the classic idea of a family clan in which one or a few key persons ("the Godfather") control the entire market. He was correct that there is no evidence indicating that removing the "Mr. Bigs" has any long-lasting effect on drug markets. Obviously, other structures are in place that allow drug markets to function even if big players are taken out of the equation (Dorn, Bucke, and Goulden 2003).

15. This label was commonly used when I was present during drug deals or when men from the previous generation showed up at the community youth center. Usually, one of them would inquire about me, and Akin (or someone else) would say, "She's our princess." That line seemed to go a long way, as further questions were never asked in front of me. Being the group's princess meant two things. First, they made sure that I was not at risk when hanging out with them—for example, Akin would pass me his car key and motion me to drive off to a safe spot whenever they got into debates with bouncers who refused us entrance into a club. Whenever he knew that a discussion could get heated or violent, he offered me the chance to leave or at least told me where to stand so that I would not get caught in the crossfire. This was not only true for Akin. One night, Rahim was so agitated and high on cocaine that he started throwing furniture around at the youth center. I was standing in a corner with Inanc when chairs came flying our way. Inanc immediately put me into a safe spot while risking being hit by the flying chairs himself. Only after I was safe did he try to calm Rahim down. Second, and more importantly, being the princess meant that I was spared the many endless discussions the young men and I had about gender roles and femininity at the beginning of my research. Essentially, it meant that they "let me be." As Akin would point out: "I can't believe no one gives you shit anymore, we are treating you like a princess."

16. As mentioned earlier, Akin was probably the only one who could have legitimately claimed such a role. However, he was strongly against taking on any formal leadership position.

17. No one, not even Akin, had reliable information about why Ulun was incarcerated. Aissa offered the following story: "Apparently, they found 80 grams of cocaine at his place and some mixing agents, but I can't believe that. He knew damn well that he was a top candidate for the police. He'd be stupid to have anything at home, let alone 80 grams. It was probably 2 and someone heard 4, and the next person said 8, and then someone heard 80. Whatever. I am sure that's all bullshit." Most of the young men, assuming that they would most likely not see Ulun again, said he had been stupid not to quit earlier, especially because he had always claimed that he wanted to live the life of a rich man in Turkey. Aissa said, "I don't understand why he did not quit earlier. He always wanted to leave. Always. But he just did not know when to stop. He got carried away. Well . . . he's got no one to blame but himself." To me, Ulun once said that he could not get carried away because he was smarter than the rest: "I am smarter than the others. I am a fox. I choose who I work with. I don't do anything myself, and I am careful. I live in a small

place. I don't drive a car. When you live big, like buy yourself a place and stuff . . . of course, the state is going to wonder where the money comes from. Don't buy anything. Save and back to Turkey, that's how you do it. The guys get carried away, just because they have a little bit of money."

18. In the beginning, I was surprised that the young men would not visit each other when someone was incarcerated. However, this was very much in line with their strong focus on the "here and now," which allowed a strict separation between their current life as drug dealers and their future life as family men (see chapter 5); essentially, someone who was not physically present was not a real part of their current life. At the same time, the young men never inquired about people who were sick. With regard to young men who were incarcerated, Lemi explained why no one visited them:

> In the beginning, it's too dangerous. No one wants to be seen in relationship with someone who just got busted. And after that, there are always new excuses: no time, no car, no approval, and so on, and so on, and so on. But, really, it's just because no one gets their ass in gear. It's like, out of sight, out of mind. And the years pass by quickly until someone gets out. And then, yeah . . . they're mad in the beginning, because no one came to visit, but that's over and forgotten in no time. Everyone knows that. Where else would you go?

19. Given that Dutch drug laws are much less prohibitive than the German ones and that marijuana can be legally purchased in that country's so-called "coffee shops," the Netherlands were always a fallback option. Despite individuals' ability to purchase drugs legally for personal consumption there, the Netherlands still has a large informal drug market. The young men never purchased drugs "legally" in the Netherlands, but instead purchased them under the table.

20. The young men avoided having clients come to their apartment, because the great majority of them still lived with their parents and siblings and wanted to keep their families out of their "professional" lives (see chapter 4).

21. Here I use the term "massage parlors/spas" to describe a German institution that is like a spa in the sense that these establishments feature saunas, hot water pools, whirlpools, and so on. It is common in Germany to visit spas naked; people go to the sauna wearing just a towel and then usually sit on the towel, naked. Most spas explicitly ask visitors to take off their bathing suits before entering. Going to the spa is a very common leisure activity, and nothing is considered odd about going to nude spas. The particular massage parlors/spas with which the young men transacted differed from these regular spas insofar as sex workers frequented them. Female visitors pay an admission fee about three times more than that paid by male visitors and can negotiate their own prices with male visitors if they engage in sexual relations. They do not have to give a percentage of their income to the owners, instead keeping everything for themselves. In contrast to the system used by brothels, these women are also not employed by the massage parlor/spa. In other words, any woman could go to these massage parlors/spas and make money on the side by selling sex.

22. Decision about where to store drugs often turned into an ethical issue for the young men. Storing drugs at home or at a relative's place was generally considered the safest strategy, but many did not want to risk of having their family home searched, arguing, as Aissa did, that their family "has to be kept out of this."

23. Another reason why the young men refrained from selling substances to outside customers was to protect the social workers. The subject of dealing cocaine and heroin, for example, was not raised in front of the social workers.

> IBOR: I don't think they even know that the guys are dealing with that stuff. They try to do this in secret, they hide the stuff pretty well and nobody would sell from here. You know, when it's pot, it's like, "Whatever, it's just pot, no one cares." But cocaine or heroin, that's a different ballgame. They don't want them to know.
>
> SANDRA: Why not?
>
> IBOR: Well, it's also . . . it's also to . . . like . . . you know, protect them. They do a lot for us and the youth center and stuff . . . it just puts them in a shitty situation if they know.
>
> SANDRA: So, you really think that they don't know?
>
> IBOR: They don't. It would be really, really hard. Almost impossible.

24. Other links exist between the formal and the informal economy; many companies operate both formally and informally and cross the formal/informal divide regularly (Paoli 2003, 146). Students and migrants are often paid under the table, as are wages for overtime hours, and certain jobs like babysitting, tutoring, and cleaning are always paid informally. In Germany, an estimated one-third of all construction workers work illegally (Pape 2005, 11) and lack any rights, benefits, or insurance. The young men sometimes discussed these possibilities for work. Nermin commented:

> The work sounded really great . . . and it was cash, you know?! But my brother [Aissa] said that I should not do it because of accidents and stuff. I'm not insured, because he did not want to register me because of the taxes and stuff. He basically said he's not going to do it because it's less money for me and for him somehow. It's a bit strange, because Enver was working there some time ago, and he was registered and insured and everything. If you work construction, things happen quickly. And my brother said that . . . you know, if I fall off the ladder or something, the dude will just claim that he doesn't know me.

25. The young men did not think of the drug trade as a "risky" business. The informal and illegal structures of the drug market made it impossible for customers and dealers to complain if they felt they had been cheated, and according to German law, the drug market has no clearly defined "victims" (Hess 2007). Customers have no interest in seeing their dealers prosecuted, because this would reveal their drug consumption (and thus their own illegal activity). It is also highly debatable whether dealers can be held responsible for short- or long-term health, psychological, or social impacts on customers' lives, so prosecutions on these grounds are unlikely. However, pro-prohibitionists in Germany argue that drugs have a negative effect on the functionality and overall health of German society, so drug dealing is prosecuted in Germany.

26. This number reflects only those offenses of which I could keep track, which I think must be very close to the actual number. The young men who were charged always reported the charge to the social workers, who acted as legal advisors. I had unlimited access to all the files in the community youth center, so I had three ways of hearing about such incidents: from the accused, from others, and from the files. I should note that some of the young men did not have any charges pressed against them during this time, while two were charged thirteen times.

CHAPTER 4

1. I deliberately use the word "belief" as opposed to "norms," "values," "morality," "cultural factors," or another similar term. Beliefs can be influenced by cultural expectations, personal values/norms, the values/norms of one's peer group or the larger society, religious beliefs, and so forth and generally involve various aspects of all of these elements.

2. In *Code of the Street*, Anderson (2000) also distinguishes between "decent" and "street." However, it remains unclear whether he attached these labels to make a value judgment or whether his sample actually used the terminology. In this study, the young men's ideas about "good" and "bad" or "pure" and "impure" were delineated within the network of the young men. They made these distinctions in order to understand themselves and their actions. As the researcher, I am simply using their own terminology.

3. Despite their insufficient factual knowledge, the young men agreed on core concepts (e.g., the purity/impurity dichotomy) that they believed to be Islamic. Their opinions about what was or was not Islamic, and what a good Muslim should be like, were shaped within the group and through group dynamics. They based their knowledge on things they had learned from their parents and grandparents, paying particular attention to what Rahim and Gezim had to say, and tried to incorporate those teachings/beliefs as Islamic principles into their everyday life (see also Kaya 2001, 159).

4. While the young men never had this experience firsthand (because none of them traveled to other Western countries during the period of my research), in their conversations, they would refer to documentaries they had watched or news reports that they had seen on Turkish TV stations.

5. One could even argue that *because* the young men did not necessarily choose drug dealing as their preferred profession but rather saw it as the best option available in a situation that did not leave them many opportunities from which to choose, the identity they formed through work was even more important. Most would have preferred to be more integrated into the German mainstream and to have well-paid jobs in the formal economy.

6. Obviously, the young men were not working on the lowest levels of the drug-dealing world and were in a position to make such choices. However, even those without many established clients or those who were short on money abided by these self-selected principles.

7. The question of whether or not the parents were informed about their sons' drug-dealing activities was beyond the scope of my research; I never interviewed parents. While the young men always insisted that their parents did not know what they were doing, they would sometimes report that their parents did not like that they were associating with the others at the center. My impression is that drug dealing was not openly discussed in the young men's families and that most of the young men lied to their parents, pretending that they were working in the formal economy (again, in an effort to come across as honorable and pure). This lie was easy to keep up, because in most families, both parents were working and left the house early in the morning. By the time they came home, the young men were still out. However, some of the young men also requested to be let into the community youth center before its actual opening time (especially in the winter) because they were pretending to work and had to leave their homes early in the morning. However, parents' tendency to give their sons a hard time about their friends was certainly an indication that they had some

idea about their sons' social milieu. At the same time, I do not believe that the parents necessarily bought their sons' claims of holding jobs in the formal economy. My sense was that avoidance was better than confrontation—open confrontation could potentially lead to disobedience on the part of the young men (by continuing to deal), which would probably have been viewed as worse than dealing in the first place.

8. The relationship between the young men and German women was anything but straightforward. Even though they strictly condemned German women for engaging in sexual activities before marriage (and for being promiscuous throughout their lives), they also benefited from this sexual liberation in that they would have casual sexual relationships with girls who were sometimes German. This does not mean that they respected the girls for making themselves available. As Jetmir explained it, the young men liked "to get out of the house" and liked having "girlfriends" who would allow them to spend nights away from their own family's small apartment, where they often shared a room with their male siblings:

> I'd say, we all have advantages, because we don't have to pay for the sex, and most of them have their own apartments and stuff—that's very practical when you need to get out of the house and stuff. But it can also be really annoying, because they always want you to meet their families and friends and kiss-kiss, and politics around that are just annoying and stuff. You know, I'd say you just don't have these kinds of problems with a prostitute. So they're good for not paying . . . but don't kid yourself, you're paying in other ways.

9. Whether or not the parents of a German girl knew about their daughter's actions did not seem to be important to the young men. They felt that parents had the duty to know exactly what their daughter was doing every minute, and neglecting that task was seen as incomprehensible to them, as Rafet expressed: Imagine my sister would spend the night at some guy's house and we would not know about it. I just can't grasp that concept at all! If my sister were to spend the night anywhere outside of my house, it would be at my aunt's. I just can't understand how you can't know where she's spending the night. I mean, they just don't care! I mean, you do have to bring them over and check everything out . . . you know, make sure everything is OK. I mean, that's your job as family, isn't it?

10. This explanation is obviously flawed, because it assumes that Muslims don't consume drugs at all.

11. Interestingly, I never got stopped during my research. The young men were only stopped a few times when I was around, and the police always ignored me. I never informed the police of my research project and thus have no explanation for this other than assuming that I was ignored either because they knew that I was doing research or because I was German.

12. In the German language, one can use a formal "you" and an informal "you." The informal you is commonly reserved for family and friends. Before using the informal you with colleagues, neighbors, and so on, one has to propose to switch to the informal you. Usually this suggestion is made by the superior person. If neither person is superior in terms of authority, the switch is commonly suggested by the older person; in interactions between men and women, it is usually suggested by the woman. Using the informal you without such an agreement—as Aissa and the police officer were doing—is considered very disrespectful.

CHAPTER 5

1. For me as a researcher, this also meant that I was sometimes out of the loop when I had not spent a few days in a row with the young men. I would then always try to hear the "news" from several of the young men to get a feeling for different perspectives on events.

2. This is very similar to the experiences described in the ethnographic literature of some other dealers who have tried to "go legit" and subsequently lost touch with their community of friends (see, e.g., Bourgois 2003).

3. As discussed in chapter 3, the young men generally did not assess their risk of incarceration to be very high. Though some (five out of fifty-five) of them did get incarcerated over the duration of my five-year fieldwork period, the threats of incarceration and even deportation did not seem to have any long-term deterrence effect. In fact, when talking about quitting dealing, "risk" never came up as a factor that might have prevented them from continuing in the drug market.

4. They also had concrete ideas about what the woman should look like, as described by Talat: "Well, if I just want to fuck someone, she should really be a hottie. I mean, you do want to have some fun, right? Sandra, honestly, don't give me that shitty look. Would you have a one-night stand with an ugly, fat guy?"

5. As Jetmir later told me, "Nobody here has girlfriends to just hang out with. I've always thought that a friendship between men and women is just not possible." Interactions with women, even with steady girlfriends, were kept outside their all-male friendship circle. When I asked why, I was given two explanations. The first was about jealousy:

   > IBOR: You never want to fight about a bitch with your friends. That's just not on. If girls are around, politics will start. That's no good for anyone.
   > SANDRA: What do you mean by that?
   > IBOR: Well, some idiots may get horny because your girl is around. And then what do you do? Beat up your friends? Or they behave totally primitively. Or whatever.

   The second explanation, expressed by several young men, was that the girls they dated did not really live up to their mutually created ideal of the "perfect woman." They spent a lot of time discussing what character traits an "ideal" woman ought to have: she must obey and please her man; she must not intrude into his private life by asking questions about his friends, family, or business; she must be good looking; she must be an excellent homemaker; and so on. All the young men seemed to agree about this ideal, but they were also aware that being in a relationship often requires both partners to make compromises. This awareness was never openly discussed as a group, only in one-on-one conversations with me, even at the beginning of my research. My "outsider" role made it easier for the young men to share information with me that they would not share with others (Fonow and Cook 1991). For example, Georgio (who was 21 years old and one of the less important members of the group) shared with me why he thought women shouldn't hang around with the men. Interestingly enough, his explanation concerned how he would be perceived if he showed up with a girl who did not adhere to the idealized picture upon which the young men agreed: "Well, then you have the guys laughing at you because they think her ass is too big or because they think she's not listening to you or whatever. I don't want that happening."

Although they talked about women constantly, the young men did not talk *with* women about their hopes and dreams or other intimate matters. Their relationships rarely lasted more than a few weeks. Over the course of my five-year study, only five men were involved in relationships that lasted longer than three months.

6. Enver is a perfect example of a young man whose successful transition out of the drug market resulted in a loss of contact with his community of friends. His marriage was arranged about three years into my fieldwork, and I barely saw him after his wedding. He took a job at the Frankfurt train station, stocking trains with food and snacks. I saw him a few times after his wedding by chance, as I visited the train station for travel. On very rare occasions, the others would report that Enver had joined them at night to go to a brothel, but I could count these instances on one hand.

7. It's also worth noting here that the young men's very explicit ideas about the purity and impurity of women served as a way to avoid facing their own fears. When I asked Aissa—who was always willing to reflect on more personal issues— why everyone wanted to marry a virgin, he offered the following explanation:

> AISSA: Well, I think that they all want a virgin and stuff *only because* she doesn't have a clue. You know, with her, they can't be horn-dogs like in a brothel, so that's why they fuck elsewhere. On top of that, they would have to really make an *effort* . . . . You know, they're all just scared. The ho doesn't tell you if you suck . . . but the wife might . . . especially when she's got some experience.
>
> SANDRA: You're saying "they"—does that mean you're not having the same fears?
>
> AISSA: Of course I do. I am just trying to explain. And I am trying to not be as radical—you must admit, I am not as radical anymore!

By introducing their wives or girlfriends to various sexual practices or by having frequent sex with them, the young men feared that the women might find pleasure in these impure actions and subsequently become sexually active outside of their relationships. They concluded that they could guarantee their partners' monogamy, and thus stability in their relationship, by keeping their relationship relatively sex-free. As Georgio said:

> OK, honestly? What the eye doesn't see, the heart doesn't grieve over, right? The more sex you have, the greater the risk that you suddenly want to experience more stuff for yourself . . . I mean sexually speaking. I do want to make her happy and stuff . . . but I wouldn't like . . . try new things with her or . . . you know . . . fuck her like I'd do with others. If you ask me, marriage is about family, not about sex. She should just be happy with normal sex when we want to have children, and that's it. I know that's different for you guys [Germans], but that's why even married women have affairs. That's just crazy!

CHAPTER 6

1. My graduate students are consistently disappointed with the concluding chapters of the ethnographies we read. Because the ethnographers have gotten so close to their study populations, my students expect them to come up with "bottom-up" approaches to solving problems, that is, approaches that target marginalization on the ground and are driven by the very people being studied. To my students, it seems logical that ethnographers should recommend changes from "within"

and "below": because these researchers study micro-level processes, one could reasonably expect them to be the best suited to come up with innovative ideas to address micro-level changes. This perception is understandable, but it is important to remember that because ethnographers have gained "lived experiences" on the ground, they have experienced firsthand what is both practical and feasible on the micro level. Ironically, then, ethnographers frequently ignore community-level policies because their experiences often teach them that such policies do not and cannot work—not because the people they're studying lack agency, but because there are greater socio-economic and structural forces at play that limit and constrain the ability of these people to "help themselves." Likewise, the interactions, exchanges, and communications of the young men in this book were often driven and shaped by what was happening above, that is, taking place in the hierarchical structure of German society. While I would like to fall back on my research experiences and interests to champion change on the ground when writing policy recommendations, the opposite often happens: my in-depth experiences tell me that solutions *cannot* simply be on the ground but instead require me to comment on and argue for structural-level "big ideas." Solving complex social problems requires strategic, sustained, and structural shifts that go well beyond the community level. Consequently, the policy recommendations I provide in this chapter do not focus on short-term "feel-good" programs offering minimal effects, but rather on sustainable economic and legal changes that could produce long-term effects.

APPENDIX

1. While the social workers prepared the young men for my presence by telling them that a female social work intern would be at the community youth center, I immediately told the young men that I was interested in their lives and was hoping to write a book about them.

2. Because the young men were heterogeneous with respect to their cultural backgrounds, they generally communicated in German, meaning that I did not have to learn another language to communicate with them (although some tried to teach me Turkish). Most of the young men said that they were more fluent in German than in their mother tongue. As Aissa said, "My parents have always spoken German to us. Bad German, but German. I always feel very awkward when visiting family in Morocco and not being able to communicate with them. It's like: 'Yeah, I am Moroccan, but I can't speak and I've never lived here.' They think you're a total moron."

3. Later in the research process, I was able to wear whatever I wanted without being subjected to negative or sexualized comments.

4. Whether or not flirting was happening was sometimes difficult to assess, because "flirting" seemed to follow different rules in the young men's world than it did in mine. Many times, they told me about interactions with women that—in their minds—indicated that the respective women were interested in them, whereas I thought to myself: "I don't think they are sending that message." As such, I was often left wondering whether Georgio, for example, would perceive walking me to the train station as flirting. This ambiguity of interactions was also related to the fact that the young men did not have any heterosocial friendships—friendships with girls seemed out of the question for them. As such, we truly had to learn to negotiate a world in which we could interact that had not existed prior to my research.

5. My role probably resembled that of Williams, who wrote, "I was kind of a big brother, able to help with homework and even babysitting, but most of all a willing and sympathetic listener" (Williams 1989, 17).
6. However, even after having hung out with the young men for a few years and having established a strong rapport with them, they would state such stereotypical opinions in one-on-one conversations, underlining the reality that they did not only say such things to impress their friends or to initially scare me off.
7. The young men used the term "Nazi" frequently and relatively loosely; they clearly did not mean Nazi in the World War II sense of the term. Instead, they used it to label different people, often Germans, who discriminated against them (i.e., immigrants). Using the term also reminded them and others of Germany's past. By using the word that hurts the German conscience more than anything else, they essentially underlined the legitimacy of their assessment that Germany and Germans were, indeed, discriminating against them. At the end of the day, "Germany fucked up before." (Akin) and so, in their eyes, it was not surprising that Germans were still discriminating against people that are different.
8. I could not change their idea that a doctorate was exclusively reserved for medical doctors. Even after several years, some young men still inquired about when I would open my practice. In their mind, I was gaining practical experience by hanging out with them before becoming a psychotherapist. (As Ferdi said: "I am sure you could not get better experience than hanging out with these crazy people. I mean, they're all fucked up and sick. You will have a very easy job when you start your practice.") Even Özgur, the only young man who had actually received a high school degree that allowed him to go to university (see chapter 3) and who had a better insight into degrees and studies, always asked me for my input based on the fact that he saw me as a psychotherapist:

    ÖZGUR: You understand that . . . all that psycho shit. So you need to help me understand why I am so aggressive.
    SANDRA: I am not trained to do this.
    ÖZGUR: Of course, you are. You're becoming a doctor. Come on, just see me as a patient.

    Despite the fact that I always corrected them, some of the young men probably continued to hold this belief.
9. At the very beginning of my research, a few of the core group members entertained the idea that I might be an undercover cop; however, they quickly dropped this conjecture, and I did not have to prove anything to dispute it. They essentially decided for themselves that I was not a police officer.
10. Just as having a different ethnicity or class background would similarly impact one's relationship with his or her research participants.

REFERENCES

Aas, Katja Franko. 2007a. *Globalization and Crime*. New York: Sage.

___. 2007b. "Analyzing a World in Motion: Global Flows Meet 'Criminology of the Other.'" *Theoretical Criminology* 11 (2):282–303.

Ackerman, Debra, William Barnett, and Kenneth Robin. 2005. *Making the Most of Kindergarten: Present Trends and Future Issues in the Provision of Full-Day Programs*. New Brunswick, NJ: National Institute for Early Education Research, Rutgers University.

Adler, Patricia. 1993. *Wheeling and Dealing*. New York: Columbia University Press.

Adler, Patricia, and Peter Adler. 1987. *Membership Roles in Field Research*. Newbury Park, CA: Sage.

Albrecht, Hans-Joerg. 2011. "Criminalization and Victimization of Immigrants in Germany." In *Racial Criminalization of Migrants in the 21st Century*, ed. Salvatore Palidda, 176–95. Surrey, UK: Ashgate.

Anderson, Elijah. 2000. *Code of the Street*. New York: W. W. Norton & Company.

Arendell, Terry. 1997. "Reflections on the Researcher-Researched Relationship: A Woman Interviewing Men." *Qualitative Sociology* 20:341–68.

Arlacchi, Pino, and Roger Lewis. 1990. *Imprenditorialità illecita e droga. Il mercato dell'eroina a Verona*. Bologna, Italy: Il Mulino.

Asselin, Marlene. 2003. "Insider Research: Issues to Consider When Doing Qualitative Research in Your Own Setting." *Journal for Nurses in Staff Development* 19:99–103.

Ateş, Seyran. 2005. *Tolerance for the Tolerant*. Berlin: Perlentaucher.

Babka von Gostomski, Christian. 2003. "Gewalt als Reaktion auf Anerkennungsdefizite? Eine Analyse bei männlichen deutschen, türkischen und Aussiedler-Jugendlichen mit dem IKG-Jugendpanel 2001." *Kölner Zeitschrift für Soziologie und Sozialpsychologie* 55 (2):253–77.

Bade, Klaus. 1984. *Auswanderer—Wanderarbeiter—Gastarbeiter: Bevölkerung, Arbeitsmarkt und Wanderung in Deutschland seit der Mitte des 19. Jahrhunderts*. Ostfildern: Scripta Mercaturae Verlag.

___. 1996. "Transnationale Migration, ethnonationale Diskussion und staatliche Migrationspolitik in Deutschland des 19. und 20. Jahrhunderts." In *Migration, Ethnizität und Konflikt: Systemfragen und Fallstudien*, ed. Klaus Bade, 403–30. Osnabrück: Universitätsverlag Rasch.

Baier, Dirk, Christian Pfeiffer, Julia Simonson, and Susann Rabold. 2009. *Jugendliche in Deutschland als Opfer und Täter von Gewalt*. Research Report No. 107. Hannover: Criminological Institute of Lower Saxony.

Baskett, Robert, Kathie Bryant, William White, and Kyle Rhoads. 2005. "Half-Day to Full-Day Kindergarten: An Analysis of Educational Change Scores and Demonstration of an Educational Research Collaboration." *Early Child Development and Care* 175 (5):419–30.

Bauman, Zygmunt. 2000. "Social Uses of Law and Order." In *Criminology and Social Theory*, ed. David Garland and Richard Sparks, 23–45. New York: Oxford University Press.

Baur, Christine, and Hartmut Häußermann. 2009. "Ethnische Segregation in deutschen Schulen." *Leviathan* 37 (3):353–66.

Beauftragte der Bundesregierung für Migration, Flüchtlinge und Integration. 2005. *Bericht über die Lage der Ausländerinnen und Ausländer in Deutschland.* Berlin, Bonn: Beauftragte der Bundesregierung für Migration, Flüchtlinge und Integration.

___. 2007. *Vielfalt fördern, Zusammenhalt stärken.* Berlin, Bonn: Beauftragte der Bundesregierung für Migration, Flüchtlinge und Integration.

Becker, Birgit, and Nicole Biedinger. 2006. "Ethnische Bildungsungleichheit zu Schulbeginn." *Kölner Zeitschrift für Soziologie und Sozialpsychologie* 58 (4):660–84.

Becker, Howard. 1955. "Marijuana Use and Social Control." In *Social Deviance 1993: Readings in Theory and Research.* Englewood Cliffs, NJ: Prentice Hall.

Berardi, Luca, and Sandra Bucerius. 2013. "Immigrant and their Children: Evidence on Generational Differences in Crime". In Sandra Bucerius and Michael Tonry *The Oxford Handbook of Ethnicity, Immigration, and Crime,* 551–81. New York: Oxford University Press.

Berk, Richard, and Joseph Adams. 1970. "Establishing Rapport with Deviant Groups." *Social Problems* 18:102–17.

Blossfeld, Hans-Peter, Wiebke Paulus, and Lydia Kleine. 2009. "Die Formation elterlicher Bildungsentscheidungen beim Übergang von der Grundschule in die Sekundarstufe I." *Zeitschrift für Erziehungswissenschaften* 12:1–23.

Bommes, Michael. 1996. "Ausbildung in Großbetrieben." In *Ausbilden statt Ausgrenzen,* ed. Ralph Kersten, Doron Kiesel, and Sener Sargut, 31–44. Frankfurt: Haag und Herchen.

___. 2004. "Migration, Belonging, and the Shrinking Inclusive Capacity of the Nation-State." In *Worlds on the Move—Globalization, Migration and Cultural Security,* ed. Jonathan Friedman and Randeria Shalini, 43–67. New York: I. B. Tauris.

Boos-Nuenning. 2000. "Gleichbehandlung durch Quotierung? Strategien zur beruflichen Eingliederung junger Zuwanderer." In *Integration und Intergrationsförderung in der Einwanderungsgesellschaft,* ed. Forschungsinstitut der Friedrich-Ebert-Stiftung, Abt. Arbeit, und Sozialpolitik, 73–90. Bonn: Friedrich Ebert Stiftung.

Bös, Matthias. 1993. "Ethnisierung des Rechts?" *Kölner Zeitschrift für Soziologie und Sozialpsychologie* 45:619–43.

Bos, Wilfried, Eva Maria Lankes, Manfred Prenzel, Knut Schwippert, Knut/Gerd Walther, and Renate Valtin, Renate. 2004. *Erste Ergebnisse aus IGLU. Schülerleistungen am Ende der vierten Jahrgangsstufe im internationalen Vergleich.* Münster/New York/München/Berlin: Waxmann.

Bourdieu, Pierre. 1984. *Distinction – A Social Critique of the Judgement of Taste.* Boston: Harvard University Press.

___. 1990. *The Logic of Practice.* Cambridge: Polity.

___. 1998. *Practical Reason: On the Theory of Action*. Stanford, CA: Stanford University Press.

___. 2004. "Gender and Symbolic Violence." In *Violence in War and Peace: An Anthology*, ed. Nancy-Scheper-Hughes and Philippe Bourgois, 339–42. Malden: Blackwell.

Bourdieu, Pierre, and Jean-Claude Passeron. 1977. *Reproduction in Education, Society and Culture*. London: Sage.

Bourdieu, Pierre, and Loic Wacquant. 1992. *An Invitation to Reflexive Sociology*. Chicago: University of Chicago Press.

Bourgois, Philippe. 2003. *In Search of Respect: Selling Crack in El Barrio*. Cambridge: Cambridge University Press.

Bourgois, Philippe, and Jeff Schonberg. 2009. *Righteous Dopefiend*. Berkeley: University of California Press.

Brannick, Teresa, and David Coghlan. 2007. "In Defense of Being 'Native': The Case of Insider Academic Research." *Organizational Research Methods* 10:59–74.

Brettfeld, Katrin, and Peter Wetzels. 2003. "Jugendliche als Opfer und Täter: Befunde aus kriminologischen Dunkelfeldstudien." In *Aggressives Verhalten bei Kindern und Jugendlichen: Ursachen, Prävention, Behandlung*, ed. Ulrike Lehmkuhl, 78–114. Göttingen: Vandenhoeck & Ruprecht.

Brubaker, Rogers. 1992. *Citizenship and Nationhood in France and Germany*. Cambridge: Harvard University Press.

___. 2001. "The Return of Assimilation? Changing Perspectives on Immigration and Its Sequels in France, Germany, and the United States." *Ethnic and Racial Studies* 24:531–48.

Bucerius, Sandra. 2007. " 'What Else Should I Do?'—Cultural Influences on the Drug Trade of Young Migrants in Germany." *Journal of Drug Issues* 37:673–98.

___. 2008. "Drug Dealers between Islamic Values, Everyday Life in Germany and Criminal Activity." *Zeitschrift für Soziologie* 3:246–65.

___. 2011. "Immigrants and Crime." In *The Oxford Handbook of Crime and Criminal Justice*, ed. Michael Tonry, 385–419. New York: Oxford University Press.

___. 2013. "Becoming a trusted outsider – Gender, Ethnicity, and Inequality in Ethnographic Research", *Journal of Contemporary Ethnography* 42:690–721.

Bundesamt für Migration und Flüchtlinge. 2011. *Das Bundesamt in Zahlen 2010 Asyl, Migration, ausländische Bevölkerung und Integration. Statistics*. Nürnberg: Bundesamt für Migration und Flüchtlinge.

Bundesanstalt für Arbeit. 1969. *Arbeitsförderungsgesetz*. Nuremberg: Bundesanstalt für Arbeit.

Bundesministerium des Innern. 2005. *Polizeiliche Kriminalstatistik 2005*. Statistics. Berlin: Bundesministerium des Innern.

___. 2006. *Polizeiliche Kriminalstatistik 2006*. Statistics. Berlin: Bundesministerium des Innern.

___. 2010. *Polizeiliche Kriminalstatistik 2010*. Statistics. Berlin: Bundesministerium des Innern.

Bundesministerium für Arbeit und Sozialforschung. 1996. *Integration und Soziales des Landes*. Nürnberg: Bundesamt für *Migration* und Flüchtlinge

Bundesministerium für Bildung und Forschung (BMBF). 2004. *Berufsbildungsbericht 2004*. Bonn, Berlin: Bundesministerium für Bildung und Forschung.

Bundesvereinigung der deutschen Arbeitgeberverbände (BDA). 1962. *B149/22374*. Bonn: BDA.

Bürgeramt, Statistik und Wahlen. 2011. *Frankfurt am Main: Statistisches Jahrbuch 2010*. Frankfurt: Stadt Frankfurt.

Castles, Stephen. 1985. *Immigrant Workers and Class Structure in Western Europe*. Oxford: Oxford University Press.

Castles, Stephen, and Mark Miller. 1998. *The Age of Migration—International Population Movements in the Modern World*. Houndsmill: MacMillan Press.

Choudhury, Tufyal. 2007. "Economic Development of Muslim Communities." In *European Islam: Challenges for Public Policy and Society*, ed. Samir Amghar, Amel Boubekeur, and Michael Emerson, 77–106. Brussels: Centre for European Policy Studies.

Coffey, Amanda. 1999. *The Ethnographic Self*. Newbury Park, CA: Sage.

Cohn-Bendit, Daniel. 1991. *Einwanderbares Deutschland oder Vertreibung aus dem Wohlstands-Paradies?* Frankfurt: Horizonte-Verlag.

Coomber, Ross, and Lisa Maher. 2006. "Street Level Drug Market Activity at Two of Australia's Primary Dealing Areas: Consideration of Organization, Cutting Practices and Violence." *Journal of Drug Issues* 36:719–53.

Cryan, John, Robert Sheehan, Jane Wiechel, and Irene Bandy-Hedden. 1992. "Success Outcomes of Full-Day Kindergarten: More Positive Behavior and Increased Achievement in the Years After." *Early Childhood Research Quarterly* 7 (2):187–203.

Curtis, Ric, and Travis Wendel. 2000. "Toward the Development of a Typology of Illegal Drug Markets." In *Illegal Drug Markets: From Research to Prevention Policy*, ed. Mike Hough and Mangai Natarajan, 121–52. Monsey, NY: Criminal Justice Press.

Curtis, Ric, Travis Wendel, and Barry Spunt. 2001. *We Deliver: The Gentrification of Drug Markets on Manhattan's Lower East Side*. New York: John Jay College of Criminal Justice.

Da Costa, Jose, and Susan Bell. 2000. "Full-Day Kindergarten at an Inner-City Elementary School: Perceived and Actual Effects." Paper presented at the Annual Conference of the American Educational Research Association, New Orleans, LA, April 25.

DeCesare, Dale. 2004. "Full-Day Kindergarten Programs Improve Chances of Academic Success: The Progress of Education Reform." *Kindergarten* 5 (4):1–6.

Denton, Barbara, and Pat O'Malley. 1999. "Gender, Trust and Drugs." *British Journal of Criminology* 39:513–30.

Desroches, Frederick. 2007. "Research on Upper Level Drug Markets." *Journal of Drug Issues* 37:827–44.

Diehm, Isabell, and Frank Olaf Radtke. 1999. *Erziehung und Migration—eine Einführung*. Stuttgart: Kohlhammer.

Ditton, Hartmut. 1992. *Ungleichheit und Mobilität durch Bildung*. Munich: Juventa.

___. 2004. "Der Beitrag von Schule und Lehrern zur Reproduktion von Bildungsungleichheit." In *Bildung als Privileg*, ed. Rolf Becker and Wolfgang Lauterbach, 243–72. Wiesbaden: VS Verlag fuer Sozialwissenschaften.

Dorn, Nicholas, Tom Bucke, and Chris Goulden. 2003. "Traffickers, Transit and Transaction." *Howard Journal of Criminal Justice* 42:348–65.

Dörrlamm, Martin 2004. "Steinbruch Drogenhilfe—Wie Crack-Raucher an einem falschen Kompromiss kratzen." In *Kokain und Crack—Pharmakodynamiken, Verbreitung und Hilfeangebote*, ed. Heino Stoever and Michael Prinzleve, 216–28. Freiburg: Lambertus.

Douglas, Mary. 1966. *Purity and Danger*. London: Routledge Classics.

Drewniak, Regine. 2004. "Ausländerkriminalität zwischen kriminologischen Binsenweisheiten und 'ideologischem Minenfeld.'" *Zeitschrift für Jugendkriminalrecht und Jugendhilfe* 15:372–78.

Duneier, Mitchell. 1999. *Sidewalk*. New York: Farrar, Straus and Giroux.

Durkheim, Emile. 2001. *The Elementary Forms of Religious Life*. New York: Oxford University Press.

Economist. 2010. "The Integration Debate in Germany: Is Multi-Kulti Dead?" *Economist*, October 22. http://www.economist.com/blogs/newsbook/2010/10/integration_debate_german=9>.

Edathy, Sebastian. 2000. *Wo immer auch unsere Wiege gestanden hat'—Parlamentarische Debatten über die deutsche Staatsbürgerschaft 1870–1999*. Frankfurt: IKO Verlag.

Einbürgerungsrichtlinien. 1977. Bonn: Einbürgerungsrichtlinien.

Engbersen, Godfried, Joanne van der Leun, and Jan de Boom. 2007. "The Fragmentation of Migration and Crime in the Netherlands." In *Crime and Justice: A Review of Research, Special Issue on Crime and Justice in the Netherlands*, ed. M. Tonry and C. J. Bijleveld, 35:389–452. Chicago: Chicago University Press.

Fagan, Jeffrey. 1991. "Drug Selling and Licit Income in Distressed Neighborhoods: The Economic Lives of Street-Level Users and Dealers." In *Drugs, Crime, and Social Isolation*, ed. Adele V. Harrell and George E. Peterson, 99–146. Washington, DC: Urban Institute Press.

Faist, Thomas. 2000. *The Volume and Dynamics of International Migration and Transnational Social Spaces*. Oxford: Oxford University Press.

Familienbericht. 2000. *Familien ausländischer Herkunft in Deutschland*. Opladen: Leske und Budrich.

Farley, Reynolds, and Richard Alba. 2002. "The New Second Generation in the United States." *International Migration Review* 36 (3):669–701.

Fay, B. 1996. *Contemporary Philosophy of Social Science*. Cambridge, UK: Blackwell.

Federal Statistical Office. 2010. *Statistisches Jahrbuch 2009 für die Bundesrepublik Deutschland*. Wiesbaden: Statistiches Bundesamt.

Ferrell, Jeff. 1998. "Criminological Verstehen." In *Ethnography at the Edge*, ed. J. Ferrell and M. Hamm, 20–42. Boston: Northeastern University Press.

Fonow, Mary, and Judith Cook. 1991. *Beyond Methodology: Feminist Scholarship as Lived Research*. Bloomington: Indiana University Press.

Freeman, Richard. 1996. "Why Do So Many Young American Men Commit Crimes and What Might We Do About It?" *Journal of Economic Perspectives* 10:25–42.

Gans, Herbert. 1968. "The Participant Observer as a Human Being." In *Institutions and the Person*, ed. H. Becker, 300–17. Chicago: Aldine.

Geertz, Clifford. 1973. *The Interpretations of Cultures*. New York: Basic Books.

Geissler, Rainer. 2004. "Die Metamorphose der Arbeitertochter zum Migrantensohn." In *Institutionalisierte Ungleichheiten*, ed. Peter Berger and Heide Kahlert, 71–100. Weinheim: Juventa.

___. 2007. "Einwanderungsland Deutschland—Herausforderungen an die Massenmedien." *Journalistik Journal* 10:11–13.

Genterczewsky, Claudia. 2008. "Kokaindealer im bürgerlichen Milieu." In *Drogenmärkte: Strukturen und Szenen des Kleinhandels*, ed. Bernd Werse, 110–36. Frankfurt: Campus.

Gerdes, Jürgen, and Thomas Faist. 2006. "Von ethnischer zu republikanischer Integration: Der Diskurs um die Reform des deutschen Staatsangehörigkeitsrechts." *Berliner Journal für Soziologie* 3:331–36.

Gesemann, Frank. 2006. *Die Integration junger Muslime in Deutschland*. Berlin: Friedrich Ebert Stiftung, Politische Akademie/Interkultureller Dialog.

Giddens, Anthony. 1984. *The Constitution of Society, Outline of the Theory of Structuration*. Cambridge: Polity Press.

Goffman, Erving. 1975. *Stigma*. Frankfurt: Suhrkamp Verlag.

Gold, Raymond. 1958. "Roles in Sociological Observations." *Social Forces* 36:217–33.

Goldberg, Andreas, and Faruk Sen. 1996. *Türken als Unternehmer. Eine Gesamtdarstellung und Ergebnisse neuerer Untersuchungen*. Opladen: Leske & Budrich.

Goldberg, Brigitta. 2006. "Freizeit und Kriminalität bei Achtklässlern mit und ohne Migrationshintergrund." In *Kriminalpolitik und ihre wissenschaftliche Grundlagen*, ed. Thomas Feltes, Christian Pfeiffer, and Gernot Steinhilper, 861–92. Heidelberg: Müller Verlag.

Gomolla, Mechthild. 2000. "Ethnisch-kulturelle Zuschreibungen und Mechanismen institutionalisierter Diskriminierung in der Schule." In *Alltag und Lebenswelten von Migrantenjugendlichen*, ed. I. Attia and H. Marburger, 49–70. Frankfurt: Iko-Verlag für Interkulturelle Kommunikation.

Gomolla, Mechthild, and Frank-Olaf Radtke. 2009. *Institutionelle Diskriminierung— eine Herstellung ethnischer Differenz in der Schule*. Opladen: Leske & Budrich.

Gottfredson, Michael, and Travis Hirschi. 1990. *A General Theory of Crime*. Stanford, CA: Stanford University Press.

Green, Simon. 2001. "Citizenship Policy in Germany." In *Towards a European Nationality*, ed. Randall Hansen and Patrick Weil, 25–51. Houndmills, UK: Palgrave.

Habermas, Jürgen. 1981. *Theorie des kommunikativen Handelns*. Frankfurt: Suhrkamp Verlag.

Hagan, John, Ron Levi, and Ronit Dinovitzer. 2007. "The Symbolic Violence of the Crime-Immigration Nexus: Migrant Mythologies in the Americas." *Criminology and Public Policy* 7:801–18.

Hagedorn, Heike. 2001. *Wer darf Mitglied werden? Einbürgerung in Deutschland und Frankreich im Vergleich*. Opladen: Leske und Budrich.

Hailbronner, Kay, Guenter Renner, and Christine Kreuzer. 1998. *Staatsangehörigkeitsrecht*. Munich: Beck.

Hansen, Randall. 2008. *A New Citizenship Bargain for the Age of Mobility? Citizenship Requirements in Europe and North America*. Washington, DC: Migration Policy Institute.

Hansen, Randall, and Patrick Weil. 2001. *Towards a European Nationality*. Houndmills, UK: Palgrave.

Hardinghaus, Barbara. 2013. "Duped by Dope: Reality Trumps Ideals in German Drug War." *Der Spiegel*, March 21.

Hayward, Keith. 2004. *City Limits*. London: Cavendish.

Heckmann, Friedrich. 1981. *Die Bundesrepublik: ein Einwanderungsland? Zur Soziologie der Gastarbeiterbevölkerung als Einwandererminorität*. Stuttgart: Klett-Cotta.

Heckmann, Friedrich, and Dominique Schnapper. 2003. *The Integration of Immigrants in European Societies*. Stuttgart: Lucius and Lucius.

Heitmeyer, Wilhelm, Joachim Müller, and Helmut Schröder. 1997. *Verlockender Fundamentalismus*. Frankfurt: Suhrkamp.

Hendricks, Nicole, Christopher Ortiz, Naomi Sugie, and Joel Miller. 2007. "Beyond the Numbers: Hate Crimes and Cultural Trauma within Arab American Immigrant Communities." *International Review of Victimology* 14:99–113.

Hess, Henner. 1992. "Rauschgiftbekämpfung und desorganisiertes Verbrechen." *Kritische Justiz* 25:315–36.

___. 2008a. "Ein drogenpolitisches Nachwort." In *Drogenmärkte: Strukturen und Szenen des Kleinhandels*, ed. Bernd Werse, 375–400. Wiesbaden: Campus Verlag.

___. 2008b. "Der illegale Drogenhandel—ein Überblick." In *Drogenmärkte: Strukturen und Szenen des Kleinhandels*, ed. Bernd Werse, 10–36. Wiesbaden: Campus Verlag.

Hill-Collins, Patricia. 1990. "Learning from the Outsider within the Sociological Significance of Black Feminist Thought." In *Beyond Methodology Feminist Scholarship as Lived Research*, ed. M. Fonow and J. Cook, 35–59. Bloomington: Indiana University Press.

Horowitz, Ruth. 1986. "Remaining an Outsider: Membership as a Threat to Research Rapport." *Journal of Contemporary Ethnography* 14:409–30.

Ismaili, Karim. 2010. "Surveying the Many Fronts of War on Immigrants in Post-9/11 U.S. Society." *Contemporary Justice Review* 13 (1):71–93.

Isserstedt, Wolfgang, Elke Middendorff, Maren Kandulla, Lars Borchert, and Michael Leszczensky. 2010. *Die wirtschaftliche und soziale Lage der Studierenden in der Bundesrepublik Deutschland 2009. 19. Sozialerhebung des Deutschen Studentenwerks durchgeführt durch HIS Hochschul-Informations-System*. Berlin: Bundesministerium für Bildung und Forschung.

Jacobs, Bruce. 1998. "Researching Crack Dealers." In *Ethnography at the Edge*, ed. Jeff Ferrell and Mark Hamm, 160–77. Boston: Northeastern University Press.

Jacobson, David. 1996. *Rights across Borders: Immigration and the Decline of Citizenship*. Baltimore: Johns Hopkins University Press.

Jankowski, Martin Sanchez. 1991. *Islands in the Street: Gang and American Urban Society*. Berkeley: University of California Press.

Jansen, Ad. 2002. *The Economics of Cannabis Cultivation in Europe*. Paper presented at the Second European Conference on Drug Trafficking, Paris, September 26.

Junger-Tas, Josine. 2001. "Ethnic Minorities, Social Integration and Crime." *European Journal on Criminal Policy and Research* 9:5–29.

Kasinitz, Philip, John Mollenkopf, Mary Waters, and Jennifer Holdaway. 2008. *Inheriting the City: The Children of Immigrants Come of Age*. Cambridge, MA: Harvard University Press.

Katz, Jack. 1988. *Seductions of Crime—A Chilling Exploration of the Criminal Mind—From Juvenile Delinquency to Cold-Blooded Murder*. New York: Basic Books.

Kauffman, Karen. 1994. "The Insider/Outsider Dilemma: Field Experience of a White Researcher 'Getting In' a Poor Black Community." *Nursing Research* 43:3.

Kaya, Ayhan. 2001. *Sicher in Kreuzberg*. Bielefeld: Transcript-Verlag.

Kelek, Necla. 2005. *Die fremde Braut. Ein Bericht aus dem Inneren des türkischen Lebens in Deutschland*. Cologne: Kiepenheuer & Witsch.

___. 2006. *Die verlorenen Söhne. Plädoyer für die Befreiung des türkisch-muslimischen Mannes*. Cologne: Kiepenheuer & Witsch.

Keskin, Hakki. 2002. "Turkey Will Be a Benefit to the European Union." In *Pro Europe: The Global Reach and Dynamic Power of the European Union*, ed. Roland Emrich and Ralf Leppin, 312–18. Brussels: Ermrich.

Klausen, Jyette. 2008. *Public Policy for European Muslims: Facts and Perceptions*. London: Institute for Strategic Dialogue.

Koch, Achim, and Martina Wasmer. 1997. "Einstellungen der Deutschen gegenüber den Zuwanderungsgruppen." In *Datenreport 1997. Zahlen und Fakten über die Bundesrepublik Deutschland*, ed. Statistisches Bundesamt, 457–67. Bonn: Bundeszentrale für politische Bildung.

Koopmans, Ruud. 1999. "Germany and Its Immigrants: An Ambivalent Relationship." *Journal of Ethnic and Migration Studies* 25:627–47.

Koopmans, Ruud, Paul Statham, Marco Guigni, and Florence Passy. 2005. *Contested Citizenship: Immigration and Cultural Diversity in Europe*. Minneapolis: University of Minnesota Press.

Lagebericht der Integrationsbeauftragten. 2012. *Bericht der Beauftragten der Bundesregierung für Migration, Flüchtlinge und Integration über die Lage der Ausländerinnen und Ausländer in Deutschland.* Berlin: Bundesregierung.

Lamont, Michele. 2000. *The Dignity of Working Men: Morality and the Boundaries of Race, Class and Immigration.* Cambridge, MA: Harvard University Press.

Langer, Antje, Rafael Behr, and Henner Hess. 2004. "Was Dir ein Stein gibt, kann Dir keine Nase geben—Crack auf der Frankfurter Drogenszene." *Forschung Frankfurt* 22:28–32.

Latour, Bruno. 2000. "When Things Strike Back." *British Journal of Sociology* 5:105–23.

Laub, John, and Robert Sampson. 2003. *Shared Beginnings, Divergent Lives.* Cambridge, MA: Harvard University Press.

Lefébvre, Henri. 1991. *The Production of Space.* Blackwell: Oxford.

Legge, Jerome. 2003. *Jews, Turks, and Other Strangers.* Madison: University of Wisconsin Press.

Lehmann, Rainer H., and Rainer Peek. 1997. *Aspekte der Lernausgangslage von Schülerinnen und Schülern der fünften Klassen an Hamburger Schulen.* Berlin: Humboldt Universitaet.

Lévi-Strauss, Claude. 1966. *The Savage Mind.* Chicago: University of Chicago Press.

Levitt, Steven, and Sudhir Venkatesh. 1998. "An Economic Analysis of Drug-Selling Gang Finances." Working Paper 6592. Cambridge, MA: National Bureau of Economic Research.

___. 2000. "An Economic Analysis of a Drug-Selling Gang's Finances." *Quarterly Journal of Economics* 115 (3):755–89.

Lieven, John. 1999. "Family Forming Migration from Turkey and Morocco to Belgium: The Demand for Marriage Partners from the Country of Origin." *International Migration Review* 33 (3):717–44.

Lopez-Gonzalez, Lorena, Veronica C. Aravena, and Robert A. Hummer. 2005. "Immigrant Acculturation, Gender and Health Behavior: A Research Note." *Social Forces* 84 (1):581–93.

Lowie, Robert. 1937. *The History of Ethnological Theory.* New York: Farrar ad Rinehart.

Lynch, James, and Rita Simon. 2002. "A Comparative Assessment of Criminal Involvement among Immigrants and Natives across Seven Nations." In *Migration, Culture Conflict and Crime*, ed. Joshua Freilich, 69–88. Aldershot, UK: Dartmouth.

Maher, Lisa. 1997. *Sexed Work.* Oxford: Clarendon Press.

Mansel, Jürgen. 2003. "Konfliktregulierung bei Straft aten—Variation des Anzeigeverhaltens nach Ethnie des Täters." In *Die Ethnisierung von Alltagskonflikten*, ed. Axel Groenemeyerand and Jürgen Mansel, 261–83. Opladen, Germany: Leske und Budrich.

Mansel, Jürgen, and Hans-Jörg Albrecht. 2003. "Migration und das kriminalpolitische Handeln staatlicher Strafverfolgungsorgane. Ausländer als polizeilich Tatverdächtigteund gerichtlich Abgeurteilte." *Kölner Zeitschrift für Soziologie und Sozialpsychologie* 55:679–715.

Marmot, Michael G., Abraham M. Adelstein, and Lak Bulusu. 1984. "Lessons from the Study of Immigrant Mortality." *Lancet* 1984 (1):1455–57.

McCain, Margaret, Fraser Mustard, and Stuart Shanker. 2007. *Early Years Study.* Toronto: Council for Early Child Development.

Mecheril, Paul. 2000. "Ist doch egal, was man macht, man ist aber trotzdem 'n Ausländer." In *Die Familie im Spannungsfeld globaler Mobilität*, ed. Horst Buchkremerm Wolf Bukow and Michaela Emmerich, 119–42. Opladen: Leske & Budrich.

___. 2003. *Politik der Unreinheit*. Wien: Passagen.

Mehrländer, Ursula, Carsteb Ascheberg, and Joerg Ueltzhöffer. 1997. *Situation der ausländischen Arbeitsnehmer und ihrer Familienangehörigen in der Bunderepublik Deutschland—Repräsentativuntersuchung '95*. Bonn: Der Bundesminister für Arbeit und Sozialordnung.

Merton, Robert. 1970. "Insiders and Outsiders: A Chapter in the Sociology of Knowledge." *American Journal of Sociology* 7:9–45.

Miller, Jody. 2000. *One of the Guys: Girls, Gangs, and Gender*. New York: Oxford University Press.

Mohamed, Rafik, and Eric Fritsvold. 2006. "Damn, It Feels Good to Be a Gangsta: The Social Organization of the Illicit Drug Trade Servicing a Private College Campus." *Deviant Behaviour* 27:97–125.

Mohammad, Fida. 1999. "Jihad as Terrorism: The Western Media and the Defamation of the Qu'ran." In *Making Trouble: Cultural Constructions of Crime, Deviance, and Control*, ed. Jeff Ferrell and Neil Websdale, 303–17. New York: Aldine de Gruyter.

Müller, Joachim. 2000. "Jugendkonflikte und Gewalt mit ethnisch-kulturellem Hintergrund." In *Bedrohte Stadtgesellschaft. Soziale Desintegrationsprozesse und ethnisch-kuslturelle Konfliktkonstellationen*, ed.Wilhelm Heitmeyer, 257–305. Weinheim: Juventa.

Mullings, Beverly. 1999. "Insider or Outsider, Both or Neither: Some Dilemmas of Interviewing in a Cross-Cultural Setting." *Geoforum* 30:337–50.

Murji, Karim. 2007. "Hierarchies, Markets and Networks." *Journal of Drug Issues* 37:781–801.

Murphy, Sheighla, Dan Waldorf, and Craig Reinarman. 1990. "Drifting into Dealing: Becoming a Cocaine Seller." *Qualitative Sociology* 13 (4):321–43.

Natarajan, Mangai, and Mathieu Belanger. 1998. "Varieties of Drug Dealing Organizations." *Journal of Drug Issues* 28:1005–26.

Neumann, Gerald. 1998. "Nationality Law in the United States and in Germany: Structure and Current Problems." In *Paths to Inclusion: The Integration of Migrants in the United States and Germany*, ed. Peter Schuck and Rainer Münz, 247–97. Providence, RI: Berghahn.

Noveck, Scott. 2007. *Does Crime Pay? An Economic Analysis of Criminal Behavior*. MA thesis, Princeton University.

Oberwittler, Dietrich. 2003. "Geschlecht, Ethnizität und sozialräumliche Benachteiligung. Überraschende Interaktionen bei sozialen Bedingungsfaktoren von Gewalt und schwerer Eigentumsdelinquenz von Jugendlichen." In *Geschlecht- und Gewaltgesellschaft*, ed. Siegfried Lamnek, 269–94. Opladen, Germany: Leske und Budrich.

Oltmer, Jochen. 2005. "Begrenzung und Abwehr: De-Globalisierung und protektionistische Migrationspolitik nach dem Ersten Weltkrieg in Deutschland und Europa." In *Grenzüberschreitungen: Differenz und Identität im Europa der Gegenwart (Forschungen zur europäischen Integration)*, ed. Holger Huget, Chryssoula Kambas, and Wolfgang Klein, 151–70. Wiesbaden: VS Verlag.

Open Society Justice Initiative. 2009. *Ethnic Profiling in the European Union: Pervasive, Ineffective, and Discriminatory*. New York: Open Society Foundations.

Organisation for Economic Co-operation and Development (OECD). 2004. *Messages from Pisa 2000*. Paris: OECD Publications.

___. 2006a. *International Immigration Outlook*. Washington DC: OECD Publications.

___. 2006b. *Where Immigrant Students Succeed*. Paris: OECD Publications.

___. 2007. "The Labour Market Integration of Immigrants in Germany." Social, Employment, and Migration Working Paper No. 47. Paris: OECD Publications.

Ostergaard-Nielsen, Eva. 2003. *Transnational Politics—Turks and Kurds in Germany.* London: Routledge.

Ousey, Graham, and Charis Kubrin. 2009. "Exploring the Connection between Immigration and Violent Crime Rates in U.S. Cities, 1980–2000." *Social Problems* 56:447–73.

Padilla, Felix. 1996. *The Gang as an American Enterprise.* New Brunswick, NJ: Rutgers University Press.

Palloni, Alberto, and Jeffrey Morenoff. 2001. "Interpreting the Paradoxical in the Hispanic Paradox: Demographic and Epidemiological Approaches." *Annals of the New York Academy of Sciences* 954:140–74.

Panayi, Panikos. 2000. *Ethnic Minorities in Nineteenth and Twentieth Century Germany— Jews, Gypsies, Poles, Turks and Others.* Essex: Pearson Education.

Paoli, Letizia. 2003. "The Informal Economy and Organized Crime." In *The Informal Economy: Threat or Opportunity in the City,* ed. Joana Shapland, Hansjörg Albrecht, Jason Ditton, Thierry Godefroy., 133–72. Freiburg im Breisgau: Edition Iuscrim.

Pape, Karin. 2005. *Informelle Ökonomie und Gewerkschaften in Deutschland.* Bonn: Global Labour Institute.

Pattillo, Mary. 1998. "Sweet Mothers and Gangbangers: Managing Crime in a Black Middle-Class Neighborhood." *Social Forces* 76:747–74.

Peek, Lori. 2005. "Becoming Muslim: The Development of a Religious Identity." *Sociology of Religion* 66:215–42.

Pfeiffer, Christian, Matthias Kleimann, and Sven Petersen. 2005. *Migration und Kriminalität. Ein Gutachten für den Zuwanderungsbeirat der Bundesregierung.* Baden-Baden, Germany: Nomos.

Pfeiffer, Christian, Michael Windizo, and Mathias Kleimann. 2004. "Die Medien, das Böse und wir. Zu den Auswirkungen der Mediennutzung auf Kriminalitätswahrnehmung." *Monatszeitschrift für Kriminologie und Strafrechtsreform* 37:415–35.

Polsky, Ned. 1967. *Hustlers, Beats, and Others.* Chicago: Aldine.

Popitz, Heinrich. 1969. *Prozesse der Machtbildung.* Tübingen: J. C. B. Mohr Verlag.

Portes, Alejandro, and Patricia Fernández-Kelly. 2008. "No Margin for Error: Educational and Occupational Achievement among Disadvantaged Children of Immigrants." *Annals of the American Academy of Political and Social Science* 620:12–36.

Portes, Alejandro, Patricia Fernández-Kelly, and William Haller. 2009. "The Adaptation of the Immigrant Second Generation in America: A Theoretical Overview and Recent Evidence." *Journal of Ethnic and Migration Studies* 35:1077–104.

Portes, Alejandro, and Dag MacLeod. 1996. "Educational Progress of Children of Immigrants: The Roles of Class, Ethnicity and School Context." *Sociology of Education* 69:255–75.

Portes, Alejandro, and Ruben Rumbaut. 2001. *Legacies: The Story of the Immigrant Second Generation.* Berkeley: University of California Press.

Powdermaker, Hortense. 1966. *Stranger and Friend.* New York: W. W. Norton & Co.

Prenzel, Manfred. 2004. "Wir ernten erste Fruechte." *Die Zeit* 51, December 9.

Presser, Lois. 2005. "Negotiating Power and Narrative in Research: Implications for Feminist Methodology." *Signs: Journal of Women in Culture and Society* 30 (4):2067–90.

Reich, Fransizka, and Özlem Gezer. 2009. "Lange hier und doch nicht da." *Stern*, April 5. http://www.stern.de/panorama/:Integration-Einwanderern-Lange/659816. html.

Reich, Kerstin. 2005. "Integrations—und Desintegrationsprozesse junger Aussiedler aus der GUS. Eine Bedingungsanalyse auf sozial-lerntheoretischer Basis." In *Kriminalwissenschaftliche Schriften*, ed., 5. Münster: LIT Verlag.

Reitz, Jeffrey. 2003. *Host Societies and the Reception of Immigrants*. San Diego: University of California, Center for Comparative Immigration Studies.

Reitz, Jeffrey, Rupa Banerjee, Mai Phan, and Jordan Thompson. 2008. "Race, Religion, and the Social Integration of New Immigrant Minorities in Canada." Toronto: University of Toronto. http://www.utoronto.ca/ethnicstudies/ RaceReligion.pdf.

Reuter, Peter. 1983. *Disorganized Crime—The Economics of the Visible Hand*. Cambridge: MIT Press.

___. 2004. *The Organization of Illegal Markets—An Economic Analysis*. Honolulu, HI: University Press of the Pacific.

Reuter, Peter, and John Haaga. 1988. *The Organization of High-Level Drug Markets*. Santa Monica, CA: Rand Corporation.

Reuter, Peter, and Robert MacCoun. 1992. "Are the Wages of Sin $30 an Hour? Economic Aspects of Street-Level Drug Dealing." *Crime and Delinquency* 38 (4):477–92.

Reuter, Peter, Robert MacCoun, and Patrick Murphy. 1990. *Money from Crime—A Study of the Economics of Drug Dealing in Washington, D.C.* Santa Monica, CA: RAND Corporation.

Rios, Victor. 2011. *Punished: Policing the Lives of Black and Latino Boys*. New York: New York University Press.

Rodriguez, Robyn. 2008. "(Dis)unity and Diversity in Post 9/11 America." *Sociological Forum* 23:379–89.

Ruggiero, Vincenzo, and Karim Khan. 2006. "British South Asian Communities and Drug Supply Networks." *International Journal of Drug Policy* 17:473–83.

Rumbaut, Ruben. 2008. "The Coming of the Second Generation: Immigration and Ethnic Mobility in Southern California." *Annals of the American Academy of Political and Social Science* 620:196–236.

Rumbaut, Ruben, and Walter Ewing. 2007. *The Myth of Immigrant Criminality and the Paradox of Assimilation*. Immigration Policy Center Special Report. Washington, DC: American Immigration Law Foundation.

Sampson, Rana. 2001. *Drug Dealing in Privately Owned Apartment Complexes*. Washington, DC: US Department of Justice, Office of Community Oriented Policing Services.

Sampson, Robert. 2008. Rethinking Crime and Immigration. *Contexts* Winter: 28–33.

Sandberg, Sveinung. 2010. "The Sweet Taste of Sin—A Muslim Drug Dealer in a Nordic Welfare State." *Journal of Scandinavian Studies in Criminology and Crime Prevention* 11 (2):103–18.

Sarrazin, Thilo. 2010a. *Deutschland schafft sich ab—Wie wir unser Land aufs Spiel setzen*. Munich: Deutsche Verlagsanstalt.

___. 2010b. "Klasse statt Masse". *Lettre International* 86:197–201.

Scheper-Hughes, Nancy. 1992. *Death without Weeping*. Berkeley: University of California Press.

Schierup, Carl-Ulrik, Peo Hansen, and Stephen Castles. 2006. *Migration, Citizenship and the European Welfare State: A European Dilemma.* London: Oxford University Press.

Schiffauer, Werner. 2004. "Cosmopolitans or Cosmopolitans." In *Worlds on the Move,* ed. Jonathan Friedman and Shalini Randaria, 93–102. London: I. B. Tauris.

Schmitt-Rodermund, Eva, and Rainer Silbereisen. 2004. "'Ich war gezwungen, alles mit der Faust zu regeln'—Delinquenz unter jugendlichen Aussiedlern aus der Perspektive der Entwicklungspsychologie." *Kölner Zeitschrift für Soziologie und Sozialpsychologie* 43:240–63.

Schönwälder, Karen. 2001. *Einwanderung und ethnische Pluralität. Politische Entscheidungen und öffentliche Debatten in Großbritannien und der Bundesrepublik von den 1950er bis zu den 1970er Jahren.* Essen: Klartext.

___. 2006. "West German Society and Foreigners in the 1960s." In *Coping with the Nazi Past: West German Debates on Nazism and Generational Conflict 1955–1975,* ed. Philipp Gassert and Alan Steinweis, 119–54. Oxford: Berghahn.

Schwalbe, Michael. 2005. "Identity Stakes, Manhood Acts, and the Dynamics of Accountability." *Studies in Symbolic Interaction* 28:65–81.

Sen, Faruk, and Andreas Goldberg. 1994. *Türken in Deutschland—Leben zwischen zwei Kulturen.* Munich: Beck Verlag.

Sherman, Lawrence. 1993. "Defiance, Deterrence and Irrelevance: A Theory of the Criminal Sanction." *Journal of Research in Crime and Delinquency* 30:445–73.

Snow, David, Robert Benford, and Leon Anderson. 1986. "Fieldwork Roles and Informational Yield." *Journal of Contemporary Ethnography* 14:377–408.

Spiegel Online. 2010. "Integration: Merkel erklärt Multikulti für gescheitert." *Spiegel Online,* October 16. http://www.spiegel.de/politik/deutschland/0,1518,723532,00.html.

Spiwak, Martin. 2008. "Furor des Wandels." *Die Zeit,* February 22.

Süddeutsche Zeitung. 1999. "Union macht gegen Bonn mobil." *Süddeutsche Zeitung,* January 4.

Sullivan, Mercer. 1989. *Getting Paid: Youth Crime and Work in the Inner City,* Ithaca: Cornell University Press.

Sutherland, Edwin. 1939. *Principles of Criminology.* Philadelphia: Lippincott.

Sykes, Gresham M., and David Matza. 1957. "Techniques of Neutralization: A Theory of Delinquency." *American Sociological Review* 22:664–70.

___. 1979. "Techniken der Neutralisierung: Eine Theorie der Delinquenz." In *Kriminalsoziologie,* ed. Fritz Sack and René König, 360–72. Wiesbaden: Akademische Verlagsgesellschaft.

Taylor, Ian. 2000. *Crime in Context: A Critical Criminology of Market Society.* Cambridge: Polity.

Tertilt, Hermann. 1996. *Turkish Power Boys.* Frankurt am Main: Suhrkamp Verlag.

Thompson, Sara, Sandra Bucerius, and Mark Luguya. 2013. "Unintended Consequences of Neighbourhood Restructuring: Uncertainty, Disrupted Social Networks and Increased Fear of Violent Victimization Among Young Adults." *British Journal of Criminology* 53 (5):719–45.

Thränhardt, Dietrich. 1994. *Ausländerinnen und Ausländer in Nordrhein-Westfalen. Die Lebenslage der Menschen aus den ehemaligen Anwerbeländern und die Handlungsm öglichkeiten der Politik.* Landessozialbericht Band 6. Düsseldorf: Ministerium für Arbeit, Gesundheit und Soziales des Landes Nordrhein-Westfalen.

Tietze, Nikola. 2001. *Islamische Identitäten—Formen muslimischer Religiosität junger Männer in Deutschland und Frankreich.* Hamburg: Hamburger Edition HIS Verlags GmbH.

Tonry, Michael. 1997. "Ethnicity, Crime, and Immigration—Comparative and Cross-National Perspectives." In *Crime and Justice*, ed. Michael Tonry, 21:1–21. Chicago and London: University of Chicago Press.

Tope, Daniel, Lindsey Chamberlain, and Marta Crowley. 2005. "The Benefits of Being There." *Journal of Contemporary Ethnography* 34:470–93.

Triadafilopolous, Triadafilos. 2006. *Beyond Nationhood: Citizenship Politics in Germany since Unification.* Working Paper Series on Controversies in Global Politics and Societies, No. 1. Toronto: Munk Centre for International Studies, Immigration and Pluralism.

Triadafilopolous, Triadafilos, and Karen Schönwälder. 2006. "How the Federal Republic Became an Immigration Country. Norms, Politics and the Failure of West Germany's Guest Worker System." *German Politics and Society* 24 (3):1–19.

Tyler, Tom. 2007. *Legitimacy and Criminal Justice: An International Perspective.* New York: Russell Sage Foundation.

Tyler, Tom, Stephen Schulhofer, and Aziz Huq. 2010. "Legitimacy and Deterrence Effects in Counterterrorism Policing." *Law and Society Review* 44:365–402.

Valdez, Avelardo, and Charles Kaplan. 2007. "Conditions that Increase Drug Market Involvement: The Invitational Edge and the Case of Mexicans in South Texas." *Journal of Drug Issues* 37 (4):893–917.

Van Gemert, Frank, and Mark Fleisher. 2005. "In the Grip of the Group; Ethnography of a Moroccan Street Gang in the Netherlands." In *European Street Groups and Troublesome Youth Groups: Findings from the Eurogang Research Program*, ed. Scott Decker and Frank Weerman, 11–30. Walnut Creek, CA: AltaMira.

Venkatesh, Sudhir. 2008. *Gang Leader for a Day.* New York: Penguin.

Vermeulen, Hans. 2010. "Segmented Assimilation and Cross-National Comparative Research on the Integration of Immigrants and their Children." *Ethnic and Racial Studies* 33 (7):1214–30.

Vigil, James Diego. 1988. *Barrio Gangs: Street Life and Identity in Southern California.* Austin: University of Texas Press.

__. 1997. *Personas Mexicanas: Chicano High Schoolers in a Changing Los Angeles.* Fort Worth, TX: Harcourt Brace.

__. 2007. *The Projects: Gang and Non-Gang Families in East Los Angeles.* Austin: University of Texas Press.

Viruell-Fuentes, Edna. 2007. "Beyond Acculturation: Immigration, Discrimination, and Health Research among Mexicans in the United States." *Social Science and Medicine* 65:1524–35.

Wadsworth, Tim. 2010. "Is Immigration Responsible for the Crime Drop? An Assessment of the Influence of Immigration on Changes in Violent Crime between 1990 and 2000." *Social Science Quarterly* 91 (2):531–53.

Waldinger, Roger, and Cynthia Feliciano. 2004. "Will the New Second Generation Experience 'Downward Assimilation'? Segmented Assimilation Re-Assessed." *Ethnic and Racial Studies* 27:376–402.

Walter, Michael, and Sebastian Trautmann. 2003. "Kriminalität junger Migranten— Strafrecht und gesellschaftliche (Des)-Integration." In *Kriminalität und Gewalt im Jugendalter: Hell- und Dunkelfeldberichte im Vergleich*, ed. Jürgen Raithel and Jürgen Mansel, 64–86. Weinheim, Germany: Juventa.

Warner, Roger. 1986. *Invisible Hand: The Marijuana Business.* New York: Beach Tree.

Weber, Max. 1947. *The Theory of Social and Economic Organization.* New York: Free Press.

___. 1964. *Soziologie—Weltgeschichtliche Analysen. Politik.* Stuttgart: Alfred Kröner Verlag.

___. 1968. *Economy and Society*, ed. Guenther Roth. New York: Bedminster.

___. 1972. *Wirtschaft und Gesellschaft*, 5th ed. Tuebingen: J. C. B. Mohr.

Wetzels, Peter, Dirk Enzmann, Eberhard Mecklenburg, and Christian Pfeiffer. 2001. *Jugendliche und Gewalt—eine repräsentative Dunkelfeldanalyse in München und acht anderen deutschen Städten.* Baden-Baden: Nomos.

Whyte, William. 1943. *Street Corner Society.* Berlin and New York: Walter de Gruyter.

Wiese, Heike. 2006. "Ich mach dich Messer—Grammatische Produktivität in Kiez-Sprache ('Kanak Sprak')." *Linguistische Berichte* 207:245–73.

Williams, David R. 2005. "The Health of U.S. Racial and Ethnic Populations." *Journals of Gerontology Series B: Psychological Sciences and Social Sciences* 60B (special issue II):53–62.

Williams, Terry. 1989. *The Cocaine Kids.* Reading, MA: Addison-Wesley.

Wilmers, Nicola, Dirk Enzmann, Dagmar Schaefer, Karin Herbers, Werner Greve, and Peter Wetzels. 2002. *Jugendliche in Deutschland zur Jahrtausendwende: Gefährlich oder gefährdet?* Baden-Baden: Nomos.

Wilson, James, and Allen Abrahamse. 1992. "Does Crime Pay?" *Justice Quarterly* 9:359–77.

Wilson, William Julius. 1987. *The Truly Disadvantaged.* Chicago: University of Chicago Press.

Windzio, Michael, and Dirk Baier. 2008. "Violent Behavior of Juveniles in a Multiethnic Society: Effects of Personal Characteristics, Urban Areas, and Immigrants' Peer Networks." *Journal of Ethnicity in Criminal Justice* 7:237–70.

Wolf, Richard, and Mihaela Tudose. 2005. *Country Report on Germany. Dimensions of Integration: Migrant Youth in Central European Countries.* Vienna: IOM Wien.

Wortley, Scot, and Julian Tanner. 2008. "Respect, Friendship, and Racial Injustice: Justifying Gang Membership in a Canadian City." In *Street Gangs, Migration, and Ethnicity*, ed. Frank Van Gemert, Dana Peterson, and Inger-Lise Lien, 192–208. Portland: Willan.

Zaitch, Damian. 2002. *Trafficking Cocaine: Colombian Drug Entrepreneurs in the Netherlands.* Den Haag, Netherlands: Kluwer Law International.

Zhou, Min, Jennifer Lee, Jody Agius Vallejo, Rosaura Tafoya-Estrada, and Yang Sao Xiong. 2008. "Success Attained, Deterred, and Denied: Divergent Pathways to Social Mobility in Los Angeles's New Second Generation." *Annals of the American Academy of Political and Social Science* 620:37–61.

INDEX

Aas, Katja Franko, 66, 72–73
Abrahamse, Allen, 159
Ackerman, Debra, 186
Acun, 93–94
Adams, Joseph, 81
addiction, 39, 210n3; crackheads and, 74, 129; junkies and, 8, 74, 87, 113, 128–134, 139, 141
Adelstein, Abraham M., 181
Adler, Patricia, 88, 108, 131, 135, 154, 193
Adler, Peter, 193
agency: future issues and, 175, 182, 187, 192; research methodology and, 8–11, 15, 48–49, 151, 175, 182, 187, 192, 220n1; social exclusion and, 48–49; structure and, 8–11
Aissa, 13; citizenship and, 56–58; drugs and, 14, 76–78, 80, 120, 122, 124–126, 129, 135, 142–143, 159–162, 210n6, 214n18, 215n23; education and, 211n9; family and, 155; future issues and, 181–182, 185, 188, 191; monthly earnings of, 160; Nermin and, 216n25; parents' use of German and, 221n2; police interactions and, 142–143; purity and, 171, 220n7; respect and, 76–78, 80, 86–89, 96, 101, 105–107, 110–112, 116, 118, 218n12; school system and, 45–49; sex and, 171, 220n7; social exclusion and, 43, 45–49, 56–58, 68, 74; trying to go legit, 188; violence and, 14
Akin, 1, 10; citizenship and, 56–58; close relationship with, 13–14, 41; deportation and, 59; drugs

and, 41–43, 76, 88, 120–122, 127, 130–134, 139–140, 148, 157–159, 162–163; 214nn16, 17,18; father of, 152; friendship and, 162; future issues and, 174, 179–180, 184, 195, 199, 202; gaining trust of, 81–83, 195–196; on Germany, 222n7; good deals and, 88; honor and, 85; leadership and, 214n17; as lifelong dealer, 163; policy solutions and, 179–180; pool and, 81, 212n2; procedure of drug deal and, 41–43; resistance to research by, 81–82; respect and, 76–77, 79–82, 85, 87–88, 93–101, 104, 107–109, 112, 114, 118–119; rocky relationship with, 80, 150; school system and, 45, 49, 54; social exclusion and, 41–43, 45, 49, 54, 59, 63, 71–74; violence and, 214n16; youth centers and, 80–82, 112
Alawites, 126
Alba, Richard, 188
Albanians: ancestral culture and, 67; arranged marriages and, 170; business partner preferences and, 92; family and, 91; greater profits of, 213n11; guest-worker families and, 27, 38; heroin and, 90–91, 104; integration and, 69; Islam and, 125; Kosovo and, 27, 114, 205n2, 208n14; stereotypes and, 5, 68
Albrecht, Hans-Joerg, 3, 35, 75
alcohol, 70, 99, 117, 132, 136, 158, 160, 203–204, 210n3
Algerians, 178
Allah, 124, 165

Department of Social Work, 11
deportation: Akin and, 59; citizenship and, 59–60; fear of, 65; immigrants and, 39, 59–60, 65, 92, 97, 99, 102, 108, 117, 163, 173, 177, 219n3; incarceration and, 59, 92, 97, 99; older generation and, 39; police and, 92; snitching and, 102; Ulun and, 102
Desroches, Frederick, 116
Deutschland schafft sich ab (Germany Abolishes Itself) (Sarrazin), 19
Diehm, Isabell, 23
discrimination: attitudes towards foreigners, 2, 4, 20–28, 34–35, 38, 40, 44, 46–47, 49, 51–53, 56, 58, 60–71, 85, 126, 137, 153, 183, 186–187, 193, 201, 207nn7,8, 209n21; *Ausländerstatus* and, 66; banks and, 63; citizenship and, 207n8; crime and, 209n21, 210n2; criminality and, 209n21; employers and, 153, 156; employment and, 189; fostering social cohesion and, 180–188; guest-worker families and, 21, 23–26, 32, 36, 40; hate crimes and, 61; impact of macro-level policies and, 39; institutional, 1, 15, 23, 32, 46, 48, 51–52; Islamophobia and, 177–179; *Kanaken* and, 1, 4, 74, 87, 114, 125–126, 136, 193; *Kanakisch* speakers and, 70; labeling and, 4, 7, 16, 35, 38, 40, 44, 52, 62, 64, 66–67, 126, 142, 167–168, 176–177, 214n16, 217n2, 222n7; Nazi term and, 222n7; Pew Global Attitudes Project and, 178–179; police and, 34–35, 43, 143–144; policy solutions for, 179–180; school system and, 1, 6, 13, 22, 30, 47, 49, 51–55, 64, 186; second-generation immigrants and, 18; social exclusion and, 43–55, 60–65, 72, 74, 167; street culture and, 6; US Memorandums of Agreement and, 190; xenophobia and, 43–44, 62, 204
Ditton, Hartmut, 49
divorce, 202
Dorn, Nicholas, 91
Dörrlamm, Martin, 39
Douglas, Mary: defilement of women and, 131; purity and, 15, 17, 129, 131, 139, 172; relative impurity and, 129, 172; sacred things and, 131, 139
Drewniak, Regine, 35
drugs: addiction and, 39, 131, 134, 210n3; Aissa and, 14, 76–78, 80, 120, 122, 124–126, 129, 135, 142–143, 159–162, 210n6, 214n18, 215n23; Akin and, 41–43, 76, 88, 120–122, 127, 130–134, 139–140, 148, 157–159, 162–163; 214nn16, 17,18; approaching buyers and, 87, 127; asking if crime pays and, 157–162; Bockenheim and, 84–86, 120, 126, 162, 213n7; business model of, 86–104; cannabis, 36–37, 79, 90, 104, 106–107, 109, 111, 113, 131; cell phones and, 72, 109; cocaine, 17, 36–37, 79, 83, 88, 90–91, 98, 100, 104, 106, 108, 110–113, 120–122, 124, 130–134, 136, 148, 151, 196, 204, 214nn16,18, 216n24; coffee shops and, 215n20; crack, 8, 39, 74, 87, 120, 129, 131, 154; cutting of, 37, 111–113; day-to-day business and, 104–106; dealing at early age, 6–7; decriminalization of, 188–189; differential associations and, 78; drifting into, 58–59; Erol and, 79, 82, 99–100, 106–109, 111–113, 117, 120–121, 128, 132–133, 141; ethnicity and, 80, 84, 87, 90–92, 213n12; family and, 155, 163, 167, 171, 215nn19,23, 217n7; fast money and, 2, 76, 105; forced into, 58; formal economy and, 113–116, 148–157; fostering social cohesion and, 180–181, 188–189; Frankfurt and, 39, 76, 213n7; future issues and, 174–181, 188–189; gangs and, 66, 137, 159, 189, 203; German laws on, 36–37; getting, 106–109; getting carried away in business of, 77–78, 80, 101, 116–119, 176, 214n18; good dealers and, 8, 16–17, 123, 125, 127–134, 144; guilt and, 89; *haram para* and, 134–135; hashish, 79, 104, 112, 131, 134; heroin, 9, 24, 36–37, 39, 79, 87, 90–91, 104–106, 111, 113, 121, 129, 131, 133–134, 139, 216; hierarchical structure and, 92–98; honor and, 120,

classes and, 184; home, 186; impact of macro-level policies and, 39; integration and, 32; language and, 175, 180, 184, 186; lower class and, 49, 185, 211nn7,9, 212n13; mandatory kindergarten and, 186, 211n10; pedagogy seminars and, 185; physical, 185; PISA and, 30–31, 58, 212n16; policy solutions for, 179–180; religious, 206n2; respect and, 19–20; social exclusion and, 45–55, 61–63, 188; social science classes and, 184; social workers and, 149; student drug users and, 11, 86–87, 106, 110, 112, 119, 128, 139; teaching profession and, 185; tutoring and, 2, 14, 216n25; vocational training and, 7, 32, 57, 79, 148–149, 153, 156; wages and, 160

employers: discrimination and, 148, 153, 156; guest-worker families and, 24, 26, 32; hiring rules and, 178; racism and, 153–156; vocational training and, 149

employment: education and, 30–33; female bosses and, 154; guest-worker families and, 30–33.see also labor

Engbersen, Godfried, 75, 177

Enlightenment, 20

Enver, 168, 170–171, 216n25, 220n6

Erol: Aissa and, 106–108; Akin and, 109; Bockenheim and, 41, 69; car ownership and, 152; drugs and, 79, 82, 99–100, 106–109, 111–113, 117, 120–121, 128, 132–133, 141; entrepreneurialism and, 155; police and, 190; social exclusion and, 41, 69, 71; Ulun and, 99–100

ethnicity, 5; attitudes toward foreigners and, 2, 4, 20–28, 34–35, 38, 40, 44, 46–47, 49, 51–53, 56, 58, 60–71, 85, 126, 137, 153, 183, 186–187, 193, 201, 207nn7,8, 209n21; citizenship and, 207n8; class and, 129; demographics and, 205n2; discrimination and, 21 (see also discrimination); drugs and, 80, 84, 87, 90–92, 213n12; future issues and, 177, 182, 186; guest workers and, 21–22, 25–27, 29, 34–35; marriage and, 213n12; parental values and, 125; profiling and, 35, 92, 142; religion and,

125; research methodology and, 201, 203–204, 222n10; social exclusion and, 53, 55, 66–68, 73, 210n2; street culture and, 9–10; trust and, 92, 213n12. *see also* specific background

ethnic profiling, 35, 92, 142

exploitation, 6, 25–26, 45, 194

Fadil, 105, 114, 128

Fagan, Jeffrey, 154

Faist, Thomas, 22

family, 120, 209n17; Albanians and, 91; aunts, 218n9; broken homes and, 70, 136; brothers, 29, 39, 69, 86, 88–89, 91, 99, 102, 106, 131, 151, 162, 173, 188, 210n6, 213n9, 216n25, 222n5; cousins, 39, 62, 69, 106–107, 131, 173; dating and, 219n5; disintegration and, 210n3; divorce and, 202; drugs and, 155, 163, 167, 171, 215nn19,23, 217n7; employment and, 150, 208n12; gangs as surrogate, 7; good families and, 146, 167–168; *haram paras* and, 134–135; honor and, 135, 138, 167, 217n7, 218n9; immigrant qualifications and, 208n12; impurity and, 134–135; informal you and, 218n12; keeping children at home and, 209n18; legitimate work and, 152; lost generation and, 4, 73, 177; marriage and, 13, 29, 137, 145–147, 164, 166–173, 208n14, 213n12, 218n8, 220nn6,7; networks and, 170; normalization and, 49; older members of, 122; organization of, 214n15; outsiders and, 163, 173; parents and, 4, 6–7, 18, 24, 27–29, 31, 43–45, 49, 51, 54–55, 59, 61, 64–72, 75, 81, 117, 123–125, 135–139, 144, 146, 149, 163–170, 173, 176–177, 181, 185, 187, 202, 209n18, 210nn5,6, 211n9, 212n14, 215n21, 217nn3,7, 218n9, 221n2; purity and, 166–167; research methodology and, 12–13, 152; respect and, 191, 201; rewards of, 155, 163, 165, 173; as sacred institution, 176; shared quarters and, 218n8; sisters, 137, 185, 193, 198, 202, 218n9; social exclusion and, 49, 64, 68–69, 71; surrogate, 7; violence in, 36

22–26; integration and, 4 (*see also* integration); Netherlands and, 181; recruitment stop and, 25; returning of, 24–26; rights of, 208n10; school system and, 22, 30–33; social exclusion and, 45, 71, 75; street culture and, 4–6

guns, 118

Gymnasium, 30–32, 45–53, 181, 184–185, 211nn7,9

Haaga, John, 108

Habermas, Jürgen, 14

habitus, 15, 58

Hagan, John, 34

Hagedorn, Heike, 23, 27–28, 43

Haldun, 42

Haller, William, 7, 47

Hansen, Randall, 23, 60

haram para, 134–135

Hardinghaus, Barbara, 36

hashish, 79, 104, 112, 131, 134

hate crimes, 61

Hauptschule, 31, 45–47, 50, 52–53, 57, 59, 211nn7,11

headscarves, 185

Heckmann, Friedrich, 22

Heitmeyer, Wilhelm, 62, 204

Hendricks, Nicole, 190

heroin: addiction and, 131; Albanians and, 90–91, 104; Bockenheim and, 87; cutting of, 37, 113; distribution rates of, 106; Frankfurt and, 39; greater risk of, 105, 131; as impure, 121; income from, 79; injection of, 9, 133; Jo and, 121; laws on, 36–37; niche market of, 91; price of, 121; prominence of, 79, 104, 129; purity of substance, 111, 134; rationalizing dealing of, 129, 139; snorting of, 133; social workers and, 216n24

Hess, Henner, 39, 92, 108

Hessen, 28, 37

Hill-Collins, Patricia, 202

Hitler, Adolph, 56

honor: Akin and, 85; drugs and, 120, 128, 144, 217n7; family and, 135, 138, 167, 217n7, 218n9; gangs and, 84–85; Germany and, 137–139, 141, 144, 201; loss of, 116, 138; respect and,

10–11, 84–85, 103, 114, 116, 120, 128, 135, 137–139, 141, 143–144, 167, 169, 201, 217n7; restoration of, 116–117; shame and, 116, 122, 135, 138; women and, 50–53, 138, 167, 169, 172

Horowitz, Ruth, 198

hostels, 185

humanism, 20

human rights, 60, 62

Hummer, Robert A., 181

Huq, Aziz, 74, 190

Ibor, 92, 107, 126, 199, 216n24, 219n5

identity: Bockenheimers and, 7–8, 17, 41, 50, 55, 69–75, 87, 106, 120, 125, 162, 175; creating a sense of belonging and, 64–73; drugs and, 87, 106, 118, 127–135, 144–145, 176; ethnic profiling and, 35, 92, 142; fluidity of researcher's, 194, 198, 201, 203–204; future issues and, 175–176, 189; German language and, 221n2; guest workers' children and, 21; honor and, 10–11, 84–85, 103, 114, 116, 120, 128, 135, 137–139, 141, 143–144, 167, 169, 201, 217n7; local identification and, 17, 44, 69, 71–74; marginalization and, 4–8 (*see also* marginalization); Muslims and, 8 (*see also* Muslims); national, 28; Nazis and, 1–2, 39, 50–51, 53–54, 62, 64–65, 70, 85, 135–136, 141–142, 155, 201, 222n7; religious, 28, 125–127, 200; research methodology and, 196–202; respect and, 87, 106, 118; sense of belonging and, 21, 40, 43–45, 55, 60, 64–74, 125, 162, 167, 175, 184, 187, 191–192, 210n4; sense of self and, 8, 16–17, 44, 64, 66, 119, 128, 176, 210n4; social exclusion and, 44–45, 55, 66, 68–71, 73–75; status symbols and, 7, 158, 166; street culture and, 4–10, 188–189; turf and, 17, 84, 116, 118, 191–192

ily, Otto, 19

immigrants, 5; *Ausländerstatus* and, 66; Berlin Wall and, 23; complexity of immigration process and, 207n6; contemporary policies on, 26–29;

3; social exclusion and, 43–44, 46, 51,
    61–62, 71–72, 210n4; violence and, 33
Internet, 36
Iranians, 5, 68
Islam, 165; Albanians and, 125; drugs
    and, 123, 136; fundamentalism and,
    62; German Islam Conference and,
    180, 185–186, 206n2; great demands
    of, 20; impurity and, 123–127, 172,
    217n3; Koran and, 123–124, 136,
    206n2; pork and, 74, 137; purity and,
    123–127, 217n3; Ramadan and, 124,
    185; Sarrazin and, 19–20, 33, 180–
    181, 184; as second-largest religion in
    Germany, 29; sex and, 124; terrorism
    and, 45; violence and, 20. *see also*
    Muslims
Islamophobia, 177–179, 182
Ismaili, Karim, 190
isolation, 5–6, 15, 20, 162
Italians: guest-worker families and, 21,
    25, 27, 29, 32–33; popularity of, 57,
    156, 207n3; social exclusion and, 57,
    156
ius sanguinis principle, 22–23
ius soli principle, 22–23

jail: crime and, 13, 39, 59, 72, 92,
    97–104, 100, 108, 117–118, 140,
    149, 163, 173, 176, 213n9, 214n18,
    215n19, 219n3; life after, 102–104;
    long-term deterrence and, 219n3;
    snitching and, 102–103; trust and,
    102–103; Ulun and, 97, 214n18;
    visitations and, 215n19
Jankowski, Martin Sanchez, 159
Jansen, Ad, 108
Jawad, 96, 131, 163
Jetmir, 91, 218n8, 219n5
Jews, 6, 20, 21, 56, 70, 194, 205n5
Jo: big deal of, 120–121; drugs and,
    1, 79, 97, 102, 117–118, 120–121,
    157–159, 198; employment in formal
    economy and, 149, 152–153, 155;
    heroin and, 121; jail and, 117, 198;
    pocket money of, 157–159; tricking
    police and, 79, 149; undercover police
    and, 118; Veli and, 1, 79, 97; violence
    and, 149
judicial sanctions, 144

Junger-Tas, Josine, 177
junkies, 8, 74, 87, 113, 128–134, 139,
    141

Kanaken, 1, 4, 74, 87, 114, 125–126,
    136, 193
Kanakisch speakers, 70
Kaner, 93, 137, 183
Kash, 105, 165–166
Kasinitz, Philip, 188
Katz, Jack, 140, 161
Kauffman, Karen, 197
Kelek, Necla, 20
Keskin, Hakki, 21
Khan, Karim, 90
kindergarten, 30, 33, 53, 186, 209n18,
    211n10
kinship, 87
Klausen, Jyette, 177–179, 183
Kleimann, Matthias, 35
Kleine, Lydia, 45
Koch, Achim, 4, 29
Koopmans, Ruud, 22–23, 187
Koran, 123–124, 136, 206n2
Kosovo, 27, 114, 205n2, 208n14
Kubrin, Charis, 181
Kurds, 126

labor: discrimination and, 189; education
    and, 30–32, 160, 164, 175; employers
    and, 24, 26, 32, 148–149, 153, 156,
    178; employment and, 30–32, 77, 81,
    148, 150, 152–153, 156–157, 163,
    175–176, 178, 189; formal economy
    and, 2, 7, 16, 21–22, 43, 62, 65, 78–
    81, 84, 91, 107, 113–116, 118–119,
    144, 148–166, 175, 177, 188–189,
    201, 206n6, 210n6, 217nn5,7; future
    issues and, 189; guest workers and,
    23 (*see also* guest workers); informal
    economy and, 2, 12, 18, 43–44, 55,
    65–66, 73, 80, 113, 118, 148, 152,
    157, 159, 163–166, 188–189, 213n11,
    216n25; low-skilled, 4; macro-level
    forces and, 2, 39; pension rights and,
    26; recruitment program and, 4, 21–
    23, 25, 183; resumes and, 149–150,
    195; skilled, 24; social exclusion and,
    61–62, 156; social insurance system
    and, 24–25; unemployment and, 23,

Neumann, Gerald, 27
New York, 5, 71, 74
Noveck, Scott, 148
Nurbay, 99
NVivo, 206n11

O'Malley, Pat, 159
Omar, 134–135
Organisation for Economic Co-operation
    and Development (OECD), 30, 33,
    178, 211n7, 212n16
Ostergaard-Nielsen, Eva, 23, 62
Ousey, Graham, 181
outsiders: family and, 163, 173; gangs
    and, 12, 88, 90; immigrants and, 16,
    47–48, 67, 163, 183, 186; marriage
    and, 173; police and, 88; research
    methodology and, 88, 194, 196–197,
    200, 202–204, 219n5; social exclusion
    and, 47–48, 67, 183, 186; social
    workers and, 88
Özgur, 2, 13–14, 32, 64, 94, 101, 151,
    184, 192–193, 198, 202, 222n8

Padilla, Felix, 148
Palloni, Alberto, 181
Panayi, Panikos, 21, 23, 43, 62
paradox of assimilation, 43
parallel societies, 6, 20, 44
Passeron, Jean-Claude, 47
Pattillo, Mary, 7
Paulus, Wiebke, 45
pension rights, 26
Petersen, Sven, 35
Pew Global Attitudes Project, 178–179
Pfeiffer, Christian, 35
police, 149; avoiding, 71–73, 77–78,
    105, 214n18; bullying by, 142–143;
    business owners and, 71; cell phones
    and, 109; citizenship records and, 28;
    cooperation with, 74, 190–191; crime
    statistics and, 34–35; discrimination
    and, 34–35, 43, 143–144; diverting
    attention of, 77; drugs and, 11–12, 41,
    77, 89–90, 93, 95, 98–99, 103, 105–
    111, 115–118, 123, 127–128, 137–
    145; escape routes from, 73; future
    issues and, 187–191; marginalization
    and, 142–143, 189–191; as outsiders,
    88; as powerless, 140; racism and,

142, 191; reports and, 37; research
    methodology and, 11, 218n11, 222n9;
    respect and, 103, 109, 118, 140,
    161, 191, 218n12; rudeness of, 143;
    as stupid, 103, 109, 118, 140–141,
    161, 189–190; surveillance and, 12,
    111, 139, 156, 191; trust and, 190;
    Turkey and, 140–141; undercover,
    71–72, 77, 98, 108, 110, 117–118,
    151, 204, 222n9; US Memorandums
    of Agreement and, 190; youth centers
    and, 12
Polish, 27
political correctness, 6, 205n5
Polsky, Ned, 201
pool, 11, 81, 149–150, 195, 199, 212n2
popes, 125
Popitz, Heinrich, 101
pork, 74, 137
Portes, Alejandro, 7, 47, 181, 188
Portuguese, 23, 25
poverty, 5–6, 210n3
Powdermaker, Hortense, 201, 203
prejudice: attitudes toward foreigners
    and, 2, 4, 20–28, 34–35, 38, 40, 44,
    46–47, 49, 51–53, 56, 58, 60–71, 85,
    126, 137, 153, 183, 186–187, 193,
    201, 207nn7,8, 209n21; banks and,
    63; guest-worker families and, 20,
    33; hate crimes and, 61; *Kanaken*
    and, 1, 4, 74, 87, 114, 125–126, 136,
    193; Sarrazin and, 19–20, 33, 180–
    181, 184; social exclusion and, 44;
    stereotypes and, 1, 3–4, 10, 35, 58, 66,
    70, 175, 182, 184, 199–200, 203–204,
    206n2, 222n6; systemic, 44
Prenzel, Manfred, 185
Presser, Lois, 198
Programme for International Student
    Assessment (PISA), 30–31, 58,
    212n16
prostitutes: drugs and, 110–111, 121,
    129, 204, 215n22; purity and, 129,
    137, 171, 218n8; sex and, 98, 110–
    111, 121, 129–130, 137, 169–171,
    204, 215n22, 218n8
purity: Aissa and, 171, 220n7; casual sex
    and, 145, 168–169, 171, 218n8; concept
    of, 15, 17, 123; cultural capital and, 149,
    154; dating and, 145; Douglas and, 15,

and, 190; research methodology and, 9, 12–14, 18, 41, 81–82, 93, 98, 193–204; undermining of, 190
Tudose, Mihaela, 44
Tunisia, 23, 178
turf, 17, 84, 116, 118, 191–192
Turkish Power Boys, 85
Turks, 2; as all-encompassing phrase, 4–5, 205n2; ancestral culture and, 67; cannabis and, 90; checkpoints and, 142; core principles and, 28–29; crime statistics of, 35; demographics of, 27; drugs and, 90–91, 102, 128, 140; Frankfurt demographics and, 38; guest-worker families and, 19–21, 23–25, 27–30, 33, 35, 38, 40; impact of macro-level policies and, 39; impurity and, 171; integration and, 69; Islamophobia and, 177–178; Kurds and, 126; marriage and, 208n14; Muslims and, 29 (*see also* Muslims); parallel societies and, 20; population growth of, 25; real, 126; social exclusion and, 42, 50, 56, 58–59, 62, 64, 67–69; social insurance system and, 24–25; stereotypes and, 5, 68, 206n2; tough police of, 140–141; Turkish treaty and, 24
tutoring, 2, 14, 216n25
TV, 7, 11, 36, 83–85, 164, 217n4
Tyler, Tom, 74, 177, 190

Ülker, 60, 141
Ulun, 97–102, 104, 107–108, 117, 214n18
Ümit, 88–89, 102, 107–110, 201
unemployment, 23, 33, 140, 178, 208n12
United States: crime rates and, 75; dealer deaths and, 117–118; fostering social cohesion and, 180–184; future issues and, 18, 180–184, 188–190, 192; guns and, 118; immigrants and, 21–22, 34–35; Los Angeles, 31; marginalization and, 5–6, 31, 188–190, 192; as melting pot, 182; Memorandums of Agreement and, 190; multiculturalism and, 5; New York, 5, 71, 74; poverty

and, 6; social exclusion and, 73, 75, 210n3; street culture and, 5–6, 9; taking responsibility for own actions and, 9; welfare and, 6
University of Frankfurt, 11, 206n10
upper class, 49, 211n9

van der Leun, Joanne, 75, 177
van Gemert, Frank, 139, 177
Veli, 1–2, 78, 79, 86, 97, 189
Venkatesh, Sudhir, 117, 122, 148, 159, 203, 206n6
Vermeulen, Hans, 44
video games, 11, 36
Vigil, James Diego, 6–7
violence: Aissa and, 14; Akin and, 214n16; alcohol and, 132; crime and, 33 (*see also* crime); demographics on, 209nn20, 21; doctors paid under the table and, 115; drugs and, 17, 39, 116, 181, 191–192, 200; gangs and, 84–86, 189, 192; gendered, 82, 149; German society and, 136; increasing rates of teenage, 35–36; integration and, 33; Islam and, 20; Jo and, 149; *Kanaken* and, 1, 4, 74, 87, 114, 125–126, 136, 193; legal obligation to report, 115; marginalization and, 189; previous generation and, 95; reunification and, 212n5; social exclusion and, 47, 55, 62–63, 70; stereotypes and, 4; symbolic, 8, 10, 15–16, 47, 55, 63, 128, 212n17; testing intruders and, 82; Ulun and, 99–100; women and, 82, 149
virgins, 167–169, 171, 173, 220n7
Viruell-Fuentes, Edna, 44
vocational training, 7, 32, 57, 79, 148–149, 153, 156

Wacquant, Loïc, 15
Wadsworth, Tim, 34
Waldinger, Roger, 44
Waldorf, Dan, 78, 122
Walter, Michael, 34–35
Warner, Roger, 108
Wasmer, Martina, 4, 29
Weber, Max, 15; Bourdieu and, 48; closed relationships and, 56; criminality and, 122–131; fear of lost privileges

and, 185; irrationality and, 121; social closure and, 15–16, 47–48, 64, 212n17; social exclusion and, 47–48, 56, 59, 64
Weil, Patrick, 23
welfare: advanced German system of, 5; drugs and, 140; exploitation of, 6, 26, 45; future issues and, 180; guest-worker families and, 19–20, 26; respect and, 19; social exclusion and, 10, 45; United States and, 6
Wendel, Travis, 87, 108
Wetzels, Peter, 3
Whyte, William, 193
Williams, David R., 181
Williams, Terry, 108, 122, 131, 135, 148, 222n5
Wilmers, Nicola, 35
Wilson, James, 159
Wilson, William Julius, 5, 205n3
Windzio, Michael, 35
Wolf, Richard, 44
women: brothels and, 110, 121, 158, 169–171, 204, 215n22, 220nn6,7; casual sex and, 145, 168–169, 171, 218n8; defilement of, 131; divorce and, 202; female bosses and, 154; female duties and, 81, 198–199; gender dynamics and, 197–200; girlfriends and, 49, 81, 86, 115, 149, 168, 170–172, 198, 218n8, 219n5, 220n7; headscarves and, 185; honor and, 167, 169; impurity and, 145, 167–168, 171, 220n7; marriage and, 13, 29, 137, 145–147, 164, 166–173, 213n12, 218n8, 220nn6,7; mistresses

and, 80; prostitutes and, 98, 110–111, 121, 129–130, 137, 169–171, 204, 215n22, 218n8; protection of, 131; purity and, 129, 131, 137, 166–172, 176, 218n8, 220n7; rape and, 82, 130, 137–138; respect and, 146, 199–200; sluts and, 50–53, 138, 169, 172; stereotypes and, 199–200, 204; violence and, 82, 149; virgin, 167–169, 171, 173, 220n7
World War II, 21, 24, 27, 205n5, 222n7
Wortley, Scot, 137, 139

xenophobia, 43–44, 62, 204

Yakut, 65, 115, 136, 145, 164
Yilmaz, 114
youth centers, 2, 170, 205n2, 217n7; Akin and, 80–82, 112, 212n2, 214n15; crime and, 194; drugs and, 3, 94–95, 111–112, 214n15, 216n24; duties at, 81; gangs and, 84; gatekeepers and, 195, 202–203; media consumption and, 36, 83; police and, 12; pool and, 81, 212n2; research methodology and, 11, 80–83, 94–95, 99–100, 115–116, 150, 159, 162, 194–198, 202, 213n13, 216n27; respect and, 92–93; social structure and, 92–93; social workers and, 11, 80, 115–116, 133, 216n27, 221n1; street culture and, 4–7
Yugoslavia, 21, 23, 25, 209n20

Zaitch, Damian, 92, 108
Zhou, Min, 188